D0160888

"Sweat"

VOLUMES IN THE SERIES

CHARLOTTE PERKINS GILMAN, "The Yellow Wallpaper"
   *Edited by Thomas L. Erskine and Connie L. Richards, Salisbury
   State University*

ZORA NEALE HURSTON, "Sweat"
   Edited by Cheryl A. Wall, Rutgers University

JOYCE CAROL OATES, "Where Are You Going,
   Where Have You Been?"
   Edited by Elaine Showalter, Princeton University

FLANNERY O'CONNOR, "A Good Man Is Hard to Find"
   Edited by Frederick Asals, University of Toronto

TILLIE OLSEN, "Tell Me a Riddle"
   *Edited by Deborah Silverton Rosenfelt, University of Maryland,
   College Park*

KATHERINE ANNE PORTER, "Flowering Judas"
   Edited by Virginia Spencer Carr, Georgia State University

LESLIE MARMON SILKO, "Yellow Woman"
   Edited by Melody Graulich, University of New Hampshire

ALICE WALKER, "Everyday Use"
   Edited by Barbara T. Christian, University of California, Berkeley

HISAYE YAMAMOTO, "Seventeen Syllables"
   Edited by King-Kok Cheung, University of California, Los Angeles

"Sweat"

ZORA NEALE HURSTON

Edited and with an introduction by
CHERYL A. WALL

Rutgers University Press
New Brunswick, New Jersey

Library of Congress Cataloging-in-Publication Data

Hurston, Zora Neale.
    Sweat / Zora Neale Hurston ; edited and with an introduction by
Cheryl A. Wall.
        p.   cm. — (Women writers)
    Includes bibliographical references.
    ISBN 0-8135-2315-X (cloth : alk. paper). — ISBN 0-8135-2316-8 (pbk. :
alk. paper)
        1. Afro-American women—Fiction. 2. Hurston, Zora Neale. Sweat.
    3. Afro-American women in literature. I. Wall, Cheryl A. II. Title.
    III. Series: Women writers (New Brunswick, N.J.)
        PS3515.U787S94   1997
        813'.52—dc20   96-31071
                                                                                              CIP

British Cataloging-in-Publication information available

This collection copyright © 1997 by Rutgers, The State University
For copyrights to individual pieces please see pages 233–234.

Manufactured in the United States of America

For my niece, Monique Alston

❏ Contents ■

Contents

 Introduction

Introduction

"Sweat" might be read as a story of a marriage in crisis in which an abused wife learns to act in self-defense. Or, it might be read as a fictional brief on behalf of southern black women in the early twentieth century, whose lot it was to "sweat" for every-body—their employers and families alike—and whose oppor-tunities for self-fulfillment were limited to the church. Many readers consider "Sweat" a carefully rendered depiction of southern black life and note that the dialogue is a faithful rep-resentation of the speech of the region and the period. Others value the story's psychological insights above the social and cultural knowledge it conveys. Still other readers perceive in "Sweat" a spiritual allegory in which the protagonist confronts a temptation that jeopardizes her soul's salvation. Placing these perspectives alongside each other raises provocative questions. Perhaps the most provocative is whether the story ends in the protagonist's triumph or defeat.

The many levels on which "Sweat" can be read make it one of Zora Neale Hurston's most enduring works. It was pub-lished in 1926, early in Hurston's career, indeed, long before she had dedicated herself to the vocation of writing. Eventually she published four novels, a memoir, two volumes of folklore, and more than fifty stories, essays, and plays. In its compact brevity, "Sweat" anticipates the thematic concerns that ani-mate much of this work. As in her greatest novel *Their Eyes Were Watching God* (1937), Hurston explores the themes of marital conflict, female exploitation, and agency. The story re-flects Hurston's abiding interest in spirituality as well. Years in advance of her travels throughout the southern United States and the Caribbean during which she conducted research on spiritual traditions in black diasporic communities, Hurston created a protagonist in "Sweat" whose religious beliefs define the terms of her psychological dilemma.

3

Perhaps the most striking continuity between "Sweat" and Hurston's later fiction is the language of the text. It bears all of the hallmarks of Hurston's signature style. At a time when African American writers were struggling to free themselves of minstrel dialect and stereotypes, Hurston wrote in a voice that was fresh and utterly distinctive. In fact, her language was not so much invented as distilled from the speech she had listened to as a child. Even in her earliest fiction, she recognized that the poetry of black folk speech might be the foundation of a new literature.

Her sense of this possibility was shared by other writers, notably Langston Hughes, James Weldon Johnson, and Jean Toomer whose achievements are synonymous with the Harlem Renaissance. Surveying the accomplishments of the new generation of writers in his landmark anthology, *The New Negro,* scholar Alain Locke praised their tendency to draw from the storehouse of folk art "something technically distinctive, something that as an idiom of style may become a contribution to the general resources of art."[1] Locke's observation responded to literary achievements, but the anthology marked a broader movement.

The Harlem Renaissance was the cultural awakening among African Americans that began at the end of the First World War, when a new generation of artists imbued with a sense of race pride wrested the attention of the American public. Musicians had led the way and throughout the next decade the sounds of men like Louis Armstrong, Duke Ellington, and Fletcher Henderson defined the age—the Jazz Age. As important as the innovators of jazz were, other musicians including blues singers like Bessie Smith and Blind Lemon Jefferson, and soloists and choral ensembles such as Roland Hayes and the Hall Johnson Choir, who brought spirituals to the concert hall, also enjoyed great popularity. Theater artists, painters, and sculptors gained attention as well.[2]

Zora Neale Hurston arrived in New York in January 1925, just as the Harlem Renaissance swung into high gear. As a student at Howard University in Washington, D.C., where Locke was a professor of philosophy, Hurston had written for the campus literary magazine. She had also attended the literary salon hosted by poet Georgia Douglas Johnson, who was at the center of a network of black women writers in Washington. Hurston's first professional publication, "Drenched in Light," appeared in *Opportunity* in December 1924, and others, including "Spunk," which Locke reprinted in *The New Negro,* quickly followed. Hurston's career was launched.

It did not take her long to find a group of kindred spirits in New York. Several of them, including poet and painter Gwendolyn Bennett, painter Aaron Douglas, Langston Hughes, avant-garde artist Richard Bruce Nugent, and critic and editor Wallace Thurman collaborated on the legendary "little magazine," *Fire!!.* Thurman led the venture to establish "A Quarterly Devoted to Younger Negro Artists." The most influential African American journals of the period were *The Crisis,* the official publication of the National Association for the Advancement of Colored People (NAACP) and *Opportunity,* the house organ of the National Urban League. Although they were the most important outlets for young writers, both were indisputably, as Hurston observed, "in literature on the side." By contrast, the editors of *Fire!!* claimed to "make no eloquent or rhetorical plea. *Fire* speaks for itself."[3]

The first issue of *Fire!!* was also the last; few copies of the elegantly produced, expensively priced journal were sold, and most were subsequently destroyed when the basement where they were stored caught fire. But several of its pieces spoke memorably. Among these were Thurman's "Cordelia the Crude: A Harlem Sketch" that outlined a young woman's descent into prostitution; Bennett's "Wedding Day," a story set in Paris that depicted the failure of an interracial romance; and "Smoke, Lilies and Jade," a stream-of-consciousness piece that explored the psyche of a young bohemian, homosexual artist in ways that were explicit enough to cause Nugent to adopt a pseudonym, Richard Bruce. In addition to "Sweat," Hurston contributed a play, "Color Struck." Its theme of racial self-hatred was as somber as the others, but its scenes of revelers from Florida towns competing in a cake-walk contest added levity.

Like the other contributions to *Fire!!,* Hurston's pieces introduced new themes and settings to African American literature. Like them, too, neither "Sweat" nor "Color Struck" sounded notes of racial protest. The conflicts in these writings could not be resolved by a NAACP lawsuit or an Urban League initiative. While racial injustice in the larger society informed the conflicts represented here, they were more profoundly the conflicts of the characters' interior lives. No piece in *Fire!!* probes psychological conflicts more deeply than "Sweat."

Unlike the other contributions to *Fire!!*, which were set in cities, Hurston's story and play took place against a rural southern backdrop. In a period when the "New Negro" was defined as an urban Northerner, Hurston set most of her work in Eatonville, Florida, an all-black village in the center of the state and Zora Hurston's hometown. While she was actually born in Notasulga, Alabama, in 1891, Hurston boasted that she was a daughter of Eatonville. She was proud of the town's historical significance, asserting that in 1886 it became "the first Negro community in America to be incorporated"[4] Her father, the Reverend John Hurston, had served three terms as mayor. But it was the town's cultural significance that Hurston most appreciated. The magnificent storytellers who gathered on the porch of Joe Clarke's store remained vivid in her memory, and they make a brief appearance in "Sweat." The sermons and the spirituals that stirred her imagination as a child inform her fiction as well. Unlike most other Harlem Renaissance writers, Hurston had known black folk culture "from the earliest rocking of [her] cradle."[5] It proved an inestimable advantage.

While the child Zora was enamored of the stories that adults in Eatonville told, she was also a voracious reader. On one occasion when two wealthy white women visited her grammar school, she read so well that the tourists sent her books when they returned home. Zora read and reread *Gulliver's Travels*, Grimms' Fairy Tales, the Greek and Roman myths, and the Norse tales. Several years later, after the death of her mother, Lucy, led to the dissolution of the family and to years of working as a maid for Zora, Hurston recalled finding a copy of Milton's complete works in a pile of trash. She read *Paradise Lost* "and luxuriated in Milton's syllables."[6] In "Sweat," Hurston alludes to the chapters in Genesis that inspired Milton's epic, but she tells her story in the idiom of Eatonville.

Despite constant financial hardship, Hurston refused to give up her quest for an education. A job as a maid to an actress in a traveling troupe brought her North, and in 1917, she was finally able to resume her schooling at Morgan Academy (now Morgan State University) in Baltimore. From there she went to Howard, where she majored in English. Poverty made it impossible for her to attend school full time, and she held various jobs including stints as a waitress and a manicurist while in Washington. Shortly after she arrived in New York, she met Annie Nathan Meyer, who arranged for Hurston's admission to Barnard College, where Meyer was a trustee. In September 1925, Hurston matriculated as a full-time student. She was thirty-four years old, although everyone assumed that she was at least ten years younger.

Hurston found her studies exhilarating, although life as Barnard's only black student posed social challenges. After taking a course from Franz Boas, who pioneered the study of anthropology in the United States, Hurston changed her major. Through what she called the "spyglass of anthropology," she began to see the culture of Eatonville in a new light. Cultural relativity was the foundational principle of anthropology. For Hurston, it meant accepting as a given that the culture of Eatonville was as good as any other. She need not apologize for the lives of the people there, neither need she protest continuously the conditions that shaped them. While she lauded the humor which graced the lives of the Eatonville citizenry, she never made jokes of them. Outside of class, Hurston conducted field work for Boas in Harlem, measuring the skulls of passers-by in a misguided effort to disprove theories of racial inferiority. She supported herself working as secretary, and later as chauffeur, for the popular white novelist, Fannie Hurst. To make ends meet, she did domestic work. In every spare moment, she wrote.

"Sweat" is by far the best of Hurston's early writings. No simplistic encounters between blacks and whites mar the credibility of the story, as was the case with "Drenched in Light." In "Sweat" blacks are seen in relation to themselves. Despite the careful attention to setting, "Sweat" transcends the category of "local color fiction," and in so doing, records a sensibility that had rarely before been expressed in American literature. It is a sensibility that had found creative expression mainly in the spirituals and the blues.

Delia Jones is a washerwoman, the family breadwinner,

and an abused wife. These roles exist in a causal relation, for Delia's work is both an economic necessity and a psychological threat to her husband Sykes. In the story Sykes seems never to work at all, and he asserts his manhood mainly by intimidating and betraying his wife. Although the story does not explore the economic motives fully, they are clearly important. No matter how onerous the labor, a black woman could always find work in the early-twentieth-century South. Black men had more difficulty. The emphasis is much more on the psychology of the characters than on their material existence. Delia is a devoutly religious woman whose faith helps her weather the storms of her marriage, while at the same time it imbues her with a meekness that makes her more vulnerable to her husband's cruelty. Conversely, when Delia gains the strength to stand up to Sykes, she jeopardizes her spiritual peace.

In the manner of Hurston's later protagonists, Delia Jones claims a self by claiming her voice, but the result is more ambiguous than for her successors, like Janie Crawford, the protagonist of *Their Eyes*. As the story opens, Sykes has returned home on a Sunday evening, a time he knows Delia will be sorting the week's laundry. Initially, he frightens her by playing on her fear of snakes. Then, he accuses her of religious hypocrisy because she is working on the Sabbath. Finally, he threatens to force her to give up her work completely. With this, "Delia's habitual meekness seemed to slip from her shoulders" and she begins to "change some words" of her own.[7]

In "talking back," Delia is practicing a cultural behavior that Hurston records frequently in both her fiction and folklore. Citing these examples in his analysis, Roger Abrahams concludes that to negotiate respect in relationships a black woman ideally "has the ability to *talk sweet* with her infants and peers but *talk smart* or *cold* with anyone who might threaten her self image." Nothing threatens Delia's sense of self more profoundly than attacks on her faith. She is compelled to talk smart to preserve her self-respect as well as to show Sykes that she intends to retain her position in their home.[8]

"Talking smart" was emphatically not a feminine value in white American culture in the 1920s. As the response of Sykes and numerous other black male characters in Hurston's writing suggests, many black men expected women to defer to male authority. But, the preponderance of examples of women "talking smart" in Hurston's writing suggests the existence of an alternative standard. The most striking example of the alternative is Big Sweet, a woman Hurston met in a sawmill camp while conducting field work in the years after writing "Sweat." The very name, "Big Sweet"—with its suggestions of physical power and sexual attractiveness, of strength and tenderness—aptly defines the ideal. Though fearsome, Big Sweet is not so much feared as respected, because the camp community draws a distinction between meanness and the defense of one's integrity. Unlike Delia Jones, Big Sweet lives outside the boundaries of social convention. For Delia, a wife and churchgoer, the risks of talking smart are high.

At first Sykes is so cowed by Delia's verbal defiance, not to mention the "defensive pose" that intimates her willingness to back up her words with action, that he does not hit her as he usually does. Yet Delia takes no joy in her victory; instead she seeks refuge in her faith. After much reflection, she is able to build a "spiritual earthworks" against Sykes. She takes comfort in the belief that "whatever goes over the Devil's back, is got to come under his belly. Sometime or ruther, Sykes, like everybody else, is gointer reap his sowing."

In this passage Hurston is able both to employ an African American aphorism and to define it for her readers. As she once rightly asserted, one of the elements that attracted attention to Hurston's fiction was the telling of the story in what she called the "idiom—not the dialect of the Negro." She would later study the idiom and summarize her findings in "Characteristics of Negro Expression." But even in her earliest writing, she relied on the idiom to give "verisimilitude to the narrative by stewing the subject in its own juice."[9] "Sweat" anticipates Hurston's conclusions that drama and the "will to adorn" are crucial elements in African American oral performance. Consider, for example, the chorus of voices rising from Joe Clarke's porch. Sykes's peers extend the strongest indictment of his cruelty: "Syke Jones aint wuth de shot an' powder hit would tek tuh kill 'em," says one. Another offers the considered conclusion that Sykes and Delia "never wuz de same in mind." Clarke's wisdom, expressed through the extended metaphor of the "cane-chew," substantiates his position as town leader. Delia's speech is less expansive and more aphoristic. Unlike the male figures on the store porch, Delia has had few opportunities to speak in public. When Roger Abrahams distinguishes presentation from performance, he alludes to the difference that gender makes.

Hurston had good reason to differentiate her use of language from "dialect," a term that evoked the caricatures of minstrelsy. The most popular entertainment in nineteenth-century America had fashioned a "stage Negro," that some white viewers mistook for their black countrymen. (Representations of black females were rare.) Audiences likewise *knew* Negro dialect, with its comic malapropisms and lachrymose sentimentality, from the minstrel stage.[10] Hurston was able to break free of the conventions of dialect, primarily because of her excellent ear for folk speech. But, the fact that she based her characters on people she knew, rather than on minstrel stereotypes, was also key. She never doubted the complexity of either their language or their lives.

The main characters in "Sweat" are named for two of Hurston's Eatonville neighbors. The United States Census of 1910 lists a Syke Jones, who with his wife Ida, had nine children; one of them was named Delia. As a fiction writer, Hurston altered the kinship relation. We should likewise assume that she invented the psychological dynamic of the marriage she depicts. What Hurston appropriated is the idiom in which the Joneses and their neighbors spoke. Then too, of course, she borrowed their names. "Sykes" (the variant spellings are in Hurston's original text) seems particularly well chosen. Not only does it carry connotations of villainy drawn from Charles Dickens's *Oliver Twist*, its sibilant sounds are especially appropriate to a "snake charmer."

Although Delia endures Sykes's cruelty in silence for an extended time, her compliance does not defuse his anger. It may in fact intensify it, for Delia's anger like all her other passion is subsumed by her faith. Even if she has turned to religion after Sykes's sexual interest in her waned, her reliance on it obviates any emotional need she has for him. Sykes's next actions test Delia's resolve. He begins to flaunt his girlfriend before the townsfolk and determines to remove Delia from the house Delia's labor has paid for. Then he brings a rattlesnake home in the hope that Delia will be terrified into leaving. The

10

snake becomes Sykes's symbol, imaging his sexuality and his evil. Manipulating the meanings associated with this symbol in Judeo-Christian tradition and in African American blues, Hurston transforms "Sweat" from a story of marital conflict to a spiritual allegory.[11] As Hurston biographer Robert Hemenway was the first to suggest, Sykes ultimately becomes a threat not so much to Delia's person as to her soul.

In a bitter final argument, Delia acknowledges Sykes's victory, or perhaps, more correctly, her defeat. Unable to sustain her stoic indifference, she confesses that she now hates Sykes as much as she once loved him. Her invective is startling: "Ah hates yuh lak uh suck-egg dog."[12] "Talking smart" in this moment fulfills the function Abrahams describes as "a means of marking a serious (or potentially serious) personal antagonism" rather than more genial verbal play. Sykes misses the signal. Although stunned by her words, he does not perceive the grave danger in which Delia's "fall" places him. If she is willing to return hate for hate, she will no longer be bound by the commandments of her faith.

The calm with which Delia pronounces her hatred is even more sinister than the invective itself. It bespeaks spiritual resignation, rather than that act of speech which cultural critic bell hooks defines as "talking back," that is, "the expression of . . . movement from object to subject—the liberated voice."[13] For Janie Crawford, "talking smart" or "specifying," as Hurston called it, represents such an act of liberation when she tells her husband Joe Starks: "Humph! Talkin' 'bout *me* lookin' old! When you pull down yo' britches, you look lak de change uh life."[14] For Delia, however, this moment of "specifying" is equally an act of self-defense and self-incrimination.

Delia struggles to hold on to her faith by attending a church service, a "loves feast," that in terms of the plot brings her temporary solace. In the discourse of the story however, the connotations of "love feast" heighten the spiritual peril of the character's situation. Derived from *agape,* one of three Greek words denoting love, specifically the understanding, redeeming love of all men, the love feast was a ritual meal shared by the early Christians in token of their love for each other; it usually preceded the Lord's Supper, or rite of communion. The tradition survives among some modern denominations, notably the

Methodist church. The service features a simple meal, usually only of bread and water, and the relation of religious experiences by various members of the congregation; it is intended to promote piety, mutual affection, and zeal.[15] Delia's participation in the love feast provides an unsettling parallel to the earlier scene in the story when she moves her church membership rather than take communion with Sykes. Can she reconcile the hatred she feels for him and the love she professes to feel for humanity?

As Delia returns home from the love feast, she sings the spiritual that will echo throughout the rest of the story:

> Jurden water, black an' col'
> Chills de body, not de soul
> An' Ah wantah cross Jordan in uh calm time.

The refrain may be a variant of lines from the spiritual, "Stan' Still Jordan": "Jordan River is chilly and cold / It will chill-a my body, but not my soul." The statement confirms the soul's safe passage to its heavenly home. No such confirmation is expressed in the story. In its theme and imagery the story's refrain echoes a number of spirituals including "Deep River," "Roll Jordan, Roll," "O, Wasn't Dat a Wide River?" and "Give-a Way, Jordan." Crossing the Jordan as a metaphor for death resonated with the creators of the spirituals, the "black and unknown bards," as James Weldon Johnson designated them, whose ancestors had crossed over the Atlantic Ocean into the death-in-life that was slavery.[16] The scriptural source of the metaphor is found in Josh. 3:8: "When ye come to the brink of the water of Jordan, ye shall stand still in Jordan." In that stillness, the soul discerned its eternal fate.

The story moves to a beautifully controlled climax. Sykes uses the snake to set a trap for Delia, but he is the one ensnared. Delia makes no effort to warn, rescue, or even comfort him. She exacts her revenge, but at a terrible spiritual cost. To describe the moment that Delia leaves Sykes to die, the narrator weaves together images of heat and cold, the sun and the river, in a way that underscores the elemental, inexorable dimensions of this tale. The narrator does not pass judgment. Yet, how will Delia, good Christian though she has tried to be, ever cross Jordan in a calm time?

Three months after "Sweat" was published, Hurston left New York City and her blossoming literary career to begin collecting folklore in Florida. Eatonville was her first stop. A research fellowship from the Department of Anthropology at Columbia University underwrote her expenses. Later she acquired a patron, a wealthy Park Avenue widow, Charlotte Osgood Mason, who supported her fieldwork. For the next six years, Hurston's primary professional identity was folklorist. Travelling throughout the South, she collected folktales, songs, sermons, children's rhymes, hoodoo curses and cures that, in her view, constituted "the arts of the people before they find out that there is any such thing as art." [17] She would eventually publish this material in 1935, in *Mules and Men,* the first volume of African American folklore published by an African American.

In 1927, while on her first expedition, Hurston married Herbert Sheen, a medical student whom she had met at Howard. The marriage lasted only a few months. A second marriage in 1939 was equally brief. Hurston never wrote about either relationship. Moreover, unlike her contemporary, novelist and editor Jessie Fauset, Hurston did not explore in fiction the competing demands of marriage and career. [18] Nevertheless, when Hurston resumed her literary career in 1933, she published "The Gilded Six-Bits," a story that depicts a marriage in which, at least initially, the partners are very much the same in mind.

This marriage inverts the portrayal in "Sweat" in other ways as well. Not only does the hardworking husband support the couple, the wife takes pleasure in performing household tasks. Most importantly, they delight in each other. The humor, verbal play, and sensuality that characterize Missy May and Joe's relationship approximate the marital ideal in Hurston's writing. Janie and her third husband Tea Cake achieve a similar union in *Their Eyes.* What is required to sustain such a relationship is the vexing question. Does it require the woman's submissiveness? Should Missy May's declaration that "if you burn me, you won't git a thing but wife ashes" be read as a statement of self-abnegation? If so, the sexual politics of "The

Gilded Six-Bits" are hopelessly reactionary. At best, the plot with its movement from female passivity to female betrayal to a reconciliation enabled by the birth of a son reflects archaic assumptions about gender. Yet, everything about this story, beginning with its title, cautions the reader that things are not always what they seem.

Viewing the couple's playful banter as an "impromptu ceremony" such as Hurston analyzes in "Characteristics for Negro Expression" allows for other possibilities. As the story opens, Missy May and Joe Banks have been married less than a year. Not surprisingly, their conversation resembles the courtship rituals that Hurston and other folklorists collected in black southern communities where "love-making" was a high art. Missy May is Joe's equal when it comes to the ability to "talk sweet," and the hyperbole of their words confirms that they are not to be taken at face value. Her boast about "wife ashes" is in the same register as his claim that he would "ruther all de other womens in de world to be dead than for you to have de toothache."

The ease and spontaneity of their banter signals the joy and mutuality of their sexual relations. This verbal play is akin to foreplay. Like the blues, it abounds in double entendres. Missy May is an equal partner in this verbal trysting too. Her status as wife does not deprive her of sexual agency. When, for example, she tells Joe that "Ah knowed you had somethin' for me in yo' clothes," she is not referring just to candy kisses. Rather, she is participating in a cultural tradition, well known among blues singers and their audiences, in which foods, especially sweets like biscuits, jelly rolls, and sugar bowls, are sexual metaphors.

As John Lowe persuasively argues, "The Gilded Six-Bits" is at heart a comic story. But it offers a serious commentary. Two clusters of metaphors—one figuring sweetness and the other money—are used to convey the deleterious effect of materialism on human relationships. Candy, chewing gum, sweet soap, potato pudding, ice cream, and sugar (as a term of endearment for Missy May) recur in the story as emblems of love. Set against them are equally frequent references to silver and gold, dollars and bits, stores and a "corperation," and to icons of U.S. industry. In the ritualized improvisation that opens the

14

story, Joe and Missy May use both money and candy kisses as tokens in a love game. Their game reflects a naivete about economics and society for which both will suffer.

Joe, whose surname is surely ironic because he understands nothing about money, is the first to be deceived by Otis D. Slemmons. He believes Slemmons's prevarications and mistakenly identifies his physical heft with financial wealth. Missy May is skeptical, as she remembers photographs she has seen of Rockefeller and Ford, in which they did not seem corpulent. Interestingly, these references, along with others to Packard and Cadillac, suggest how much the influences of the larger society penetrate life in Eatonville. Only the white candy store owner, who has made sweetness a salable commodity, is naive enough to think that black communities are untouched by the white world which surrounds them. To be sure, the narrator seems inclined to wish that such isolation were possible, but recognizes that it is not.

In the beginning, Missy May is unimpressed by Slemmons, and by the rich white men on whom he models himself. She prefers Joe's unaffected nobility. Eventually, though, Slemmons wears down her defenses, and she too is tempted by his false gold. Her deception provokes the crisis that threatens the marriage. The lure of materialism has alienated Joe and Missy May from each other and from themselves. The story's saddest moment comes when Joe leaves the gilded coin under her pillow as payment for sex. A subtle reference connects this moment to the larger forces of history. The bit of chain that remains attached to the coin is a metonym of slavery, which in turn constituted the ultimate commodification of human beings and disfigurement of relationships.

When Joe and Missy May resume the ceremony of the candy and the coins—this time with the understanding that experience provides—they triumph over much more than the comic villainy of Otis D. Slemmons. They perform an act of resistance against a soul-destroying system of oppression, here symbolized by the G and G Fertilizer works, the enterprise that provides the economic foundation of the story's black settlement. In "The Gilded Six-Bits," as throughout Hurston's writing, the drama, "will to adorn," and the impromptu ceremonies of everyday life affirm the survival of the human spirit.

In addition to the two short stories, this volume contains "Research," an excerpt from Hurston's memoir, *Dust Tracks on a Road,* that describes her fieldwork and her relationship with her patron, Mrs. Charlotte Osgood Mason. The deference Hurston shows Mason exposed her to scathing criticism from some of her black peers. By contrast, the description of her fieldwork in Polk County, Florida, which is among the most evocative in her writing, won wide praise. Of particular interest is the account of her introduction to Big Sweet. The example of Big Sweet would inform the creation of Janie Crawford, a protagonist who, unlike Delia Jones, is able to defend her integrity without jeopardizing her soul.

"Characteristics of Negro Expression" sets forth Hurston's theories of African American speech, music, and dance. Hurston abstracted the theories from her field notes and published them in Nancy Cunard's 1934 anthology, *Negro.* "Characteristics" is also a valuable guide to Hurston's own aesthetic practice; it offers an uncommonly useful framework in which to interpret her fiction.

Forty years after "Characteristics" was published, folklorist Roger Abrahams found in Hurston's writing invaluable sources for his article, "Negotiating Respect: Patterns of Presentation among Black Women." Abrahams is more interested than Hurston in analyzing social roles, as he focuses on black women's interaction with men, children, and each other. While his ideas concerning black matriarchy will strike many as erroneous, his detailed observations of women's speech acts illuminate moments in both "Sweat" and "The Gilded Six-Bits."

A selection of blues and spirituals provides another context for "Sweat." Blind Lemon Jefferson's "Black Snake Moan" exemplifies the sexual symbolism of the snake, while the five spirituals offer variations of the crossing Jordan metaphor. Hurston's biblical knowledge informs just about everything she wrote. Since allusions to the opening chapters of Genesis recur in "Sweat," those chapters are reprinted here from the King James version.

Henry Louis Gates's "Zora Neale Hurston and the Speakerly Text," a section excerpted from a chapter in his influential book *The Signifying Monkey,* surveys the social and literary history that mitigated against the use of black vernacular English by African American writers. "The Gilded Six-Bits," which follows Gates's essay, is a sterling example of what was gained once this linguistic resource could be mined.

Published in 1977, Robert Hemenway's *Zora Neale Hurston: A Literary Biography* reconstructed the fragments of Hurston's life and offered an illuminating critique of her writing. His analysis of "Sweat" is brief but highly suggestive, as the other critiques of the story in this volume confirm.

"The Artist in the Kitchen: The Economics of Creativity in Hurston's 'Sweat'" locates the story in the context of social history. Kathryn Seidel argues that Delia Jones's plight is representative of that of southern black women of the period. She is especially interested in pursuing the ways that economic hardship impinges on artistic expression.

Reading "The Gilded Six-Bits" in tandem with the earlier story, Paul Laurence Dunbar's "The Lynching of Jube Benson," novelist Gayl Jones identifies the technical innovations that allowed Hurston to break out of the conventions of dialect. If Dunbar draws black characters within a frame controlled by a white narrator, Hurston cracks the frame and begins to let her characters tell their own stories.

In an excerpt from his book, *Jump at the Sun: Zora Neale Hurston's Cosmic Comedy,* John Lowe analyzes the humor in both "Sweat" and "The Gilded Six-Bits." His careful attention to language and to textual nuances pays rich dividends. As deftly as he uncovers the humor in "Sweat," he discerns the muted spiritual echoes in "The Gilded Six-Bits."

Mary Helen Washington hones in on the problematic development of the female hero in Hurston's writing. "I Love the Way Janie Left Her Husbands" draws its contrasts between John Pearson, the male protagonist of *Jonah's Gourd Vine,* and Janie Crawford. Even in the representation of Janie, Washington finds, the female hero is not entirely free to speak.

Despite her impressive accomplishments, Hurston died in obscurity in January 1960. Thirteen years later, novelist Alice Walker went "Looking for Zora." The essay which closes this volume constitutes both an incisive critique of and an eloquent tribute to a writer whose pioneering efforts helped lay the foundation for the current renaissance among African American women writers.

□ *Notes* ■

1. "Negro Youth Speaks," in *The New Negro,* ed. Alain Locke (1925; reprint, New York: Atheneum, 1992), 51.

2. Two notable histories of the Harlem Renaissance are Nathan Huggins, *Harlem Renaissance* (New York: Oxford University Press, 1971) and David Levering Lewis, *When Harlem Was in Vogue* (New York: Alfred A. Knopf, 1981).

3. A facsimile edition of *Fire!!* with an introduction by scholar Arnold Rampersad, was printed in 1982. For more on Hurston's involvement, see Robert Hemenway, *Zora Neale Hurston: A Literary Biography* (Urbana: University of Illinois Press, 1977), pp. 43–50.

4. Hurston, *Dust Tracks on a Road* (1942; reprint, New York: HarperCollins, 1991), p. 1.

5. Hurston, *Mules and Men* (1935; reprint, New York: HarperCollins, 1990), p. 1. For biographical information, see Hemenway, *Zora Neale Hurston* and Cheryl A. Wall, *Women of the Harlem Renaissance* (Bloomington: Indiana University Press, 1995), pp. 138–199.

6. *Dust Tracks,* p. 92.

7. The phrase "to change words" recurs in Hurston's writing. Derived from a form of the word "exchange," in which the weakly stressed syllable has been dropped, it denotes the speaker's determination to engage in dialogue.

8. See Abrahams's article, "Negotiating Respect: Patterns of Presentation among Black Women," in this volume.

9. From "Art and Such," an essay written for the Florida Federal Writers' Project in 1938 and reprinted in *Zora Neale Hurston: Folklore, Memoirs & Other Writings* edited by Cheryl A. Wall (New York: Library of America, 1995), p. 910.

10. For more on the history and significance of minstrelsy, see Huggins, *Harlem Renaissance,* chapter 6; Eric Lott, *Love and Theft: Blackface Minstrelsy and the American Working Class* (New York: Oxford University Press, 1993), and Robert C. Toll, *Blacking Up: The Minstrel Show in Nineteenth Century America* (New York: Oxford University Press, 1974).

11. The snake is also a predominant symbol in African spiritual traditions. See Hurston's introduction to *Moses, Man of the Mountain* (1938; reprint, New York: HarperCollins, 1991).

12. The phrase is known to lexicographers. According to the *American Dialect Dictionary* (New York: Thomas Y. Crowell, 1944), egg-sucking denotes mean and base; it is usually used in attribution, especially "suck-egg dog," and less often "suck-egg mule."

13. bell hooks, *Talking Back: Thinking Feminist, Thinking Black* (Boston: South End Press, 1989), p. 9.

14. *Their Eyes Were Watching God* (1937; reprint, New York: HarperCollins, 1990), p. 75.

15. Definitions of love feast are taken from the Oxford English Dictionary and Jonathan Crowther, *Portraiture of Methodism: or, The History of the Wesleyan Methodists* (London, 1815), pp. 282–283.

16. Johnson memorialized the creators of the spirituals in his poem, "O Black and Unknown Bards," which he included in his anthology, *The Book of American Negro Poetry* (1931; reprint, New York: Harcourt, 1969), pp. 123–24. He also edited *The Book of American Negro Spirituals* (1925, 1926; reprint, New York: Viking Press, 1940).

17. "Folklore and Music," from "The Florida Negro," *Zora Neale Hurston: Folklore, Memoirs & Other Writings,* p. 876.

18. Fauset's first novel *There Is Confusion* (1924; reprint, Boston: Northeastern University Press, 1989) explores this tension in detail. Nella Larsen portrayed a marriage in crisis in her 1929 novel, *Passing* (Reprint, New Brunswick, Rutgers University Press, 1986). The bourgeois class position of Fauset's and Larsen's characters stands in sharp contrast to that of the characters in Hurston's stories.

❑ Chronology ■

1891	Born January 7, in Notasulga, Macon County, Alabama, to Lucy Ann (Potts) and John Hurston.
1894–1895	Moves to Eatonville, Florida, an all-black town five miles north of Orlando that she identifies proudly as "the first Negro community in America to be incorporated."
1904	After mother's death, family disperses, and Hurston is sent to school in Jacksonville.
1918	Enters Howard University in September, after years of working as a domestic in various locations.
1924	Publishes "Drenched in Light," a short story, in *Opportunity*, a national magazine sponsored by the Urban League.
1925	Moves to New York City as the Harlem Renaissance takes flight; enters Barnard College where she studies anthropology in the fall.
1926	Collaborates with Gwendolyn Bennett, Langston Hughes, and Wallace Thurman on *Fire!!;* "Sweat" appears in the only issue.
1927	Begins fieldwork in Florida, where she marries Herbert Sheen; marriage is short-lived.
1934	First novel, *Jonah's Gourd Vine,* based loosely on the lives of her parents.
1935	*Mules and Men,* the first volume of African American folklore compiled by a black American.
1936	Awarded a Guggenheim Fellowship to study "Obeah" practices in the West Indies.
1937	Her masterpiece *Their Eyes Were Watching God,* a novel that charts a black woman's journey to selfhood, garners positive reviews with the notable exceptions of Alain Locke and Richard Wright.

1938	*Tell My Horse,* a volume based on fieldwork in Jamaica and Haiti.
1939	*Moses, Man of the Mountain* uses the Old Testament to allegorize the history of black Americans; marries Albert Price; marriage is short-lived.
1942	The memoir *Dust Tracks on a Road* mentions neither marriage and is generally evasive about the facts of Hurston's life.
1942–1948	Becomes a frequent contributor to mainstream magazines such as *American Mercury* and *Saturday Evening Post;* political views grow increasingly conservative.
1948	Publishes *Seraph on the Suwanee,* a novel whose characters are all white; is thoroughly demoralized when she is indicted on a false morals charge.
1949	Indictment is dismissed when Hurston proves that she was out of the country when the alleged crime took place.
1950	Wire service reports "Famous Negro Author Working as a Maid."
1954	Continues working for years on biography of Herod the Great that like much of her writing of the last decade is rejected by publishers; writes widely reprinted letter to the Orlando *Sentinel* condemning the 1954 Supreme Court Brown vs. Topeka decision which ruled segregated schools unconstitutional because she does not believe that black children need to go to school with whites in order to learn.
1960	Dies in a welfare home on January 28, in Fort Pierce, Florida; buried in an unmarked grave in a segregated cemetery.
1973	Author Alice Walker purchases a tombstone that memorializes Hurston as "A Genius of the South."

☐ Sweat

▢ Sweat

It was eleven o'clock of a Spring night in Florida. It was Sunday. Any other night, Delia Jones would have been in bed for two hours by this time. But she was a washwoman, and Monday morning meant a great deal to her. So she collected the soiled clothes on Saturday when she returned the clean things. Sunday night after church, she sorted and put the white things to soak. It saved her almost a half-day's start. A great hamper in the bedroom held the clothes that she brought home. It was so much neater than a number of bundles lying around.

She squatted on the kitchen floor beside the great pile of clothes, sorting them into small heaps according to color, and humming a song in a mournful key, but wondering through it all where Sykes, her husband, had gone with her horse and buckboard.

Just then something long, round, limp and black fell upon her shoulders and slithered to the floor beside her. A great terror took hold of her. It softened her knees and dried her mouth so that it was a full minute before she could cry out or move. Then she saw that it was the big bull whip her husband liked to carry when he drove.

She lifted her eyes to the door and saw him standing there bent over with laughter at her fright. She screamed at him.

From *Zora Neale Hurston: Novels and Stories,* ed. Cheryl Wall (New York: Library of America, 1995).

"Sykes, what you throw dat whip on me like dat? You know it would skeer me—looks just like a snake, an' you knows how skeered Ah is of snakes."

"Course Ah knowed it! That's how come Ah done it." He slapped his leg with his hand and almost rolled on the ground in his mirth. "If you such a big fool dat you got to have a fit over a earth worm or a string, Ah don't keer how bad Ah skeer you."

"You ain't got no business doing it. Gawd knows it's a sin. Some day Ah'm gointuh drop dead from some of yo' foolishness. 'Nother thing, where you been wid mah rig? Ah feeds dat pony. He ain't fuh you to be drivin' wid no bull whip."

"You sho' is one aggravatin' nigger woman!" he declared and stepped into the room. She resumed her work and did not answer him at once. "Ah done tole you time and again to keep them white folks' clothes outa dis house."

He picked up the whip and glared at her. Delia went on with her work. She went out into the yard and returned with a galvanized tub and set it on the wash-bench. She saw that Sykes had kicked all of the clothes together again, and now stood in her way truculently, his whole manner hoping, *praying,* for an argument. But she walked calmly around him and commenced to re-sort the things.

"Next time, Ah'm gointer kick'em outdoors," he threatened as he struck a match along the leg of his cor-duroy breeches.

Delia never looked up from her work, and her thin, stooped shoulders sagged further.

"Ah ain't for no fuss t'night Sykes. Ah just come from taking sacrament at the church house."

He snorted scornfully. "Yeah, you just come from

de church house on a Sunday night, but heah you is gone to work on them clothes. You ain't nothing but a hypocrite. One of them amen-corner Christians—sing, whoop, and shout, then come home and wash white folks' clothes on the Sabbath."

He stepped roughly upon the whitest pile of things, kicking them helter-skelter as he crossed the room. His wife gave a little scream of dismay, and quickly gathered them together again.

"Sykes, you quit grindin' dirt into these clothes! How can Ah git through by Sat'day if Ah don't start on Sunday?"

"Ah don't keer if you never git through. Anyhow, Ah done promised Gawd and a couple of other men, Ah ain't gointer have it in mah house. Don't gimme no lip neither, else Ah'll throw 'em out and put mah fist up side yo' head to boot."

Delia's habitual meekness seemed to slip from her shoulders like a blown scarf. She was on her feet; her poor little body, her bare knuckly hands bravely defying the strapping hulk before her.

"Looka heah, Sykes, you done gone too fur. Ah been married to you fur fifteen years, and Ah been takin' in washin' fur fifteen years. Sweat, sweat, sweat! Work and sweat, cry and sweat, pray and sweat!"

"What's that got to do with me?" he asked brutally.

"What's it got to do with you, Sykes? Mah tub of suds is filled yo' belly with vittles more times than yo' hands is filled it. Mah sweat is done paid for this house and Ah reckon Ah kin keep on sweatin' in it."

She seized the iron skillet from the stove and struck a defensive pose, which act surprised him greatly, coming from her. It cowed him and he did not strike her as he usually did.

"Naw you won't," she panted, "that ole snaggle-toothed black woman you runnin' with ain't comin' heah to pile up on *mah* sweat and blood. You ain't paid for nothin' on this place, and Ah'm gointer stay right heah till Ah'm toted out foot foremost."

"Well, you better quit gittin' me riled up, else they'll be totin' you out sooner than you expect. Ah'm so tired of you Ah don't know whut to do. Gawd! How Ah hates skinny wimmen!"

A little awed by this new Delia, he sidled out of the door and slammed the back gate after him. He did not say where he had gone, but she knew too well. She knew very well that he would not return until nearly daybreak also. Her work over, she went on to bed but not to sleep at once. Things had come to a pretty pass!

She lay awake, gazing upon the debris that cluttered their matrimonial trail. Not an image left standing along the way. Anything like flowers had long ago been drowned in the salty stream that had been pressed from her heart. Her tears, her sweat, her blood. She had brought love to the union and he had brought a longing after the flesh. Two months after the wedding, he had given her the first brutal beating. She had the memory of his numerous trips to Orlando with all of his wages when he had returned to her penniless, even before the first year had passed. She was young and soft then, but now she thought of her knotty, muscled limbs, her harsh knuckly hands, and drew herself up into an unhappy little ball in the middle of the big feather bed. Too late now to hope for love, even if it were not Bertha it would be someone else. This case differed from the others only in that she was bolder than the others. Too late for everything except her little home. She had built it for her old days, and planted one by one the trees and flowers there. It was lovely to her, lovely.

Somehow, before sleep came, she found herself saying aloud: "Oh well, whatever goes over the Devil's back, is got to come under his belly. Sometime or ruther, Sykes, like everybody else, is gointer reap his sowing." After that she was able to build a spiritual earthworks against her husband. His shells could no longer reach her. *Amen*. She went to sleep and slept until he announced his presence in bed by kicking her feet and rudely snatching the covers away.

"Gimme some kivah heah, an' git yo' damn foots over on yo' own side! Ah oughter mash you in yo' mouf fuh drawing dat skillet on me."

Delia went clear to the rail without answering him. A triumphant indifference to all that he was or did.

II

The week was as full of work for Delia as all other weeks, and Saturday found her behind her little pony, collecting and delivering clothes.

It was a hot, hot day near the end of July. The village men on Joe Clarke's porch even chewed cane listlessly. They did not hurl the cane-knots as usual. They let them dribble over the edge of the porch. Even conversation had collapsed under the heat.

"Heah come Delia Jones," Jim Merchant said, as the shaggy pony came 'round the bend of the road toward them. The rusty buckboard was heaped with baskets of crisp, clean laundry.

"Yep," Joe Lindsay agreed. "Hot or col', rain or shine, jes ez reg'lar ez de weeks roll roun' Delia carries 'em an' fetches 'em on Sat'day."

"She better if she wanter eat," said Moss. "Syke Jones ain't wuth de sot an' powder hit would tek tuh kill 'em. Not to *huh* he ain't."

"He sho' ain't," Walter Thomas chimed in. "It's too bad, too, cause she wuz a right pretty li'l trick when he got huh. Ah'd uh mah'ied huh mahseff if he hadnter beat me to it."

Delia nodded briefly at the men as she drove past.

"Too much knockin' will ruin *any* 'oman. He done beat huh 'nough tuh kill three women, let 'lone change they looks," said Elijah Moseley. "How Syke kin stom-muck dat big black greasy Mogul he's layin' roun' wid, gits me. Ah swear dat eight-rock couldn't kiss a sardine can Ah done thowed out de back do' 'way las' yeah."

"Aw, she's fat, thass how come. He's allus been crazy 'bout fat women," put in Merchant. "He'd a' been tied up wid one long time ago if he could a' found one tuh have him. Did Ah tell yuh 'bout him come sidlin' roun' *mah* wife—bringin' her a basket uh pee-cans outa his yard fuh a present? Yessir, mah wife! She tol' him tuh take 'em right straight back home, 'cause Delia works so hard ovah dat washtub she reckon everything on de place taste lak sweat an' soapsuds. Ah jus' wisht Ah'd a' caught 'im 'roun' dere! Ah'd a' made his hips ketch on fiah down dat shell road."

"Ah know he done it, too. Ah sees 'im grinnin' at every 'oman dat passes," Walter Thomas said. "But even so, he useter eat some mighty big hunks uh humble pie tuh git dat li'l 'oman he got. She wuz ez pritty ez a speck-led pup! Dat wuz fifteen years ago. He useter be so ske-ered uh losin' huh, she could make him do some parts of a husband's duty. Dey never wuz de same in de mind."

"There oughter be a law about him," said Lindsay. "He ain't fit tuh carry guts tuh a bear."

Clarke spoke for the first time. "Tain't no law on earth dat kin make a man be decent if it ain't in 'im. There's plenty men dat takes a wife lak dey do a joint uh sugar-cane. It's round, juicy an' sweet when dey gits it. But dey squeeze an' grind, squeeze an' grind an' wring tell dey wring every drop uh pleasure dat's in 'em out. When dey's satisfied dat dey is wrung dry, dey treats 'em jes' lak dey do a cane-chew. Dey throws 'em away. Dey knows whut dey is doin' while dey is at it, an' hates theirselves fuh it but they keeps on hangin' after huh tell she's empty. Den dey hates huh fuh bein' a cane-chew an' in de way."

"We oughter take Syke an' dat stray 'oman uh his'n down in Lake Howell swamp an' lay on de rawhide till they cain't say Lawd a' mussy. He allus wuz uh ovah-bearin niggah, but since dat white 'oman from up north done teached 'im how to run a automobile, he done got too biggety to live—an' we oughter kill 'im," Old Man Anderson advised.

A grunt of approval went around the porch. But the heat was melting their civic virtue and Elijah Moseley began to bait Joe Clarke.

"Come on, Joe, git a melon outa dere an' slice it up for yo' customers. We'se all sufferin' wid de heat. De bear's done got *me!*"

"Thass right, Joe, a watermelon is jes' whut Ah needs tuh cure de eppizudicks," Walter Thomas joined forces with Moseley. "Come on dere, Joe. We all is steady customers an' you ain't set us up in a long time. Ah chooses dat long, bowlegged Floridy favorite."

"A god, an' be dough. You all gimme twenty cents and slice away," Clarke retorted. "Ah needs a col' slice m'self. Heah, everybody chip in. Ah'll lend y'all mah meat knife."

The money was all quickly subscribed and the huge melon brought forth. At that moment, Sykes and Bertha arrived. A determined silence fell on the porch and the melon was put away again.

Merchant snapped down the blade of his jackknife and moved toward the store door.

"Come on in, Joe, an' gimme a slab uh sow belly an' uh pound uh coffee—almost fuhgot 'twas Sat'day. Got to git on home." Most of the men left also.

Just then Delia drove past on her way home, as Sykes was ordering magnificently for Bertha. It pleased him for Delia to see.

"Git whutsoever yo' heart desires, Honey. Wait a minute, Joe. Give huh two bottles uh strawberry soda-water, uh quart uh parched ground-peas, an' a block uh chewin' gum."

With all this they left the store, with Sykes reminding Bertha that this was his town and she could have it if she wanted it.

The men returned soon after they left, and held their watermelon feast.

"Where did Syke Jones git da 'oman from no-how?" Lindsay asked.

"Ovah Apopka. Guess dey musta been cleanin' out de town when she lef'. She don't look lak a thing but a hunk uh liver wid hair on it."

"Well, she sho' kin squall," Dave Carter contributed. "When she gits ready tuh laff, she jes' opens huh mouf an' latches it back tuh de las' notch. No ole granpa alligator down in Lake Bell ain't got nothin' on huh."

III

Bertha had been in town three months now. Sykes was still paying her room-rent at Della Lewis'—the only house in town that would have taken her in. Sykes took her frequently to Winter Park to 'stomps'. He still assured her that he was the swellest man in the state.

"Sho' you kin have dat li'l ole house soon's Ah git dat 'oman outa dere. Everything b'longs tuh me an' you sho' kin have it. Ah sho' 'bominates uh skinny 'oman. Lawdy, you sho' is got one portly shape on you! You kin git *anything* you wants. Dis is *mah* town an' you sho' kin have it."

Delia's work-worn knees crawled over the earth in Gethsemane and up the rocks of Calvary many, many times during these months. She avoided the villagers and meeting places in her efforts to be blind and deaf. But Bertha nullified this to a degree, by coming to Delia's house to call Sykes out to her at the gate.

Delia and Sykes fought all the time now with no peaceful interludes. They slept and ate in silence. Two or three times Delia had attempted a timid friendliness, but she was repulsed each time. It was plain that the breaches must remain agape.

The sun had burned July to August. The heat streamed down like a million hot arrows, smiting all things living upon the earth. Grass withered, leaves browned, snakes went blind in shedding and men and dogs went mad. Dog days!

Delia came home one day and found Sykes there before her. She wondered, but started to go on into the house without speaking, even though he was standing in the kitchen door and she must either stoop under his arm or ask him to move. He made no room for her. She noticed a soap box beside the steps, but paid no particular attention to it, knowing that he must have brought it there. As she was stooping to pass under his outstretched arm, he suddenly pushed her backward, laughingly.

"Look in de box dere Delia, Ah done brung yuh somethin'!"

She nearly fell upon the box in her stumbling, and when she saw what it held, she all but fainted outright.

"Syke! Syke, mah Gawd! You take dat rattlesnake 'way from heah! You *gottuh*. Oh, Jesus, have mussy!"

"Ah ain't got tuh do nuthin' uh de kin'—fact is Ah ain't got tuh do nothin' but die. Tain't no use uh you puttin' on airs makin' out lak you skeered uh dat snake—he's gointer stay right heah tell he die. He wouldn't bite me cause Ah knows how tuh handle 'im. Nohow he wouldn't risk breakin' out his fangs 'gin *yo* skinny laigs."

"Naw, now Syke, don't keep dat thing 'round tryin' tuh skeer me tuh death. You knows Ah'm even feared uh earth worms. Thass de biggest snake Ah evah did see. Kill 'im Syke, please."

"Doan ast me tuh do nothin' fuh yuh. Goin' 'round tryin' tuh be so damn asterperious. Naw, Ah ain't gonna kill it. Ah think uh damn sight mo' uh him dan you! Dat's a nice snake an' anybody doan lak 'im kin jes' hit de grit."

The village soon heard that Sykes had the snake, and came to see and ask questions.

"How de hen-fire did you ketch dat six-foot rattler, Syke?" Thomas asked.

"He's full uh frogs so he cain't hardly move, thass how Ah eased up on 'm. But Ah'm a snake charmer an' knows how tuh handle 'em. Shux, dat ain't nothin'. Ah could ketch one eve'y day if Ah so wanted tuh."

"Whut he needs is a heavy hick'ry club leaned real heavy on his head. Dat's de bes' way tuh charm a rattlesnake."

"Naw, Walt, y'all jes' don't understand dese diamon' backs lak Ah do," said Sykes in a superior tone of voice.

The village agreed with Walter, but the snake stayed on. His box remained by the kitchen door with its screen wire covering. Two or three days later it had digested its meal of frogs and literally came to life. It rattled at every movement in the kitchen or the yard. One day as Delia came down the kitchen steps she saw his chalky-white fangs curved like scimitars hung in the wire meshes. This time she did not run away with averted eyes as usual. She stood for a long time in the doorway in a red fury that grew bloodier for every second that she regarded the creature that was her torment.

That night she broached the subject as soon as Sykes sat down to the table.

"Syke, Ah wants you tuh take dat snake 'way fum heah. You done starved me an' Ah put up widcher, you done beat me an Ah took dat, but you done kilt all mah insides bringin' dat varmint heah."

Sykes poured out a saucer full of coffee and drank it deliberately before he answered her.

"A whole lot Ah keer 'bout how you feels inside uh out. Dat snake ain't goin' no damn wheah till Ah gits ready fuh 'im tuh go. So fur as beatin' is concerned, yuh ain't took near all dat you gointer take ef yuh stay 'round *me*."

Delia pushed back her plate and got up from the table. "Ah hates you, Sykes," she said calmly. "Ah hates you tuh de same degree dat Ah useter love yuh. Ah done took an' took till mah belly is full up tuh mah neck. Dat's de reason Ah got mah letter fum de church an' moved mah membership tuh Woodbridge—so Ah don't haftuh take no sacrament wid yuh! Ah don't wantuh see yuh 'round me atall. Lay 'round wid dat 'oman all yuh wants tuh, but gwan 'way fum me an' mah house. Ah hates yuh lak uh suck-egg dog."

Sykes almost let the huge wad of corn bread and collard greens he was chewing fall out of his mouth in amazement. He had a hard time whipping himself up to the proper fury to try to answer Delia.

"Well, Ah'm glad you does hate me. Ah'm sho' tiahed uh you hangin' ontuh me. Ah don't want yuh. Look at yuh stringey ole neck! Yo' rawbony laigs an' arms is enough tuh cut uh man tuh death. You looks jes' lak de devvul's doll-baby tuh *me*. You cain't hate me no worse dan Ah hates you. Ah been hatin' *you* fuh years."

"Yo' ole black hide don't look lak nothin' tuh me, but uh passle uh wrinkled up rubber, wid yo' big old yeahs flappin' on each side lak uh paih uh buzzard wings. Don't think Ah'm gointuh be run 'way fum mah house neither. Ah'm goin' tuh de white folks 'bout *you,* mah young man, de very nex' time you lay yo' han's on me. Mah cup is done run ovah." Delia said this with no signs of fear and Sykes departed from the house, threatening her, but made not the slightest move to carry out any of them.

That night he did not return at all, and the next day being Sunday, Delia was glad she did not have to quarrel before she hitched up her pony and drove the four miles to Woodbridge.

She stayed to the night service—'love feast'— which was very warm and full of spirit. In the emotional winds her domestic trials were borne far and wide so that she sang as she drove homeward,

> Jurden water, black an' col
> Chills de body, not de soul
> An' Ah wantah cross Jurden in uh calm time.

She came from the barn to the kitchen door and stopped.

"Whut's de mattah, ol' Satan, you ain't kickin' up yo' racket?" She addressed the snake's box. Complete silence. She went on into the house with a new hope in its birth struggles. Perhaps her threat to go to the white folks had frightened Sykes! Perhaps he was sorry! Fifteen years of misery and suppression had brought Delia to the place where she would hope *anything* that looked towards a way over or through her wall of inhibitions.

She felt in the match-safe behind the stove at once for a match. There was only one there.

"Dat niggah wouldn't fetch nothin' heah tuh save his rotten neck, but he kin run thew whut Ah brings quick enough. Now he done toted off nigh on tuh haff uh box uh matches. He done had dat 'oman heah in mah house, too."

Nobody but a woman could tell how she knew this even before she struck the match. But she did and it put her into a new fury.

Presently she brought in the tubs to put the white things to soak. This time she decided she need not bring the hamper out of the bedroom; she would go in there and do the sorting. She picked up the pot-bellied lamp and went in. The room was small and the hamper stood hard by the foot of the white iron bed. She could sit and reach through the bedposts—resting as she worked.

"*Ah wantah cross Jurden in uh calm time.*" She was singing again. The mood of the 'love feast' had returned. She threw back the lid of the basket almost gaily. Then, moved by both horror and terror, she sprang back toward the door. *There lay the snake in the basket!* He moved sluggishly at first, but even as she turned round and round, jumped up and down in an insanity of fear, he began to stir vigorously. She saw him pouring his awful beauty from the basket upon the bed, then she seized the lamp and ran as fast as she could to the kitchen. The wind from the open door blew out the light and the darkness added to her terror. She sped to the darkness of the yard, slamming the door after her before she thought to set down the lamp. She did not feel safe even on the ground, so she climbed up in the hay barn.

There for an hour or more she lay sprawled upon the hay a gibbering wreck.

Finally she grew quiet, and after that same coherent thought. With this stalked through her a cold, bloody rage. Hours of this. A period of introspection, a space of retrospection, then a mixture of both. Out of this an awful calm.

"Well, Ah done de bes' Ah could. If things ain't right, Gawd knows tain't mah fault."

She went to sleep—a twitch sleep—and woke up to a faint gray sky. There was a loud hollow sound below. She peered out. Sykes was at the wood-pile, demolishing a wire-covered box.

He hurried to the kitchen door, but hung outside there some minutes before he entered, and stood some minutes more inside before he closed it after him.

The gray in the sky was spreading. Delia descended without fear now, and crouched beneath the low bedroom window. The drawn shade shut out the dawn, shut in the night. But the thin walls held back no sound.

"Dat ol' scratch is woke up now!" She mused at the tremendous whirr inside, which every woodsman knows, is one of the sound illusions. The rattler is a ventriloquist. His whirr sounds to the right, to the left, straight ahead, behind, close under foot—everywhere but where it is. Woe to him who guesses wrong unless he is prepared to hold up his end of the argument! Sometimes he strikes without rattling at all.

Inside, Sykes heard nothing until he knocked a pot lid off the stove while trying to reach the match-safe in the dark. He had emptied his pockets at Bertha's.

The snake seemed to wake up under the stove and Sykes made a quick leap into the bedroom. In spite of the gin he had had, his head was clearing now.

"Mah Gawd!" he chattered, "ef Ah could on'y strack uh light!"

The rattling ceased for a moment as he stood paralyzed. He waited. It seemed that the snake waited also.

"Oh, fuh de light! Ah thought he'd be too sick"— Sykes was muttering to himself when the whirr began again, closer, right underfoot this time. Long before this, Sykes' ability to think had been flattened down to primitive instinct and he leaped—onto the bed.

Outside Delia heard a cry that might have come from a maddened chimpanzee, a stricken gorilla. All the terror, all the horror, all the rage that man possibly could express, without a recognizable human sound.

A tremendous stir inside there, another series of animal screams, the intermittent whirr of the reptile. The shade torn violently down from the window, letting in the red dawn, a huge brown hand seizing the window stick, great dull blows upon the wooden floor punctuating the gibberish of sound long after the rattle of the snake had abruptly subsided. All this Delia could see and hear from her place beneath the window, and it made her ill. She crept over to the four-o'clocks and stretched herself on the cool earth to recover.

She lay there. "Delia, Delia!" She could hear Sykes calling in a most despairing tone as one who expected no answer. The sun crept on up, and he called. Delia could not move—her legs were gone flabby. She never moved, he called, and the sun kept rising.

"Mah Gawd!" She heard him moan, "Mah Gawd fum Heben!" She heard him stumbling about and got up from her flower-bed. The sun was growing warm. As she approached the door she heard him call out hopefully, "Delia, is dat you Ah heah?"

She saw him on his hands and knees as soon as she reached the door. He crept an inch or two toward her—all that he was able, and she saw his horribly swollen neck and his one open eye shining with hope. A surge of pity took strong to support bore her away from that eye that must, could not, fail to see the tubs. He would see the lamp. Orlando with its doctors was too far. She could scarcely reach the chinaberry tree, where she waited in the growing heat while inside she knew the cold river was creeping up and up to extinguish that eye which must know by now that she knew.

Background to the Story

Research

Research is formalized curiosity. It is poking and prying with a purpose. It is a seeking that he who wishes may know the cosmic secrets of the world and they that dwell therein.

I was extremely proud that Papa Franz felt like sending me on that folklore search. As is well known, Dr. Franz Boas of the Department of Anthropology of Columbia University, is the greatest anthropologist alive, for two reasons. The first is his insatiable hunger for knowledge and then more knowledge; and the second is his genius for pure objectivity. He has no pet wishes to prove. His instructions are to go out and find what is there. He outlines his theory, but if the facts do not agree with it, he would not warp a jot or dot of the findings to save his theory. So knowing all this, I was proud that he trusted me. I went off in a vehicle made out of corona stuff.

My first six months were disappointing. I found out later that it was not because I had no talents for research, but because I did not have the right approach. The glamor of Barnard College was still upon me. I dwelt in marble halls. I knew where the material was all right. But, I went about asking, in carefully accented Barnardese, "Pardon me, but do you know any folk-tales or folk-songs?" The men and women who had whole treasuries of material just seeping through their pores looked at me and shook their heads. No, they had never heard of anything like that around there. Maybe it was over in the next county. Why didn't I try over there? I did, and got the selfsame answer. Oh, I got a few little items. But compared with what I did later, not enough to make a flea a waltzing jacket. Considering the mood of my going south, I went back to New York with my heart beneath my knees and my knees in some lonesome valley.

_____

From *Dust Tracks on a Road: An Autobiography* (1942; reprint ed. New York: HarperCollins, 1991).

I stood before Papa Franz and cried salty tears. He gave me a good going over, but later I found that he was not as disappointed as he let me think. He knew I was green and feeling my oats, and that only bitter disappointment was going to purge me. It did.

What I learned from him then and later, stood me in good stead when Godmother, Mrs. R. Osgood Mason, set aside two hundred dollars a month for a two-year period for me to work.

My relations with Godmother were curious. Laugh if you will, but there was and is a psychic bond between us. She could read my mind, not only when I was in her presence, but thousands of miles away. Both Max Eastman and Richmond Barthe have told me that she could do the same with them. But, the thing that delighted her was the fact that I was her only Godchild who could read her thoughts at a distance. Her old fingers were cramped and she could not write, but in her friend Cornelia Chapin's exact script, a letter would find me in Alabama, or Florida, or in the Bahama Islands and lay me by the heels for what I was *thinking*. "You have broken the law," it would accuse sternly. "You are dissipating your powers in things that have no real meaning," and go on to lacerate me. "Keep silent. Does a child in the womb speak?"

She was just as pagan as I. She had lived for years among the Plains Indians and had collected a beautiful book of Indian lore. Often when she wished to impress upon me my garrulity, she would take this book from the shelf and read me something of Indian beauty and restraint. Sometimes, I would feel like a rabbit at a dog convention. She would invite me to dinner at her apartment, 399 Park Avenue, and then she, Cornelia Chapin, and Miss Chapin's sister, Mrs. Katherine Garrison Biddle would all hem me up and give me what for. When they had given me a proper straightening, and they felt that I saw the light, all the sternness would vanish, and I would be wrapped in love. A present of money from Godmother, a coat from Miss Chapin, a dress from Mrs. Biddle. We had a great deal to talk about because Cornelia Chapin was a sculptor, Katherine Biddle, a poet, and Godmother, an earnest patron of the arts.

Then, too, she was Godmother to Miguel Covarrubias and Langston Hughes. Sometimes all of us were there. She has

44

several paintings by Covarrubias on her walls. She summoned us when one or the other of us returned from our labors. Miguel and I would exhibit our movies, and Godmother and the Chapin family, including brother Paul Chapin, would praise us and pan us, according as we had done. Godmother could be as tender as mother-love when she felt that you had been right spiritually. But anything in you, however clever, that felt like insincerity to her, called forth her well-known "That is nothing! It has no soul in it. You have broken the law!" Her tongue was a knout, cutting off your outer pretenses, and bleeding your vanity like a rusty nail. She was merciless to a lie, spoken, acted or insinuated.

She was extremely human. There she was sitting up there at the table over capon, caviar and gleaming silver, eager to hear every word on every phase of life on a saw-mill "job." I must tell the tales, sing the songs, do the dances, and repeat the raucous sayings and doings of the Negro farthest down. She is altogether in sympathy with them, because she says truthfully they are utterly sincere in living.

My search for knowledge of things took me into many strange places and adventures. My life was in danger several times. If I had not learned how to take care of myself in these circumstances, I could have been maimed or killed on most any day of the several years of my research work. Primitive minds are quick to sunshine and quick to anger. Some little word, look or gesture can move them either to love or to sticking a knife between your ribs. You just have to sense the delicate balance and maintain it.

In some instances, there is nothing personal in the killing. The killer wishes to establish a reputation as a killer, and you'll do as a sample. Some of them go around, making their announcements in singing:

> I'm going to make me a graveyard of my own,
> I'm going to make me a graveyard of my own,
> Oh, carried me down on de smoky road,
> Brought me back on de coolin' board,
> But I'm going to make me a graveyard of my own.

And since the law is lax on these big saw-mill, turpentine and railroad "jobs," there is a good chance that they never will be jailed for it. All of these places have plenty of men and women who are fugitives from justice. The management asks no questions. They need help and they can't be bothered looking for a bug under every chip. In some places, the "law" is forbidden to come on the premises to hunt for malefactors who did their malefacting elsewhere. The wheels of industry must move, and if these men don't do the work, who is there to do it?

So if a man, or a woman, has been on the gang for petty-thieving and mere mayhem, and is green with jealousy of the others who did the same amount of time for a killing and had something to brag about, why not look around for an easy victim and become a hero, too? I was nominated like that once in Polk County, Florida, and the only reason that I was not elected, was because a friend got in there and staved off old club-footed Death.

Polk County! Ah!
Where the water tastes like cherry wine,
Where they fell great trees with axe and muscle.

These poets of the swinging blade! The brief, but infinitely graceful, dance of body and axe-head as it lifts over the head in a fluid arc, dances in air and rushes down to bite into the tree, all in beauty. Where the logs march into the mill with its smokestacks disputing with the elements, its boiler room reddening the sky, and its great circular saw screaming arrogantly as it attacks the tree like a lion making its kill. The log on the carriage coming to the saw. A growling grumble. Then contact! Yeelld-u-u-ow! And a board is laid shining and new on a pile. All day, all night. Rumble, thunder and grumble. Yee-ee-ow! Sweating black bodies, muscled like gods, working to feed the hunger of the great tooth. Polk County!

Polk County. Black men laughing and singing. They go down in the phosphate mines and bring up the wet dust of the bones of pre-historic monsters, to make rich land in far places, so that people can eat. But, all of it is not dust. Huge ribs, twenty feet from belly to backbone. Some old-time sea monster caught in the shallows in that morning when God said, "Let's make some more dry land. Stay there, great Leviathan! Stay there as a memory and a monument to Time." Shark-teeth as wide as the hand of a working man. Joints of backbone three feet high, bearing witness to the mighty monster of the deep when the Painted Land rose up and did her first dance with the morning sun. Gazing on these relics, forty thousand years old and more, one visualizes the great surrender to chance and change when these creatures were rocked to sleep and slumber by the birth of land.

Polk County. Black men from tree to tree among the lordly pines, a swift, slanting stroke to bleed the trees for gum. Paint, explosives, marine stores, flavors, perfumes, tone for a violin bow, and many other things which the black men who bleed the trees never heard about.

Polk County. The clang of nine-pound hammers on railroad steel. The world must ride.

Hah! A rhythmic swing of the body, hammer falls, and another spike driven to the head in the tie.

> Oh, Mobile! Hank!
> Oh, Alabama! Hank!
> Oh, Fort Myers! Hank!
> Oh, in Florida! Hank!
> Oh, let's shake it! Hank!
> Oh, let's break it! Hank!
> Oh, let's shake it! Hank!
> Oh, just a hair! Hank!

The singing-liner cuts short his chant. The straw-boss relaxes with a gesture of his hand. Another rail spiked down. Another offering to the soul of civilization whose other name is travel.

Polk County. Black men scrambling up ladders into orange trees. Singing, laughing, cursing, boasting of last night's love, and looking forward to the darkness again. They do not say embrace when they mean that they slept with a woman. A behind is a behind and not a form. Nobody says anything about incompatibility when they mean it does not suit. No bones are made about being fed up.

I got up this morning, and I knowed I didn't want it,
Yea! Polk County!
You don't know Polk County like I do
Anybody been there, tell you the same thing, too.
Eh, rider, rider!
Polk County, where the water tastes like cherry wine.

Polk County. After dark, the jooks. Songs are born out of feelings with an old beat-up piano, or a guitar for a mid-wife. Love made and unmade. Who put out dat lie, it was supposed to last forever? Love is when it is. No more here? Plenty more down the road. Take you where I'm going, woman? Hell no! Let every town furnish its own. Yeah, I'm going. Who care anything about no train fare? The railroad track is there, ain't it? I can count tires just like I been doing. I can ride de blind, can't I?

Got on de train didn't have no fare
But I rode some
Yes I rode some
Got on de train didn't have no fare
Conductor ast me what I'm doing there
But I rode some.
Yes I rode some.
Well, he grabbed me by de collar and he led me to de door
But I rode some
Yes I rode some.
Well, he grabbed me by de collar and he led me to de door
He rapped me over de head with a forty-four
But I rode some
Yes I rode some.

Polk County in the jooks. Dancing the square dance. Dancing the scronch. Dancing the belly-rub. Knocking the right hat off the wrong head, and backing it up with a switch-blade.
"Fan-foot, what you doing with my man's hat cocked on *your* nappy head? I know you want to see your Jesus. Who's a whore? Yeah I sleeps with my mens, but they pays me. I wouldn't be a fan-foot like you—just on de road somewhere.

48

Runs up and down de road from job to job making pay-days. Don't nobody hold her! Let her jump on me! She pay her way on me, and I'll pay it off. Make time in old Bartow jail for her."

Maybe somebody stops the fight before the two switch-blades go together. Maybe nobody can. A short, swift dash in. A lucky jab by one opponent and the other one is dead. Maybe one gets a chill in the feet and leaps out of the door. Maybe both get cut badly and back off. Anyhow, the fun of the place goes on. More dancing and singing and buying of drinks, parched peanuts, fried rabbit. Full drummy bass from the piano with weepy, intricate right-hand stuff. Singing the memories of Ella Wall, the Queen of love in the jooks of Polk County. Ella Wall, Planchita, Trottin' Liza.

It is a sad, parting song. Each verse ends up with:

Quarters Boss! High Sheriff? Lemme git gone from here!
Cold, rainy day, some old cold, rainy day
I'll be back, some old cold, rainy day.
Oh de rocks may be my pillow, Lawd!
De sand may be my bed
I'll be back some old cold, rainy day.

"Who run? What you running from the man for, nigger? Me, I don't aim to run a step. I ain't going to run unless they run me. I'm going to live anyhow until I die. Play me some music so I can dance! Aw, spank dat box, man!! Them white folks don't care nothing bout no nigger getting cut and kilt, nohow. They ain't coming in here. I done kilt me four and they ain't hung me yet. Beat dat box!"

"Yeah, but you ain't kilt no women, yet. They's mighty particular 'bout you killing up women."

"And I ain't killing none neither. I ain't crazy in de head. Nigger woman can kill all us men she wants to and they don't care. Leave us kill a woman and they'll run you just as long as you can find something to step on. I got good sense. I know I ain't got no show. De white mens and de nigger women is running this thing. Sing about old Georgy Buck and let's dance off of it. Hit dat box!"

Old Georgy Buck is dead
Last word he said
I don't want no shortening in my bread.
Rabbit on de log
Ain't got no dog
Shoot him wid my rifle, bam! bam!

And the night, the pay night rocks on with music and gambling and laughter and dancing and fights. The big pile of cross-ties burning out in front simmers down to low ashes before sun-up, so then it is time to throw up all the likker you can't keep down and go somewhere and sleep the rest off, whether your knife has blood on it or not. That is, unless some strange, low member of your own race has gone and pimped to the white folks about something getting hurt. Very few of those kind are to be found.

That is the primeval flavor of the place, and as I said before, out of this primitive approach to things, I all but lost my life.

It was in a saw-mill jook in Polk County that I almost got cut to death.

Lucy really wanted to kill me. I didn't mean any harm. All I was doing was collecting songs from Slim, who used to be her man back up in West Florida before he ran off from her. It is true that she found out where he was after nearly a year, and followed him to Polk County and he paid her some slight attention. He was knocking the pad with women, all around, and he seemed to want to sort of free-lance at it. But what he seemed to care most about was picking his guitar, and singing.

He was a valuable source of material to me, so I built him up a bit by buying him drinks and letting him ride in my car.

I figure that Lucy took a pick at me for three reasons. The first one was, her vanity was rubbed sore at not being able to hold her man. That was hard to own up to in a community where so much stress was laid on suiting. Nobody else had offered to shack up with her either. She was getting a very limited retail trade and Slim was ignoring the whole business. I had store-bought clothes, a lighter skin, and a shiny car, so she saw wherein she could use me for an alibi. So in spite of public knowledge of the situation for a year or more before I came, she was telling it around that I came and broke them up. She was going to cut everything off of me but "quit it."

Her second reason was, because of my research methods I had dug in with the male community. Most of the women liked me, too. Especially her sworn enemy, Big Sweet. She was scared of Big Sweet, but she probably reasoned that if she cut Big Sweet's protégée it would be a slam on Big Sweet and build up her own reputation. She was fighting Big Sweet through me.

Her third reason was, she had been in little scraps and been to jail off and on, but she could not swear that she had ever killed anybody. She was small potatoes and nobody was paying her any mind. I was easy. I had no gun, knife or any sort of weapon. I did not even know how to do that kind of fighting.

Lucky for me, I had friended with Big Sweet. She came to my notice within the first week that I arrived on location. I heard somebody, a woman's voice "specifying" up this line of houses from where I lived and asked who it was.

"Dat's Big Sweet" my landlady told me. "She got her foot up on somebody. Ain't she specifying?"

She was really giving the particulars. She was giving a "reading," a word borrowed from the fortune-tellers. She was giving her opponent lurid data and bringing him up to date on his ancestry, his looks, smell, gait, clothes, and his route through Hell in the hereafter. My landlady went outside where nearly everybody else of the four or five hundred people on the "job" were to listen to the reading. Big Sweet broke the news to him, in one of her mildest bulletins that his pa was a double-humpted camel and his ma was a grass-gut cow, but even so, he tore her wide open in the act of getting born, and so on and so forth. He was a bitch's baby out of a buzzard egg.

My landlady explained to me what was meant by "putting your foot up" on a person. If you are sufficiently armed—enough to stand off a panzer division—and know what to do with your weapons after you get 'em, it is all right to go to the house of your enemy, put one foot up on his steps, rest one elbow on your knee and play in the family. That is another way of saying play the dozens, which also is a way of saying low-rate your enemy's ancestors and him, down to the present moment for reference, and then go into his future as far as your imagination leads you. But if you have no faith in your personal courage and confidence in your arsenal, don't try it. It is a risky pleasure. So then I had a measure of this Big Sweet.

"Hurt who?" Mrs. Bertha snorted at my fears. "Big Sweet? Humph! Tain't a man, woman nor child on this job going to tackle Big Sweet. If God send her a pistol she'll send him a man. She can handle a knife with anybody. She'll join hands and cut a duel. Dat Cracker Quarters Boss wears two pistols round his waist and goes for bad, but he won't break a breath with Big Sweet lessen he got his pistol in his hand. Cause if he start anything with her, he won't never get a chance to draw it. She ain't mean. She don't bother nobody. She just don't stand for no foolishness, dat's all."

Right away, I decided that Big Sweet was going to be my friend. From what I had seen and heard in the short time I had been there, I felt as timid as an egg without a shell. So the next afternoon when she was pointed out to me, I waited until she was well up the sawdust road to the Commissary, then I got in my car and went that way as if by accident. When I pulled up beside her and offered her a ride, she frowned at me first, then looked puzzled, but finally broke into a smile and got in.

By the time we got to the Commissary post office we were getting along fine. She told everybody I was her friend. We did not go back to the Quarters at once. She carried me around to several places and showed me off. We made a date to go down to Lakeland come Saturday, which we did. By the time we sighted the Quarters on the way back from Lakeland, she had told me, "You sho is crazy!" Which is a way of saying I was witty. "I loves to friend with somebody like you. I aims to look out for you, too. Do your fighting for you. Nobody better not start nothing with you, do I'll get my switch-blade and go round de hambone looking for meat."

We shook hands and I gave her one of my bracelets. After that everything went well for me. Big Sweet helped me to collect material in a big way. She had no idea what I wanted with it, but if I wanted it, she meant to see to it that I got it. She pointed out people who knew songs and stories. She wouldn't stand for balkiness on their part. We held two lying contests, story-telling contests to you, and Big Sweet passed on who rated the prizes. In that way, there was no argument about it.

So when the word came to Big Sweet that Lucy was threatening me, she put her foot up on Lucy in a most particular manner and warned her against the try. I suggested buying a knife for defense, but she said I would certainly be killed that way.

"You don't know how to handle no knife. You ain't got dat kind of a sense. You wouldn't even know how to hold it to de best advantage. You would draw your arm way back to stop her, and whilst you was doing all dat, Lucy would run in under your arm and be done; cut you to death before you could touch her. And then again, when you sure 'nough fighting, it ain't enough to just stick 'em wid your knife. You got to ram it in to de hilt, then you pull *down*. They ain't no more trouble after dat. They's *dead*. But don't you bother 'bout no fighting. You ain't like me. You don't even sleep with no mens. I wanted to be a virgin one time, but I couldn't keep it up. I needed the money too bad. But I think it's nice for you to be like that. You just keep on writing down them lies. I'll take care of all de fighting. Dat'll make it more better, since we done made friends."

She warned me that Lucy might try to "steal" me. That is, ambush me, or otherwise attack me without warning. So I was careful. I went nowhere on foot without Big Sweet.

Several weeks went by, then I ventured to the jook alone. Big Sweet let it be known that she was not going. But later she came in and went over to the cooncan game in the corner. Thinking I was alone, Lucy waited until things were in full swing and then came in with the very man to whom Big Sweet had given the "reading." There was only one door. I was far from it. I saw no escape for me when Lucy strode in, knife in hand. I saw sudden death very near that moment. I was paralyzed with fear. Big Sweet was in a crowd over in the corner, and did not see Lucy come in. But the sudden quiet of the place made her look around as Lucy charged. My friend was large and portly, but extremely light on her feet. She sprang like a lioness and I think the very surprise of Big Sweet being there when Lucy thought she was over at another party at the Pine Mill unnerved Lucy. She stopped abruptly as Big Sweet charged. The next moment, it was too late for Lucy to start again. The man who came in with Lucy tried to help her out, but two other men joined Big Sweet in the battle. It took on amazingly. It seemed that anybody who had any fighting to do, decided to settle-up then and there. Switch-blades, ice-picks and old-fashioned razors were out. One or two razors had already been bent back and thrown across the room, but our fight was the main attraction. Bit Sweet yelled to me to run. I really ran, too. I ran out of the place, ran to my room, threw my things in the car and left the place. When the sun came up I was a hundred miles up the road, headed for New Orleans.

Characteristics of Negro Expression

Drama

The Negro's universal mimicry is not so much a thing in itself as an evidence of something that permeates his entire self. And that thing is drama.

His very words are action words. His interpretation of the English language is in terms of pictures. One act described in terms of another. Hence the rich metaphor and simile.

The metaphor is of course very primitive. It is easier to illustrate than it is to explain because action came before speech. Let us make a parallel. Language is like money. In primitive communities actual goods, however bulky, are bartered for what one wants. This finally evolves into coin, the coin being not real wealth but a symbol of wealth. Still later, even coin is abandoned for legal tender, and still later cheques for certain usages.

Every phase of Negro life is highly dramatized. No matter how joyful or how sad the case there is sufficient poise for drama. Everything is acted out. Unconsciously for the most part of course. There is an impromptu ceremony always ready for every hour of life. No little moment passes unadorned.

Now the people with highly developed languages have words for detached ideas. That is legal tender. "That-which-we-squat-on" has become "chair." "Groan-causer" has evolved into "spear" and so on. Some individuals even conceive of the equivalent of cheque words, like "ideation" and "pleonastic." Perhaps we might say that *Paradise Lost* and *Sartor Resartus* are written in cheque words.

From *Negro: An Anthology,* ed. Nancy Cunard (London: Wishart, 1934).

The primitive man exchanges descriptive words. His terms are all close fitting. Frequently the Negro, even with detached words in his vocabulary—not evolved in him but transplanted on his tongue by contact—must add action to it to make it do. So we have "chop-axe," "sitting-chair," "cook-pot" and the like because the speaker has in his mind the picture of the object in use. Action. Everything illustrated. So we can say the white man thinks in a written language and the Negro thinks in hieroglyphics.

A bit of Negro drama familiar to all is the frequent meeting of two opponents who threaten to do atrocious murder one upon the other.

Who has not observed a robust young Negro chap posing upon a street corner, possessed of nothing but his clothing, his strength, and his youth? Does he bear himself like a pauper? No, Louis XIV could be no more insolent in his assurance. His eyes say plainly "Female, halt!" His posture exults "Ah, female, I am the eternal male, the giver of life. Behold in my hot flesh all the delights of this world. Salute me, I am strength." All this with a languid posture, there is no mistaking his meaning.

A Negro girl strolls past the corner lounger. Her whole body panging* and posing. A slight shoulder movement that calls attention to her bust, that is all of a dare. A hippy undulation below the waist that is a sheaf of promises tied with conscious power. She is acting out "I'm a darned sweet woman and you know it."

These little plays by strolling players are acted out daily in a dozen streets in a thousand cities, and no one ever mistakes the meaning.

Will to Adorn

The will to adorn is the second most notable characteristic in Negro expression. Perhaps his ideas of ornament does not attempt to meet conventional standards, but it satisfies the soul of its creator.

---

* From "pang."

In this respect the American Negro has done wonders to the English language. This is true, but it is equally true that he has made over a great part of the tongue to his liking and has his revision accepted by the ruling class. No one listening to a Southern white man talk could deny this. Not only has he softened and toned down strongly consonanted words like "aren't" to "ain't" and the like, he has made new force words out of old feeble elements. Examples, of this are "ham-shanked," "battle-hammed," "double-teen," "bodaciously," "muffle-jawed."

But the Negro's greatest contribution to the language is: (1) the use of metaphor and simile; (2) the use of the double descriptive; (3) the use of verbal nouns.

1.   Metaphor and Simile

One at a time, like lawyers going
to heaven.
You sho is propaganda.
Sobbing hearted.
I'll beat you till: (a) rope like okra,
(b) slack like lime, (c) smell like
onions.
Fatal for naked.
Kyting along.
That's a rope.
Cloakers—deceivers.
Regular as pig-tracks.
Mule blood—black molasses.
Syndicating—gossiping.
Flambeaux—cheap cafe (lighted by flambeaux).
To put yo'self on de ladder.

2.   The Double Descriptive

High-tall.
Little-tee-ninchy (tiny).
Low-down.
Top-superior.
Sham-polish.
Lady-people.

Kill-dead.
Hot-boiling.
Chop-axe.
Sitting-chairs.
De watch wall.
Speedy-hurry.
More great and more better.

3. Verbal Nouns

She features somebody I know.
Funeralize.
Sense me into it.
Puts the shamery on him.
'Taint everybody you kin confidence.
I wouldn't friend with her.
Jooking—playing piano or guitar as
it is done in Jook-houses (houses of
ill-fame).
Uglying away.
I wouldn't scorn my name all up on you.
Bookooing (beaucoup) around—showing off.
Won't stand a broke.
She won't take a listen.
He won't stand straightening.
That is such a compliment.
That's a lynch.

The stark, trimmed phrases of the Occident seem too bare for the voluptuous child of the sun, hence the adornment. It arises out of the same impulse as the wearing of jewelry and the making of sculpture—the urge to adorn.

On the walls of the homes of the average Negro one always finds a glut of gaudy calendars, wall pockets and advertising lithographs. The sophisticated white man or Negro would tolerate none of these, even if they bore a likeness to the Mona Lisa. No commercial art for decoration. Neither the calendar nor the advertisement spoils the picture for this lowly man. He sees the beauty in spite of the declaration of the Portland Cement Works or the butcher's announcement. I saw in Mobile a room in which there was an over-stuffed mohair living-room suite, an imitation mahogany bed and chifferobe, a console victrola. The walls were gaily papered with Sunday supplements of the *Mobile Register*. There were seven calendars and three wall pockets. One of them was decorated with a lace doily. The mantel-shelf was covered with a scarf of deep home-made lace, looped up with a huge bow of pink crepe paper. Over the door was a huge lithograph showing the Treaty of Versailles being signed with a Waterman fountain pen.

It was grotesque, yes. But it indicated a desire for beauty. And decorating a decoration, as in the case of the doily on the gaudy wall pocket, did not seem out of place to the hostess. The feeling back of such an act is that there can never be enough of beauty, let alone too much. Perhaps she is right. We each have our standards of art, and thus we are all interested parties and so unfit to pass judgment upon the art concepts of others.

Whatever the Negro does of his own volition he embellishes. His religious service is for the greater part excellent prose poetry. Both prayers and sermons are tooled and polished until they are true works of art. The supplication is forgotten in the frenzy of creation. The prayer of the white man is considered humorous in its bleakness. The beauty of the Old Testament does not exceed that of a Negro prayer.

Angularity

After adornment the next most striking manifestation of the Negro is Angularity. Everything that he touches becomes angular. In all African sculpture and doctrine of any sort we find the same thing.

Anyone watching Negro dancers will be struck by the same phenomenon. Every posture is another angle. Pleasing, yes. But an effect achieved by the very means which a European strives to avoid.

The pictures on the walls are hung at deep angles. Furniture is always set at an angle. I have instances of a piece of furniture in the *middle* of a wall being set with one end nearer the wall than the other to avoid the simple straight line.

Asymmetry

Asymmetry is a definite feature of Negro art. I have no samples of true Negro painting unless we count the African shields, but the sculpture and carvings are full of this beauty and lack of symmetry. It is present in the literature, both prose and verse. I offer an example of this quality in verse from Langston Hughes:

I ain't gonna mistreat ma good gal any more,
I'm just gonna kill her next time she makes me sore.

I treats her kind but she don't do me right,
She fights and quarrels most every night.

I can't have no woman's got such low-down ways
Cause de blue gum woman ain't de style now'days.

I brought her from the South and she's goin on back,
Else I'll use her head for a carpet tack.

It is the lack of symmetry which makes Negro dancing so difficult for white dancers to learn. The abrupt and unexpected changes. The frequent change of key and time are evidences of this quality in music (Note the St. Louis Blues).

The dancing of the justly famous Bo-Jangles and Snake Hips are excellent examples.

The presence of rhythm and lack of symmetry are paradoxical, but there they are. Both are present to a marked degree. There is always rhythm, but it is the rhythm of segments. Each unit has a rhythm of its own, but when the whole is assembled it is lacking in symmetry. But easily workable to a Negro who is accustomed to the break in going from one part to another, so that he adjusts himself to the new tempo.

Dancing

Negro dancing is dynamic suggestion. No matter how violent it may appear to the beholder, every posture gives the impression that the dancer will do much more. For example, the performer flexes one knee sharply, assumes a ferocious face mask, thrusts the upper part of the body forward with clenched fists, elbows taut as in hard running or grasping a thrusting blade. That is all. But the spectator himself adds the picture of ferocious assault, hears the drums and finds himself keeping time with the music and tensing himself for the struggle. It is compelling insinuation. That is the very reason the spectator is held so rapt. He is participating in the performance himself—carrying out the suggestions of the performer.

The difference in the two arts is: the white dancer attempts to express fully; the Negro is restrained, but succeeds in gripping the beholder by forcing him to finish the action the performer suggests. Since no art can ever express all the variations conceivable, the Negro must be considered the greater artist, his dancing is realistic suggestion, and that is about all a great artist can do.

Negro Folklore

Negro folklore is not a thing of the past. It is still in the making. Its great variety shows the adaptability of the black man: nothing is too old or too new, domestic or foreign, high or low, for his use. God and the Devil are paired, and are treated no more reverently than Rockefeller and Ford. Both of these men are prominent in folklore. Ford being particularly strong, and they talk and act like good-natured stevedores or mill-hands. Ole Massa is sometimes a smart man and often a fool. The automobile is ranged alongside of the oxcart. The angels and the apostles walk and talk like section hands. And through it all walks Jack, the greatest culture hero of the South; Jack beats them all—even the Devil, who is often smarter than God.

CULTURE HEROES

The Devil is next after Jack as a culture hero. He can outsmart everyone but Jack. God is absolutely no match for him. He is good-natured and full of humour. The sort of person one may count on to help out in any difficulty.

Peter the Apostle is third in importance. One need not look far for the explanation. The Negro is not a Christian really. The primitive gods are not deities of too subtle inner reflection; they are hard-working bodies who serve their devotees just as laboriously as the suppliant serves them. Gods of physical violence, stopping at nothing to serve their followers. Now of all the apostles, Peter is the most active. When the other ten fell back trembling in the garden, Peter wielded the blade on the posse. Peter first and foremost in all action. The gods of no peoples have been philosophic until the people themselves have approached that state.

The rabbit, the bear, the lion, the buzzard, the fox are culture heroes from the animal world. The rabbit is far in the lead of all the others and is blood brother to Jack. In short, the trickster-hero of West Africa has been transplanted to America.

John Henry is a culture hero in song, but no more so than Stacker Lee, Smokey Joe or Bad Lazarus. There are many, many Negroes who have never heard of any of the song heroes, but none who do not know John (Jack) and the rabbit.

EXAMPLES OF FOLKLORE AND THE MODERN CULTURE HERO

Why de Porpoise's Tail is on Crosswise

Now, I want to tell you 'bout de porpoise. God had done made de world and everything. He set de moon and de stars in the sky. He got de fishes of de sea, and de fowls of de air completed. He made de sun and hung it up. Then He made a nice gold track for it to run on. Then He said, "Now, Sun, I got everything made but Time. That's up to you. I want you to start out and go round de world on dis track just as fast as you kin make it. And de time it takes you to go and come, I'm going to call day and night." De Sun went zoomin' on cross de elements. Now, de porpoise was hanging round there and heard God what he told de Sun, so he decided he'd take dat trip round de world hisself. He looked up and saw de Sun kytin' along, so he lit out too, him and dat Sun!

So de porpoise beat de Sun round de world by one hour and three minutes. So God said, "Aw naw, this aint gointer do! I didn't mean for nothin' to be faster than de Sun!" So God run dat porpoise for three days before he runs him down and caught him, and took his tail off and put it crossways to slow him up. Still he's de fastest thing in de water. And dat's why de porpoise got his tail on crossways.

62

Rockefeller and Ford

Once John D. Rockefeller and Henry Ford was woofing at each other. Rockefeller told Henry Ford he could build a solid gold road round the world. Henry Ford told him if he would he would look at it and see if he liked it, and if he did he would buy it and put one of his tin lizzies on it.

Originality

It has been said so often that the Negro is lacking in originality that it has almost become a gospel. Outward signs seem to bear this out. But if one looks closely its falsity is immediately evident.

It is obvious that to get back to original sources is much too difficult for any group to claim very much as a certainty. What we really mean by originality is the modification of ideas. The most ardent admirer of the great Shakespeare cannot claim first source even for him. It is his treatment of the borrowed material.

So if we look at it squarely, the Negro is a very original being. While he lives and moves in the midst of a white civilization, everything that he touches is re-interpreted for his own use. He has modified the language, mode of food preparation, practice of medicine, and most certainly the religion of his new country, just as hc adapted to suit himself the Sheik haircut made famous by Rudolph Valentino.

Everyone is familiar with the Negro's modification of the whites' musical instruments, so that his interpretation has been adopted by the white man himself and then re-interpreted. In so many words, Paul Whiteman is giving an imitation of a Negro orchestra making use of white-invented musical instruments in a Negro way. Thus has arisen a new art in the civilized world, and thus has our so-called civilization come. The exchange and re-exchange of ideas between groups.

Imitation

The Negro, the world over, is famous as a mimic. But this in no way damages his standing as an original. Mimicry is an art in itself. If it is not, then all art must fall by the same blow that strikes it down. When sculpture, painting, dancing, literature neither reflect nor suggest anything in nature or human experience we turn away with a dull wonder in our hearts at why the thing was done. Moreover, the contention that the Negro imitates from a feeling of inferiority is incorrect. He mimics for the love of it. The group of Negroes who slavishly imitate is small. The average Negro glories in his ways. The highly educated Negro the same. The self-despisement lies in a middle class who scorns to do or be anything Negro. "That's just like a Nigger" is the most terrible rebuke one can lay upon this kind. He wears drab clothing, sits through a boresome church service, pretends to have no interest in the community, holds beauty contests, and otherwise apes all the mediocrities of the white brother. The truly cultured Negro scorns him, and the Negro "farthest down" is too busy "spreading his junk" in his own way to see or care. He likes his own things best. Even the group who are not Negroes but belong to the "sixth race," buy such records as "Shake dat thing" and "Tight lak dat." They really enjoy hearing a good bible-beater preach, but wild horses could drag no such admission from them. Their ready-made expression is: "We done got away from all that now." Some refuse to countenance Negro music on the grounds that it is niggerism, and for that reason should be done away with. Roland Hayes was thoroughly denounced for singing spirituals until he was accepted by white audiences. Langston Hughes is not considered a poet by this group because he writes of the man in the ditch, who is more numerous and real among us than any other.

But, this group aside, let us say that the art of mimicry is better developed in the Negro than in other racial groups. He does it as the mocking-bird does it, for the love of it, and not because he wishes to be like the one imitated. I saw a group of small Negro boys imitating a cat defecating and the subsequent toilet of the cat. It was very realistic, and they enjoyed it as much as if they had been imitating a coronation ceremony. The dances are full of imitations of various animals. The buzzard lope, walking the dog, the pig's hind legs, holding the mule, elephant squat, pigeon's wing, falling off the log, seabord (imitation of an engine starting), and the like.

64

Absence of the Concept of Privacy

It is said that Negroes keep nothing secret, that they have no reserve. This ought not to seem strange when one considers that we are an outdoor people accustomed to communal life. Add this to all-permeating drama and you have the explanation.

There is no privacy in an African village. Loves, fights, possessions are, to misquote Woodrow Wilson, "Open disagreements openly arrived at." The community is given the benefit of a good fight as well as a good wedding. An audience is a necessary part of any drama. We merely go with nature rather than against it.

Discord is more natural than accord. If we accept the doctrine of the survival of the fittest there are more fighting honors than there are honors for other achievements. Humanity places premiums on all things necessary to its well-being, and a valiant and good fighter is valuable in any community. So why hide the light under a bushel? Moreover, intimidation is a recognized part of warfare the world over, and threats certainly must be listed under that head. So that a great threatener must certainly be considered an aid to the fighting machine. So then if a man or woman is a facile hurler of threats, why should he or she not show their wares to the community? Hence, the holding of all quarrels and fights in the open. One relieves one's pent-up anger and at the same time earns laurels in intimidation. Besides, one does the community a service. There is nothing so exhilarating as watching well-matched opponents go into action. The entire world likes action, for that matter. Hence prize-fighters become millionaires.

Likewise love-making is a biological necessity the world over and an art among Negroes. So that a man or woman who is proficient sees no reason why the fact should be moot. He swaggers. She struts hippily about. Songs are built on the power to charm beneath the bed-clothes. Here again we have individuals striving to excel in what the community considers an art. Then if all of his world is seeking a great lover, why should he not speak right out loud?

It is all in a view-point. Love-making and fighting in all their branches are high arts, other things are arts among groups where they brag about their proficiency just as brazenly as we do about these things that others consider matters for conversation behind closed doors. At any rate, the white man is despised by Negroes as a very poor fighter individually, and a very poor lover. One Negro, speaking of white men, said, "White folks is alright when dey gits in de bank and on de law bench, but dey sho' kin lie about wimmen folks."

I pressed him to explain. "Well you see, white mens makes out they marries wimmen to look at they eyes, and they know they gits em for just what us gits em for. 'Nother thing, white mens say they goes clear round de world and wins all de wimmen folks way from they men folks. Dat's a lie too. They don't win nothin, they buys em. Now de way I figgers it, if a woman don't want me enough to be wid me, 'thout I got to pay her, she kin rock right on, but these here white men don't know what to do wid a woman when they gits her—dat's how they come they gives they wimmen so much. They got to. Us wimmen works jus as hard as us does an come home an sleep wid us every night. They own wouldn't do it and its de mens fault. Dese white men done fooled theyself bout dese wimmen.

"Now me, I keeps me some wimmens all de time. Dat's whut dey wuz put here for—us mens to use. Dat's right now, Miss. Y'll wuz put here so us mens could have some pleasure. Course I don't run round like heap uh men folks. But if my old lady go way from me and stay mor'n two weeks, I got to git me somebody, ain't I?"

The Jook

Jook is the word for a Negro pleasure house. It may mean a bawdy house. It may mean the house set apart on public works where the men and women dance, drink and gamble. Often it is a combination of all these.

In past generations the music was furnished by "boxes," another word for guitars. One guitar was enough for a dance; to have two was considered excellent. Where two were playing one man played the lead and the other seconded him. The first player was "picking" and the second was "framming," that is, playing chords while the lead carried the melody by dexterous finger work. Sometimes a third player was added, and he played a tomtom effect on the low strings. Believe it or not, this is excellent dance music.

Pianos soon came to take the place of the boxes, and now player-pianos and victrolas are in all of the Jooks.

Musically speaking, the Jook is the most important place in America. For in its smelly, shoddy confines has been born the secular music known as blues, and on blues has been founded jazz. The singing and playing in the true Negro style is called "jooking."

The songs grow by incremental repetition as they travel from mouth to mouth and from Jook to Jook for years before they reach outside ears. Hence the great variety of subject-matter in each song.

The Negro dances circulated over the world were also conceived inside the Jooks. They too make the round of Jooks and public works before going into the outside world.

In this respect it is interesting to mention the Black Bottom. I have read several false accounts of its origin and name. One writer claimed that it got its name from the black sticky mud on the bottom of the Mississippi River. Other equally absurd statements gummed the press. Now the dance really originated in the Jook section of Nashville, Tennessee, around Fourth Avenue. This is a tough neighborhood known as Black Bottom—hence the name.

The Charleston is perhaps forty years old and was danced up and down the Atlantic seaboard from North Carolina to Key West, Florida.

The Negro social dance is slow and sensuous. The idea in the Jook is to gain sensation, and not so much exercise. So that just enough foot movement is added to keep the dancers on the floor. A tremendous sex stimulation is gained from this. But who is trying to avoid it? The man, the woman, the time and place have met. Rather, little intimate names are indulged in to heap fire on fire.

These too have spread to all the world.

The Negro theatre, as built up by the Negro, is based on Jook situations, with women, fighting and drinking. Shows like "Dixie to Broadway" are only Negro in cast, and could just as well have come from pre-Soviet Russia.

Another interesting thing—Negro shows before being

tampered with did not specialize in octoroon chorus girls. The girl who could hoist a Jook song from her belly and lam it against the front door of the theatre was the lead, even if she were as black as the images of hell. The question was "Can she jook?" She must also have a good belly wobble, and her hips must, to quote a popular work song, "Shake like jelly all over and be so broad, Lawd, Lawd, and be so broad." So that the bleached chorus is the result of a white demand and not the Negro's.

The woman in the Jook may be nappy headed and black, but if she is a good lover she gets there just the same. A favorite Jook song of the past has this to say:

> Singer: It aint good looks dat takes you through dis world.
> Audience: What is it, good mama?
> Singer: Elgin* movements in your hips. Twenty years guar-
> antee.

And it always brought down the house too.

> Oh de white gal rides in a Cadillac,
> De yaller girl rides de same,
> Black gal rides in a rusty Ford
> But she gits dere just de same.

The sort of woman her men idealize is the type put forth in the theatre. The art-creating Negro prefers a not too thin woman who can shake like jelly all over as she dances and sings, and that is the type he put forth on the stage. She has been banished by the white producer and the Negro who takes his cue from the white.

Of course a black woman is never the wife of the upper class Negro in the North. This state of affairs does not obtain in the South, however. I have noted numerous cases where the wife was considerably darker than the husband. People of some substance, too.

This scornful attitude towards black women receives mouth sanction by the mud-sills.

---

* Elegant (?). [from the Elgin Watch, Ed.]

Even on the works and in the Jooks the black man sings disparagingly of black women. They say that she is evil. That she sleeps with her fists doubled up and ready for action. All over they are making a little drama of waking up a yaller* wife and a black one.

A man is lying beside his yaller wife and wakes her up. She says to him, "Darling, do you know what I was dreaming when you woke me up?" He says, "No honey, what was you dreaming?" She says, "I dreamt I had done cooked you a big fine dinner and we was setting down to eat out de same plate and I was setting on yo' lap jus huggin you and kissin you and you was so sweet."

Wake up a black woman, and before you kin git any sense into her she be done up and lammed you over the head four or five times. When you git her quiet she'll say, "Nigger, know whut I was dreamin when you woke me up?"

You say, "No honey, what was you dreamin?" She says, "I dreamt you shook yo' rusty fist under my nose and I split yo' head open wid a axe."

But in spite of disparaging fictitious drama, in real life the black girl is drawing on his account at the commissary. Down in the Cypress Swamp as he swings his axe he chants:

> Dat ole black gal, she keeps on grumblin,
> New pair shoes, new pair shoes,
> I'm goint to buy her shoes and stockings
> Slippers too, slippers too.

Then adds aside: "Blacker de berry, sweeter de juice."

To be sure the black gal is still in power, men are still cutting and shooting their way to her pillow. To the queen of the Jook!

Speaking of the influence of the Jook, I noted that Mae West in "Sex" had much more flavor of the turpentine quarters than she did of the white bawd. I know that the piece she played on the piano is a very old Jook composition. "Honey let yo' drawers hang low" had been played and sung in every Jook in

---

* Yaller (yellow), light mulatto

the South for at least thirty-five years. It has always puzzled me why she thought it likely to be played in a Canadian bawdy house.

Speaking of the use of Negro material by white performers, it is astonishing that so many are trying it, and I have never seen one yet entirely realistic. They often have all the elements of the song, dance, or expression, but they are misplaced or distorted by the accent falling on the wrong element. Everyone seems to think that the Negro is easily imitated when nothing is further from the truth. Without exception I wonder why the black-face comedians *are* black-face; it is a puzzle—good comedians, but darn poor niggers. Gershwin and the other "Negro" rhapsodists come under this same axe. Just about as Negro as caviar or Ann Pennington's athletic Black Bottom. When the Negroes who knew the Black Bottom in its cradle saw the Broadway version they asked each other, "Is you learnt dat *new* Black Bottom yet?" Proof that it was not *their* dance.

And God only knows what the world has suffered from the white damsels who try to sing Blues.

The Negroes themselves have sinned also in this respect. In spite of the goings up and down on the earth, from the original Fisk Jubilee Singers down to the present, there has been no genuine presentation of Negro songs to white audiences. The spirituals that have been sung around the world are Negroid to be sure, but so full of musicians' tricks that Negro congregations are highly entertained when they hear their old songs so changed. They never use the new style songs, and these are never heard unless perchance some daughter or son has been off to college and returns with one of the old songs with its face lifted, so to speak.

I am of the opinion that this trick style of delivery was originated by the Fisk Singers; Tuskegee and Hampton followed suit and have helped spread this misconception of Negro spirituals. This Glee Club has gone on so long and become so fixed among concert singers that it is considered quite authentic. But I say again, that not one concert singer in the world is singing the songs as the Negro songmakers sing them.

If anyone wishes to prove the truth of this let him step into some unfashionable Negro church and hear for himself.

To those who want to institute the Negro theatre, let me

say it is already established. It is lacking in wealth, so it is not seen in the high places. A creature with a white head and Negro feet struts the Metropolitan boards. The real Negro theatre is in the Jooks and the cabarets. Self-conscious individuals may turn away the eye and say, "Let us search elsewhere for our dramatic art." Let 'em search. They certainly won't find it. Butter Beans and Susie, Bo-Jangles and Snake Hips are the only performers of the real Negro school it has ever been my pleasure to behold in New York.

Dialect

If we are to believe the majority of writers of Negro dialect and the burnt-cork artists, Negro speech is a weird thing, full of "arms" and "Ises." Fortunately, we don't have to believe them. We may go directly to the Negro and let him speak for himself.

I know that I run the risk of being damned as an infidel for declaring that nowhere can be found the Negro who asks "am it?" nor yet his brother who announces "Ise uh gwinter." He exists only for a certain type of writers and performers.

Very few Negroes, educated or not, use a clear clipped "I." It verges more or less upon "Ah." I think the lip form is responsible for this to a great extent. By experiment the reader will find that a sharp "i" is very much easier with a thin taut lip than with a full soft lip. Like tightening violin strings.

If one listens closely one will note too that a word is slurred in one position in the sentence but clearly pronounced in another. This is particularly true of the pronouns. A pronoun as a subject is likely to be clearly enunciated, but slurred as an object. For example: "You better not let me ketch yuh."

There is a tendency in some localities to add the "h" to "it" and pronounce it "hit." Probably a vestige of Old English. In some localities "if" is "ef."

In story telling "so" is universally the connective. It is used even as an introductory word, at the very beginning of a story. In religious expression "and" is used. The trend in stories is to state conclusions; in religion, to enumerate.

I am mentioning only the most general rules in dialect because there are so many quirks that belong only to certain localities that nothing less than a volume would be adequate.

☐ ROGER D. ABRAHAMS ■

Negotiating Respect: Patterns of Presentation among Black Women

Studies of hero tales show how male values are embodied in narrative form. And we know (through negative evidence) how the male ideal of women is projected in such tales—chiefly with regard to inaction, constancy, and a willing subordination. But how women assert their image and values as women is seldom found in the folklore literature. We know even less about the verbal traditions of black women in particular.

However, a fairly large body of information about such sex-specific expressive capacities can be found in the autobiographical writings of black women themselves and in social scientific descriptions, a literature that tells us something about the content, if not always the devices and techniques, of black female presentations. To get at this material from a folkloristic perspective, it is necessary to analyze more conversational traditions than folklorists are generally committed to studying. Presentational devices are not unique to black women or characteristic of them but are common to all segments of the black community and as such they need to be studied to gain a fuller knowledge of what is unique to the female repertoire of presentational strategies and styles. This essay will attempt to unite the concerns of role theory and commonsense social structure as pursued by symbolic interactionists with the more usual perspectives of a performance-centered theory of folkloristics.

From *Journal of Folklore* 83 (1975): 58–80.

"Testimonies" and "Accounts" in Folkloristics

To this point, I have been using the term *presentation* for certain formulaic devices to distinguish them in some dimension from *performances*. Presentational routines are as formulaic and as subject to being learned and passed on through oral transmission as performances of traditional songs or tales, but they are not so self-consciously rendered. Rather they arise in the midst of, and as part of, the apparently spontaneous interpersonal exchanges of everyday interactions.

The kind of presentational device I focus on has been noticed in the sociological literature before. For instance, a recent study of hitchhikers develops upon the term *rap*, which the author impressionistically defines as "a purposeful reconstruction of past and present directed at explaining, enhancing and embellishing a fantasized future. This reconstruction of 'who I am' and 'where I was' in terms of 'what I will do' is an advertisement of self to significant others, with both parties aware that the presentation is, to a large extent, fantasy [i.e., fiction]."[1]

A *rap* or any other kind of presentational routine is closely related to Erving Goffman's conception of *acting out a line*. This he defines as "a pattern of verbal and nonverbal acts by which [a person] expresses his view of a situation and through this his evaluation of the participants, especially himself."[2] Acting out a line is done to assert and maintain face, "the positive social value a person claims for himself by the line others assume he has taken during a particular contact."[3] Further, "The line maintained by and for a person during contact with others tends to be of a legitimate institutionalized kind,"[4] and it is precisely the institutionalized dimension that is of interest from a folkloristic perspective, for it is just such learnable and transmittable notions of order through enactment (especially in performance) that provide an impetus for those traditional items that have been the stock in trade of our discipline.

Goffman, however, does not dwell on the formulaic and institutionalized dimension of these routines so much as the way in which their familiar order provides a means of maintaining one's image in interactional encounters and negotiations. The formulaic order in a *line,* Goffman implies, somehow in-

74

duces a sense of expressive order—"an order that regulates the flow of events . . . so that anything that appears to be expressed by them will be consistent with his face."[5] Any group might then be studied both with regard to the options of *face* with which an individual is presented as part of the socialization and enculturation process and with regard to the related *lines* or *routines* available to be learned and replayed by him.

Discussing the establishment of personal and social identities in terms of such lines and routines may seem somewhat mechanical; however, the process is far from rigid for a number of reasons. Although there is a formulaic dimension to routines, each role has a number of such devices available, which may be combined for a wide range of effects. Further, there are numerous styles by which the lines may be enacted and a number of scenes in which they may be employed, each calling for modifications of strategy.

Finally, and most important, a distinction might be made between *filling* and *playing* a role. "Filling a role" would arise when there is a slot in the social structure, and interactions are dominated by the status relationship of the participants. There is a strong sense of the obligatory in the carrying out of such relationships; in fact, one could argue that the possibility of pursuing a line is ruled out in favor of ritualized routines that articulate and maintain decorum. "Playing a role," on the other hand, would carry a sense of optation to it. Lines become possible, and alternative approaches arise with regard to self-presentation and relationship establishment. But the presence of such options lays the individual open to the charge of "play-acting" if the role is not played successfully, or if it is successful but later proves to be inconsistent.

Lines are employed, then, primarily in relationships in which status is to be negotiated. In fact, one of the uses of the most overtly formulaic lines is to announce that one is "in play," that is, available for the type of identity negotiation most characteristic of egalitarian relationships, in which flexibility of line and spontaneity of approach are stressed.

The distinction between *filling* and *playing* roles is similar to one made by symbolic interactionists between "instrumental" and "expressive" role definition: the former arises from institutional role-assigning, the latter from a more personalistic approach. Given the egalitarian cast of American society, we have a tendency to downgrade or mask out instrumental role-taking. But, as I will argue here, Euro-Americans employ a great many more instrumental formulae in establishing family and community relationships than do Afro-Americans. Even those who most demand serious respect in the community carefully signal that they are available for role play—that the licensed dimension of playful activity may be employed as a means of negotiation with them.

There are set scenarios (often given names) in which the routines associated with the range of role formulation are situated. These events or scenes associated with role filling commonly turn on judgmental occasions, ones in which character is attacked or maintained through techniques of apology, self-assertion, or talk about others. This would include such routines as *putting up an argument, accounting for oneself, making a spiel* (or a *pitch*), *giving an excuse, gossiping, catting,* or (from black talk) *getting on someone's case.* These do not just name a type of presentation but a recurrent interactional situation and the kinds of strategies it employs. They are essentially serious, as opposed to scenes of role playing involving joking and other such licensed inversions. These other more playful routines, since they may involve greater displays of wit and even open contest, come closer to overt performances. But they are not framed and marked as performances because they involve routines that arise in conversational contexts as part of the apparently spontaneous flow of interaction and are used to assert one's perceived role, to focus or realign one's face in relation to others in the conversation and, by extension, in the narrator's network of relations. In the case of alignment, the sort of line one enacts to establish an identity with others we might call *testimony.*[6] Where interactants already know each other, and their need to realign this personal sense of identity arises from some disruption, we might speak of an *account,* as in "giving an account of oneself."[7]

Such presentational routines are as formulaic and repetitive as performances; we know this implicitly because when we encounter them we "know what's coming." But because they commonly arise in those more conversational contexts in which spontaneity is the norm and the formulaic is to be masked, this range of presentation is not foregrounded as it is in jokes or even anecdotes, not as intensely framed, and there are fewer markers which announce that a performance is taking place. The social fiction is maintained that not only demands the appearance of spontaneity in such talk but also signals a willingness to focus on content features to the exclusion of stylistic considerations—what we seem to mean when we say we are "just talking." To stylize is to call attention to formal and formulaic features and, thus, to make the speaker appear nonspontaneous and therefore not to be listened to or trusted in a conversationally defined situation. Though not as overtly marked, presentations are certainly as full of commonplaces and formulae as, say, jokes except that although they are preformulated and learned, they are employed in a more "open" manner, that is, in nonfixed sequences. We may therefore regard them as traditional arguments or rationalizations. These are the kinds of interactional devices that come to the folklorist's attention only when they achieve concentration and focus in such fixed-form genres as proverbs. We then recognize them as traditional because they call attention simultaneously to both the form and the content of the device.[8]

Devices of this sort will become of greater interest to folklorists as we investigate performance in everyday life, and especially the traditional presentations of women. At least with regard to black women, I have found this expanded notion of a common body of such learned devices of communication useful in understanding more fully the relationship between performance forms and styles and the social structure as perceived by members of Afro-American communities. I will consider a number of formulaic devices reported from black women's interactions and relate them to perceived Afro-American social segmentation and ways by which values (that is, ideals and norms on both the overt and covert levels) are put into action.

I do so recognizing the limitations of using reported materials that are not, for the most part, actual transcriptions of conversational exchanges. Although the language of the materials is often conversational, and thus the same formulae of argument and idea continually emerge, they are presented in autobiographical accounts in the reportorial voice and often in the past tense. In the sociological and anthropological literature, on the other hand, we are given, for the most part, distillations of reported attitudes and communication behaviors; these are even farther away from formulaic presentations. However, given the dearth of reported interactions and what I perceive to be the need to fill in the interactional portrait of the communicational life in postagrarian black communities,[9] it has seemed useful to proceed, if only to provide an outline of the recurrent scenes and settings by which black women give testimonies and accounts of their role as women. I do this recognizing that asserting one's face as a woman is, of course, only one of the types of roles (though certainly one of the most important) available to individual black women.

The essence of the negotiation involved in asserting one's role lies in a woman being both sweet and tough depending upon her capacity to define and reasonably manipulate the situation. Ideally she has the ability to *talk sweet* with her infants and peers but *talk smart* or *cold* with anyone who might threaten her self-image. She expects both good behavior and bad at all times and has routines prepared for handling and capitalizing on both. Acting and being regarded as *respectable* is not a static condition in any way; quite the contrary, the ladies most respected are often those who maintain themselves at the center of the action.

Many ethnographers of black communities have noted the importance of such routines in the assertion and maintenance of role. Ulf Hannerz, for instance, notes of the members of one neighborhood in Washington, D.C., that their opinions are often "based not only on their individual experiences but also on the interpretations their associates make for them." These interpretations are embodied in what Hannerz calls "public imagery" or "collective representations," a "motif collection into which individual experiences are fitted." Furthermore, this "culture of common sense" then provides "a screen through which impressions are sifted, as individuals become trained to take particular note of these phenomena which match or can be brought to match public images."[10]

Though Hannerz goes on to point out a few of these collective representations in the female repertoire, the great majority of his anecdotal data come from men, and this is characteristic of the ethnographic literature. Of the numerous studies we have of black life, only the studies from the Pruitt-Igoe (St. Louis) Project offer much data on female attitudes and approaches; even these deal little with the specifics of interaction, the attitudinal content being distilled from the observed conversations.[11]

Nevertheless, both males and females give a range of formulaic testimonies to values of respect and their connection with home and with the female head of the household. In this article, I will survey the ways in which respectability is asserted and maintained in those social situations in which this norm-image is under test: while childrearing in the home; among peers; in male-female interactions. Respectability is not something a person *is;* rather it is an ideal-image that is conceived and put into action through a complex enactment of motives. Though the focus will be on strategies and directions of female presentation and maintenance of roles, the data called upon here will also cast light on those communication registers and varieties of speech regarded as situationally appropriate within the lives of black women. This suggests that further field research in this area should involve the techniques and perspectives of the ethnography of communication.

The Affirming Negations in the Opposition of the House and the Street

A problem attending the description of black presentational strategies arises from the essential differences between Euro-Americans and Afro-Americans in the systems of communication and in images of social and cultural order. These differences are especially notable in the means by which perceived oppositions are handled; in Euro-American communicational practices, we tend to minimize antagonism, to encapsulate it in "scenes," effecting closure within the scenes so that "bad feelings" are not carried away from the confrontation. Among Afro-Americans, such oppositions tend to be viewed as constant contrarieties, antagonisms that cannot be eliminated and in fact may be used to effect a larger sense of cultural affirmation of community through a dramatization of opposing forces.

We may be dealing here with a specific rendering of a cultural universal, for every culture seems to have some way of "naming" and presenting its recurrent conflicts. The very idea of drama is predicated on the process of rendering oppositions of values or allegiances playfully and interactively. Furthermore, inherent in any meaningful drama is the process Hegel saw residing in the term *aufheben,* which means at one and the same time to negate and to affirm.[12] The negation or self-cancellation occurs on the apparently temporal level, while the affirmation arises out of the embodiment and celebration of these opposing ideas or forces. It is precisely in the way a culture chooses to dramatize these oppositions that it asserts its own characteristic patterns of life style as well as art style.

This seems important to note here, because the kind of negotiation carried on by black women through their repertoire of self-presentational routines is in many ways similar to the more stylized black performances enacted by other members of the community as well. Life-affirming is carried on in such a world through an open-ended dramatization of conflicts in values and allegiances, and it is through such dramatizations that black life is invested with vigor, as well as with expressions of anxiety.

No theme of conflict is more constant in black life than the independence and consequent opposition of the sexes. Put in its simplest terms, women are expected to be psychologically, socially, and economically independent of men. But also (and simultaneously) verbalized is an ideal of sexual interdependence, both in courtship and marriage and in the system of willingness to place oneself in the position to manipulate and be manipulated. It is precisely this simultaneous statement of independence and interdependence that results in what I will call a special Afro-American *aufheben,* that is, a unique way of affirming through the enactment of oppositions.[13] We might approach the discussion of these opposing forces through sexual dimorphisms. We could express the opposition in terms of locus, through the emic contrasting of the private *home* and the public *street* worlds. Or, to put it in value terms, we could phrase it as the competition between respectability- and reputation-seeking norms. Though they are never coterminous, there is a constant sense of relationship between male values, reputation-seeking, and the public world, and between women, respectability, and the home.

80

However, it cannot be overstressed that black children are taught to fend for and "to go for" themselves in both the house and the street worlds, even while they are taught the value—indeed, the necessity—of cooperation. We can understand this balancing of the motives of self-reliance and cooperation quite simply by observing that black children are taught at quite an early age the entire range of housekeeping activities to assure their self-reliance in later life; but they learn to carry them out as part of the functioning cooperative unit of the household. Perhaps the point can be better made by looking at an equivalent of "going for yourself": *doing your thing.* In black talk, this does not mean acting independently of the group but rather asserting yourself *within* the group, especially in performances. Specifically, doing your thing seems to have originally meant entering into a performance by adding your voice to the ensemble, by playing off against the others, as each instrument does in jazz, for instance. A crucial part of the black aesthetic involves this voice overlap and interlock effect; everyone gets to do his own individual "thing" even while contributing to the overall sense of the whole. This, it seems to me, is the peculiar Afro-American sense of *aufheben,* the means by which opposition is transformed into affirmation. Negotiation for respectability must be viewed thus not as an attempt to sing some songs of respectability to the exclusion of alternatives, but rather as an effort to maintain a melody line against (and therefore defined by) those other voices setting up a sometimes cacophonous opposition.

By this I do not mean that there is no woman within black communities who will always assert herself in respect-seeking terms. Some will, to be sure, but these are the very ones most people will tend to regard as "uppity." The women most respected seem to be those who recognize respectability norms and decorous behaviors as negotiable. There is a good deal of legendary lore about just such women, and, in a study of stories associated with them, one of my black students calls such characters "Madame Queens," [14] describing them not only in terms of their integrity, strong will, and the sense of order they take into every encounter, but also by their need to demonstrate these qualities through dramatic interactions with those who differ, who oppose their will and sense of order.

81

Respectability hardly equates with the imposition of order through silence and hauteur. Firm distinctions are maintained then between being respectable and being *uppity, dicty, saddity*.[15] The former calls for maintaining self-respect through the willful imposition of order in monitoring behavior; the latter set involves setting oneself above others through a mistaken social sense that decorum is more important than vitality. And such values are embodied not only in the dramatized respectability of these ladies, but also in the many stories concerning the exploits of the most successful of these Madame Queens.

We have few studies of such exemplary stories because folkloristic interest in memorates is relatively recent. One fugitive work of J. Mason Brewer, *Aunt Dicy Tales*,[16] gives a number of representative stories concerning an older black slave who after emancipation is able to maintain her snuff-dipping habit by her willfulness and cunning, all the while proclaiming and maintaining her respectability. Similarly, Katherine L. Morgan's stories of her own family's legends concern an ancestor named Caddy, who established her integrity through the dramatizing of her values, by thumbing her nose in highly dramatic public style at those who would confront her with an insult.[17]

Such stories illustrate the flexible and highly personalistic approach to interactions characteristic of Afro-American societies in which, as noted before, the expressive or personalistic rather than the instrumental or institutional dimension of role validation is stressed. Black joke traditions underline this in portraying various hypocrisies (even to the point of satirizing grandma as being sexually wanton).[18] Though these particular stories exist primarily in the male repertoire and reflect a male perspective, the point they make is that no role automatically carries power or respect, whether preacher, old master, or "grandma." Respect is something which must constantly be earned, negotiated.

Dramatization occurs in confrontations with those who challenge respect—with men (especially *street men* or *players*), with children, and with other women. In each social situation, set expressions and strategies indicate that the best protection against such assaults is to expect the worst. Thus, one of the most commonly encountered routines expressing the moral dominant stance of women asserts in some way that all (or most) men are untrustworthy and bad. One of Hannerz's informants notes, for instance, that "Men talk too much and drink too much and work too little. . . . These men always get into trouble the way they act, or they get someone else in trouble. Always something bad in their minds. Talking sweet to women, and then they don't do a thing for them when they're in trouble."[19]

Similarly, though speaking in the past tense, Ossie Guffy gives another formulation of this argument: "Lots of black people fall back on the comforting thought that the Lord will provide. To a black man, I suspect that the Lord is a black woman."[20]

This image of men is encouraged by the men them-selves, so that one often finds the same accounts of misbehavior used by both sexes, but for different reasons. For instance, both women and men describe the male propensity to play around sexually as "the dog in him," that is, pure, uncontrollable animal instinct. Thus, one of Hannerz's female informants notes, "Sure they're all sweet to start with, and you have a good time together, but then they start running around with another woman the moment you turn your back. You hear people say every man has a dog in him? That ain't no joke you know."[21] Another discussion between men invokes the same argument, but this time as an excuse: "Men have a little bit of dog in them, you know. That's why they can't leave the women alone."[22]

Men have a great deal to do with maintaining the image of female respectability, even when they regard actual respect-seeking behavior as insincere or hypocritical. They support the image for a number of reasons: to maintain a good environment for raising their children; to maintain a locus which continues to represent a life-style alternative that can be turned to if and when they choose to give up their reputation-seeking ways; to provide a given model of behavior that can be depended upon when a man wants to manipulate a woman. But with regard to this last ploy, just as men evince their badness in order to en-hance their reputation, women will define the strength and force of their respectability by successfully contending against such men.

The locus of respectability is the home; the operation of the household is both the real and the symbolic means by which these overt social values are put into practice. But black talk commonly recognizes that this private sphere of activity will be under constant attack from the more public "street" world and that it is in the inevitable confrontation between these worlds that a female is able to enact being a woman.

In a marvelous piece of portraiture, Maya Angelou describes her mother in her autobiography *I Know Why the Caged Bird Sings*. After discussing how her mother maintained herself financially as a public character, she notes that, in spite of her mother's availability for rough joking from other street-people, "everyone knew that although she cussed freely as she laughed, no one cussed around her, and certainly no one cussed her."[23] This set of distinctions demonstrates one of the problems encountered by black women whenever they must go into a public situation, for some attempt will commonly be made by them to balance the need to present themselves as successful public interactants with the need to maintain the sense of female respectability that is the ideal of feminine "face" in the community. As Beverly Stoeltje's informant "Evelyn" analyzes it (in another recent study), there is an important behavioral distinction between acting *at home* and *on the street,* a distinction that goes beyond the places where interactions take place to the style by which exchanges are carried out.

> The "lady on the street" is . . . they could call it a pick-up lady. She is on the street, man after man, day after day. Just as I get up and go to the job, she gets up and goes to the street.
>
> But you take a lady *at home* that goes out, very seldom would accept a drink from a man outside. If they buy you a drink, they think you are sittin' waiting for a pick-up. But if a lady go out by herself and sit in a particular place, she's looking for a pickup and she consider herself a lady on the street.
>
> The lady *at home* is a very independent lady. She leaves home, . . . knowing where her kids is, and knowing that 12:30 or 1:00 o'clock it's nice to come home . . . knowing that everything was taken care of at home. . . . The lady on the street . . . she leaves home with nothing and it's nothing at home either. . . . Nine chances out of ten they give the kids up, or they don't even have time, they leave 'em at a baby sitter's

on Thursday night and don't see 'em until the next Thursday.
The lady at home knows she have to go home at a certain hour
to even respect her kids, draggin' in and out at all times of the
night. And a lady on the street will bring 'em in to her apartment, where a lady at home respect her household. . . .[24]

Thus, at least for this one informant, being *at home* does
not mean staying at home but maintaining the integrity of the
household in the face of possible incursions from the street; her
respect for the home begets respect from the others in it but
must be asserted in many nonhome situations.[25]

This dichotomy between house and street is certainly far
from unique to black communities; as in other groups, the basic
distinction is between private and public realms and their associated behaviors. Also not uncommonly, the two worlds become identified to some extent with the age and sex of their
citizens, the household world being associated with the very
young, the old, and with women, the street with adolescents
and young adults and primarily with men. Herbert Gans describes much the same complex as a lower-class phenomenon
in a study of working class Italian-Americans.[26] It is not this distinction of worlds that is distinctively black, then, but the types
and styles of interactions carried on within and between the
denizens of the two domains. Blacks regard different styles of
communication behaviors as appropriate to these two worlds.

The most important distinction between the household
and the street world turns on the roles and the role types available in the two realms. In the home one's role is generally determined by family relationships. Roles are assigned according
to where one stands vis-à-vis the distribution of power and re-
sponsibility within the household. Generally, even with a resident paterfamilias, in the Afro-American family it is *Momma*
who delegates responsibilities, because her respectability is
judged by how effectively her household is run. She must both
encounter, and guard her private world from, the incursions of
the more public streets, incursions that constantly threaten
from many sides. In this, her values on being *treated respectably* come into conflict all too often with the values of those in
the street life, whose names depend on reputation rather than

respectability.[27] *Maintaining a rep,* and especially a *high rep,* means acting with a display style and spending one's resources in a manner that threatens Momma in many ways.

Momma is not the only one who is basically ambivalent about the street and its public life. From the perspective of Momma and her values, everything on the street provides a threat to her respectability; any kind of rudeness, excessive noise, or playing may be viewed by her as an attack. But to many, and especially the young men and women, the street world (which includes other public places) is *where the action is* and where one is expected to have fun. Though men find it easier to handle street situations, even they must be wary at all times of the threats coming from such a world. On the street, one is constantly in danger of being *hustled,* of having a *game run* on him. Anyone who goes public (especially in the cities) is open to such *trickification.*

> You know yourself, man, when you walk out in the streets you have to be ready. Everybody walking out there is game on everybody else. If you don't watch what you're doing, before you know it you're going to be put in a trick bag. . . . It's true where the members are found [i.e., wherever Blacks are congregating]. Our people are always plotting and scheming.[28]

This kind of account could be given by male or female. In this specific case, it was uttered by a man threatened by the street not so much for himself but for his wife, whom he felt had been sheltered from the tricks and thus had been easily taken in. (This is one example of why and how men attempt to maintain the respect image for women.) He goes on to argue that for a man, it is easy to adopt the street attitude of "Do unto others before they do unto you,"[29] but for a woman it is more difficult, and she can lose her *name* as a result.

> I have heard reports that my wife is running around . . . it really does hurt me because I wonder how she could have time to be a mother and a player at the same time. . . . It is impossible for a woman to take care of her child and be out in the streets at the same time. . . . *I would rather have us fighting and fuss-*

*ing all the time and have her with me than to have her get a
bad name by being out on the streets.*[30]

Such arguments are so familiar and formulaic that they begin
to seem almost proverbial (although lacking the conciseness of
form). Perhaps because of the very repetitive nature of such
arguments they are seldom reported with fidelity to the situation and to progression of a communicative interaction. But
values and life-styles alternatives are learned and celebrated
more through such routines and the commonplaces of their argument than through formal stories

Negotiating at Home with Children

Being a mother does not make one a *Momma,* even when one
begins to set up a household of one's own. The role must be
acted upon appropriately or the rest of the community will not
recognize a woman in that role. If a woman maintains her
family connections, she must continue to respect her Momma,
and that means acting appropriately when in her own home as
well as in her Momma's. Otherwise her Momma may be accused of raising her children improperly (though she may argue
in her own defense that she can't control what happens outside
her own home). Just how this operates is explained by one of
Carol Stack's informants in discussing her first baby, which she
had at nineteen.

> I was really wild in those days, out on the town all hours of
> the night, and every night and weekend I layed my girl on my
> mother. I wasn't living home at the time, but mama kept Chris-
> tine most of the time. One day mama up and said I was making
> a fool of her and she was going to take my child and raise her
> right. She said I was immature and had no business being a
> mother the way I was acting. All my mama's people agreed and
> there was nothing I could do. So mama took my child.[31]

This records both an attitude and a commonly encountered routine on the part of Momma or some other lady
presenting herself as respectable, in distinction to a younger

woman too much on the streets. As one Momma in a parallel situation put it succinctly, "I'm not gonna have those babies out in the street. They're gonna stay here even if [their mother] moves out. I'll not have it, not knowing who's taking care of them."[32] Again, what is a fixed account in the repertoire of one person (the young mother) becomes both a testimony and a different sort of account in the presentation of another. But they both reflect the same ideal and public image.

Respectability is expressed not only in such testimonies but also in the strategies and styles of communication insisted upon as appropriate in the house or some other place regarded as respectable, such as church, or even lodge. One of the routines of respectability involves monitoring others' presentational techniques. In general, women are expected to be more restrained than men in their talk, less loud, less public, and much less abandoned. They speak in a register closer to standard conversational English than do the men. Girls are lectured by both Daddy and Momma on never talking loudly or cursing, not even when involved in street encounters. As Louise Meriwhether explained it: "Daddy didn't even want me to say darn. He was always telling me: 'It's darn today, damn tomorrow, and next week it'll be goddamn. You're going to grow up to be a lady, and ladies don't curse.'"[33] Any kind of public talk may not be respectably ladylike to a man. Zora Neale Hurston has one of her male characters note of his wife when someone asks her during a public occasion to give a speech: "mah wife don't know nothin' 'bout no speechmaking. Ah never married her for nothin' lak dat. She's uh woman and her place is in de home." (But the novel relates how a lady learns to speak in the development of her self-respect.)[34]

The house as the locus of a woman's sense of respectability causes Momma to monitor constantly her own as well as others' talk there. Silence is also highly valued in children (especially in the presence of Momma). What Virginia Heyer Young notes of mother-toddler interactions is by other accounts characteristic of mother-child communications in general. At the point of changing from infant (*lap-baby*) to toddler (*knee-baby*), a perceptible shift occurs, in which, among other things, the speaking variety seems to be altered, and "Children speak less to adults and get along adequately with 'Yes'm' and 'No'm.' " [35]

Within the home the child is expected to observe and, in learning tasks, to emulate the maternal figure. This means that whenever Momma is present, a child will watch what she does and observe her reactions. He will test her constantly but also will expect to be reprimanded by the strong glance, by the direct question concerning his actions, or by admonitions.

In this ambience words between adults and children are extremely restricted; few words are used, and tasks are broken down into small units "with brief directions for each short task following on the completion of the previous one." [36] In the situation in which the mother's respectability is constantly felt to be tested, any repeated communication—verbal or otherwise—is loaded with significance. Mother's words are highly weighted in such a system, giving her directive power with an economy of means.

That is not to say that there is no interaction between mother and child, only that interactions are nonreciprocal. Imperatives are given, informational questions asked, but seldom is either used to instigate verbal communication so much as to produce action on the part of the child. This means, among other things, that "Parents are not in the habit of asking questions to which they already know the answer . . . neither do [they] indulge in pleasantries." [37]

The value placed on silence in the home (on the part of children) is one facet of an elaborate ideal of deference, which includes learning proper modes of address, how and when to act in the presence of adults, and how and where to look (mutely) when being addressed by an older person. [38] Thus, one of the most important routines by which a woman defines her respectable sex-role is by speaking little with the mouth and a great deal with the eyes, the arms and shoulders, the whole set of the body.

Neither Momma (nor other adults) will be expected always to behave in accord with their own ideals in talking style or in actions. One has the feeling, from discussions with a wide range of black people and from perusing the literature, that consonance between actual and ideal behavior was and is greater in country and small-town black life than in the cities— in spite of jokes to the contrary. But this may be an operation of our very American pastoral sympathies, our desire to maintain an image of our agrarian past as a time when we lived more harmoniously, more in tune with both nature and our social ideals. In any case, the child observes early and often that there are at least two standards of behavior in front of Momma, one for children and one for adults; though their own noise is despised, the environment is filled with other noises, against which they learn to play. Further, numerous kinds of aggressive verbal behaviors go on in front of Momma, and in fact Momma engages in them. These behaviors are denied children, at least until they attain young adult status—and even then they will probably have to fight for the right.

To this point in this section I have focused on the respect routines between Momma and children. But a strong counter-valent tendency is noted in the literature: children are encouraged from the earliest age to be aggressive, even hostile, to Momma. This encouragement is related to the standard maternal account for any kind of misbehavior, namely that children are often "born bad," with all the ambiguous meaning of *badness* in black talk.[39]

For instance, children are encouraged to fight back if they learn how to do so properly, by acting linguistically as adults. Ward points out that "while children may be punished for crying and making too much noise, they are not responsible for what might be thought of as 'linguistic offenses,' sassiness, for example. A child who adopts the same tone and phrases as his mother will be laughed at . . . a child's cursing or profanity [too] is interpreted as funny."[40]

Indeed, this kind of competitive spirit between parents and children in which the child shows an adult ability (even to the point of hitting his mother) is in many cases applauded, in spite of the obvious challenge to authority and respectability. This acting like an adult is one of the features characteristic of the highly approved role of *little mama* or *nurse mama* but is also a motive with boys.[41] The approval stems from the ambivalence toward acting bad, meaning not only to act disrespectfully but to do so by displaying self-reliance.

90

However, children hear not only that all children are bad, but that so are all men, and so are all women. Young girls, as they are taught their household work-skills, are also taught that they had better learn them well because chances are they are going to have to run households on their own since men cannot be trusted to do their share or to stay in one place very long. And young boys are given the same argument about girls as the reason for them to learn the entire range of household maintenance tasks. This encourages children to learn and practice these tasks well, and thus enables Momma to maintain her sense of respectability. But it also teaches children that the only kind of relationship, indeed the only kind of love, on which one can depend is that of Momma for her children.

Saying that one expects the doings of all these others to be *bad* is, then, among other things to evaluate from the perspective of the house and its leader. Whether this means that there is a real expectation of badness on the part of all others is hardly important (if it could be ascertained). In this Afro-American perspective, the overt explanation of bad behavior will be something like, "Well that's the way men (or women or children or even Negroes) are." Rather than masking alternative (perhaps deviant) behaviors, the black approach seems to be to expect anything and to develop techniques for capitalizing on the good and perhaps the bad as well. Whatever the causes for this pattern of expectation, one effect is that among blacks action (and talk) is constantly being judged, and generally from the perspective of respectability values. This makes it all the more important that Momma's household stand up well under scrutiny, lest she receive the ill judgment of her peers and community.

One of the components of this argument is that not only order but also work become identified with home and Momma, play and action with the streets. Such associations are important for a number of reasons, not least of which is that when one of her children is working outside the home it should be in part to help Momma with the bills. This obligation (as many have noted) operates as a norm throughout one's life and supplies men with one of their consistent routines of making a bow toward respectability values. For instance, Friedland and

Nelkin note in their study of the culture of black migratory laborers:

> People believe that, regardless of how little money one earns, one must financially support "mother." They may disrespect their wives and women, but mothers seem sacrosanct. George sends his mother $20.00 every week. He says his mother is much more important to him than his fiancée because "you can have lots of wives but you only have one mother. . . ." James said even though he couldn't stand his mother, he sent her $20.00 every week. "My mother was the one who brought me into this world and I owe her for it."[42]

Negotiating with Men

Giving money is one important way a man shows his respect for a woman, particularly one who is taking care of his children, whether she is Momma, or his *old lady,* or his wife. This is especially so because the contrary pull faced by many men is the need to maintain their male friendship networks and develop a good reputation.[43] In a situation of scarce resources, the willingness to respect a woman and her household needs becomes a matter of being able to attain the basic necessities. Certainly, then, one of the central requirements for asserting respectability is the ability to maintain the household as a home.[44] Unfortunately, almost nothing in the literature concerns the interactions of men and women already in a household-keeping kind of arrangement. What we do have reported are those areas surveyed above in which women discuss the generic failures of men—and one can assume that many of the same formulaic arguments arise (though from different perspectives) in arguments with a husband or "old man."

Such problems are part of a larger man-woman contest that is carried on both in the home and in more public settings. With younger girls, contact with males is a very deep part of their definition of themselves as maturing women. In her study of black adolescent females, Joyce Ladner notes: "Girls realize early that one of the ways to achieve the status of a woman is to learn the more complex game that is involved in male-female

92

relationships. There are appropriate things to say and ways to behave at appropriate times in the interchange of communication and contact."[45] Furthermore, it is through relationships with men that girls achieve womanhood status not only in men's eyes, but in the eyes of their own peers and of adults generally as well.

With regard to how maturing girls operate in male-female situations, Ladner points out two general types: those who are "childish," sincere and innocent, and the more sophisticated type, who "rather frequently engage . . . in manipulative strategies . . . [who] had learned the rules of the game and devised [their] own strategies. . . ."[46] Both types depend upon the female making herself available for public interactions with men. The naïve type would then be so defined by an essentially *sweet-talking* approach on the part of the man, with a minimum of vocal response on the woman's part. The sophisticate, on the other hand, asserts her self-sufficiency through an answering style, one which relies on joking *smart talk* to assert distance and make room for her own manipulation.

These alternatives seem to have operated for some time in Afro-American communities in the United States, as can be observed in the southern courtship scenes found in fictional renderings; Alston Anderson describes one, a sweet-talking procedure:

> One day I was standing outside the barbershop with some of the boys. Miss Florence come by on her way home from the schoolhouse, and they got to signifying:
> "Mmmmmmm-*mph!* What a fine day *this* is!"
> "Yes, Lawd, it sho is."
> "My, my, what a *purty* day!"
> "How do, Miss Florence!"
> "How do you do."
> "Yes, Lawd, I'd sleep in the streets fawdy days and fawdy nights for a day like *that!*"
> "Y'all hush your signifying," I said. "That there's a *lady*, and I won't have y'all signifying 'bout her like that."
> I said it in a tone of voice that wasn't loud, but I knew she heard it. Next time I seen her she had a nice little smile for me, but I acted like nothing had ever happened.[47]

Courtship patterns in the South were primarily characterized by males adopting the eloquent "fancy talk" variety of speaking as a means of paying respect, discoursing in a code replete with latinate words and an appropriately expansive style of delivery.[48] This style of talking was commonly employed by men and by the young of both sexes whenever they were in a place, like church or school, which was regarded by the community as one in which proper (that is, ideal household) behaviors were appropriate. But it is also found in totally male groups as one register in which a man-of-words may *run the changes*, demonstrating his verbal abilities.[49] Puckett, reviewing the literature on courtship, noted that "the suitor with a retinue of grandiose words had a decided advantage, and many plantations had an old slave experienced in the words and ways of courtship to instruct young gallants in the way in which they should go in the delicate matter of winning the girl of their choice."[50] He provides us with a number of examples of the kinds of speeches to use on such occasions.

This was not the only approach to such male-female talking-relationships in the South, however. Equally characteristic seems to have been the bantering street encounter such as the acting-out courtships reported by Hurston in a number of her works, in which eloquence becomes mixed with tomfoolery and *smart talk:*

> . . . here comes Bootsie, and Teadi and Big 'oman down the street making out they are pretty by the way they walk. They have got that fresh, new taste about them like young mustard greens in the spring, and the young men on the porch are just bound to tell them about it and buy them some treats.
>
> "Heah come mah order right now," Charlie Jones announces and scrambles off the porch to meet them. But he has plenty of competition. A pushing, shoving show of gallantry. They all beg the girls to just buy anything they can think of. Please let them pay for it. Joe is begged to wrap up all the candy in the store and order more. All the peanuts and soda water—everything!
>
> "Gal, Ah'm crazy 'bout you," Charlie goes on to the entertainment of everybody. "Ah'll do anything in the world except work for you and give you mah money."

> The girls and everybody else help laugh. They know it's not courtship. It's acting-out courtship and everybody is in the play.[51]

The scene proceeds with further mock-courtship in which the men vie, in elevated hyperbole, over who will get the hand of one of the girls. Daisy. It ends on this note:

> "Daisy, Ah'll take uh job cleanin' out de Atlantic Ocean fuh you any time you say you so desire." There was a great laugh and then they hushed to listen.
>
> "Daisy," Jim began, "You know mah heart and all de ranges uh mah mind. And you know if Ah wuz ridin' up in uh earoplane way up in de sky and Ah looked down and seen you walkin' and knowed you'd have tuh walk ten miles tuh git home, Ah'd step backward offa dat earoplane just to walk home wid you."[52]

If a woman places herself in a public situation, she is in jeopardy of having to contend with men and their *jive* (or to use the southern term, *high pro*). What is a serious variety of communication in the enclosed settings of home or church becomes a playful one in the more open context of porch and road and country store. If a woman's sense of respectability is challenged in such a situation, she may fight fire with fire, becoming as verbally open and aggressive as her contenders, resorting to a very tendentious sort of *smart talking*. Hurston again provides us with a description of such a scene, which begins with a man seriously kidding the heroine, Janie, as she waits on him in a store.

> "I god almighty! A woman stay round uh store till she get old as Methusalem and still can't cut a little thing like a plug of tobacco! Don't stand dere rollin' yo' pop eyes at me wid yo' rump hangin' nearly to you' knees!"
>
> "Nah, Ah ain't no young gal no mo' but den Ah ain't no old woman neither. Ah reckon Ah looks mah age too. But Ah'm uh woman every inch of me, and Ah knows it. Dat's uh whole lot more'n *you* kin say. You big-bellies round here and put out a lot of brag, but 'tain't nothin' to it but yo' big voice. Humph! Talkin'

'bout *me* lookin' old! When you pull down yo' britches, you look lak de change uh life."[53]

Elevated "fancy talking" has not been totally lost in the flight from the South, but it becomes mixed in with other varieties, as one way in which a young man may *run the changes* while *rapping* to a woman. For instance, Claudia Mitchell-Kernan reports a conversation she had with some young men in a park, in which talking fancy talk and talking smart are resorted to by both man and woman (in this case the author herself).

I: Baby, you a real scholar. I can tell you want to learn. Now if you'll just cooperate a li'l bit, I'll show you what a good teacher I am. But first we got to get into my area of expertise.

R: I may be wrong but seems to me we already in your area of expertise.

I: You ain' so bad yourself, girl. I ain't heard you stutter yet. You a li'l fixated on your subject though. I want to help a sweet thang like you all I can. I figure all that book learning you got must mean you been neglecting other areas of your education.

II: Talk that talk! . . .

R: Why don't you let me point out where I can best use your help.

I: Are you sure you in the best position to know?
(laughter)

I: I'mo leave you alone, girl. Ask me what you want to know. Tempus fugit, baby.[54]

This fashion of interaction that includes talking smart is just one of a number of black types of speaking which involve an agonistic motive and the use of cleverness. Smartness may be found in the repertoires of men, women, and children, but it does seem to be especially important in women's talk both with each other and with men. Furthermore, it seems to arise as a means of marking a serious (or potentially serious) personal antagonism, thus distinguishing it from the overtly playful yet often agonistic *talkin' shit* or *woofin'*.[55]

"Talking smart" routines develop in male-female inter-actions in a range of situations—from the totally public badi-nage in which the interactants entertain on-lookers while they establish joking as the basis of their relationship to the dyadic interaction between two already deeply involved participants in which the smart talk is intended to produce strategic advantage (and thus to modify the behavior of the man). Strong women develop reputations for their talking ability. As Maya Angelou reports it, her mother was one of these.

> The good Lord gave her a mind and she intended to use it to support her mother and her children. She didn't need to add "And have a little fun along the way."
> In the street the people were genuinely happy to see her. "Hey, baby, what's the news?"
> "Everything's steady, baby, steady."
> "I can't win, 'cause of the shape I'm in." (Said with a laugh that belied the content.)
> "You all right, momma?"
> "Aw, they tell me the whitefolks still in the lead." (Said as if that was not quite the whole truth.) . . .
> With all her jollity, Vivian Baxter [her mother] had no mercy. There was a saying in Oakland at the time which, if she didn't say it herself, explained her attitude. The saying was, "Sympathy is next to shit in the dictionary, and I can't even read." Her temper was not diminished with the passing of time, and when a passionate nature is not eased with moments of compassion, melodrama is likely to take the stage.[56]

The message is clear: if you have anything to do with such a woman, especially as a man, don't expect to be able to beat her at the talking game, at *signifying*. Thus, smartness becomes one way of maintaining distance and demonstrating the kind of *cool* that contributes to respect behavior. With the data provided by Mitchell-Kernan and Stoeltje, and from the fiction of Zora Neale Hurston and more recently Toni Cade Bambara,[57] one gets the impression that there is a different style and strategy of female signifying in which personal re-proach is put into impersonal attack form. Mitchell-Kernan, in her discussion of *signifying,* provides most of her examples from woman-humor, and they are of this less immediately personal and aggressive sort. For instance, she reports a conversation between a husband and wife:

> Wife: Where are you going?
> Husband: I'm going to work.
> Wife: . . . a suit, tie and white shirt. You didn't tell me you got a promotion.[58]

Talking Sweet and Smart to Each Other

The female style of signifying is, of course, not restricted to male-female encounters but may be employed in any situation of competition or conflict in which women find themselves. Nowhere does the available data seem less satisfactory than in the area of women talking smart among themselves, as a kind of female equivalent of "talking shit." Fiction by black women writers like Hurston and Bambara strongly suggests that the same devices of talking smart are used, but more playfully, in some peer-group interactions. See especially the latter's tour de force short story, "The Johnson Girls."[59] There is a difference of tone between these depictions and those describing similar rapping among black men, but without much more observational data it is not possible to detail what this difference is— other than the frequency of indirect and metaphoric phrasing and a less prolonged agonistic tone (that is, the contest elements seem to last for a shorter duration in women's talk). Also, additional data are needed to judge what importance such interactions have in the maintenance of the respect dimension of being female.

What we do know is that discussion of each other's behavior does go on between and among women, in front of each other and otherwise, and that such talk provides a running commentary on how individuals adhere to respect ideals or depart from them. Not all such talk is demeaning. As Hannerz depicts the situation, women are threatened when one of their number dramatizes herself as departing from the norms of respectability. "It is the women who complain most frequently about the disorderliness of specific individuals or of their neighborhood in general." [60] To do so is to give testimonial to their adherence to the respectable female role expectations. This is a kind of "gossiping" household performance that keeps "the public imagery of the 'good woman' going by speaking favorably about female behavior and morals more often than not, and by finding excuses for female infractions of mainstream behavior when confronted with evidence more often than they do for men." [61] Gossiping, then, does not just mean *bad-mouthing*. Women talking about the business of other women comment both approvingly and disapprovingly, all the while creating the impression of constant surveillance of behavior.

There is some question about the register and style in which such talking is carried out. Age and situational factors are important, but under certain circumstances the women may use a different register of speaking than is found in their communication with men or children. Hannerz describes these "sociable conversations" between women when they are commenting favorably about each other as being carried on in a "tone of relaxed sweetness, sometimes bordering on the saccharine, which contrasts sharply with the heated arguments of the male peer group." [62] This may be so when sweet talking among women occurs in the house; the arguments and discussions of men are carried out in the more public arena of the street world, where *playing* and *loud-talking*—"talk loud and draw a crowd"—may provide a reputation-maintaining device.

The ones most threatened by gossip are, of course, those who are heads of households, and they go to some lengths to maintain their names; name, in such circumstances, extends to a woman's house, which includes her man, and her children, insofar as their doings relate to the maintenance of the household. Just where the line is drawn is often a fine problem, as this conversation reported by Hylan Lewis from a Piedmont black community indicates. Lewis' informant is discussing her daughter's illegitimate children and the gossip excited by them:

> I had to lay Miss A—out about talking about my daughter and her three babies. I told her that although she had got them babies, that not nary one was got in my house; she got them away from my house; nobody, I mean nobody, can accuse me of

letting some man lie up in my house with my daughter. . . . *I keeps my house decent.* What they does outside, I can't help that. I'm going to take care of them as long as I is able.[63]

A woman, then, has to be cognizant of the fact that her behavior is going to be discussed, especially with regard to how she keeps her household under control.[64] On the other hand, this same gossip network accords her vocal acclaim in the behaviors they judge to be appropriate.

Furthermore, a woman does not have to abide by the judgment of the network. She may simply ignore such pressures, especially if she has made the decision to be on the streets, *playing*. Or she may continue to behave as she deems right but to provide accounts for her behavior in a court that generally allows a good deal of latitude if these accounts are indeed forthcoming. Or she may adopt an in-between position, giving an account to one member of the network with whom she feels most secure. In extreme situations, she may dramatically give counter testimony or a justifying account of ultimate respectability to a person who has chosen to use supposed behavior in her own testimony for respect.[65]

Numerous means of defense against gossip may not only argue back but propose alternative interpretations of what is meant by behaving respectably and what therefore leads to being accorded respectability by the community or by some of its members.[66] Though "Mouth-Almighties" exist, they are not just malicious gossipers; they provide a means of dramatizing one dimension of behavior in the dynamic of the black cultural system. They are purveyors of "words walking without masters"[67] but in a fuller sense than Hurston seems to have meant by that phrase. The words are those of community and of traditional image, and if they sometimes hurt they also act as part of a communication system that has maintained a sense of community in some trying times.

Respectability and Black Culture

I have been discussing the feasibility of studying social structure through learned interaction patterns that exist both on the level of role relationships and on that of style and the formalized content of communications. These are "learned" in the sense that individuals draw upon formulaic routines as a means of typing themselves and others. In this way I hoped to establish for women the same kind of continuities between talking styles and ascribed role and status as I have attempted in previous descriptions of self-dramatizations of black men. Here, however, the subject has to some degree resisted such a performance-centered folkloristic perspective, for we have so very few data concerning the communication and performance habits of women. We know something of the importance of women being able to answer a rap with a rap and to maintain self-respect through a control over the speaking going on in their presence through such means as smart talk and maintaining silence.

Clearly, respectability is an important role feature to negotiate as a woman matures. Because respect is equated in certain situations with money and attention to family maintenance, this negotiation may be carried on as a necessity of life. Looking at it from the larger performance perspective, negotiations are clearly also an important way in which some of the crucial dimensions of the contrarieties of black culture are asserted and maintained. Respect is never simply an attitude that brings about a monitoring of behavior in the presence of a respectable woman; it is also an ideal susceptible to being tested and the source of an important, and often entertaining, drama, which invests black life with its constant sense of adaptability, endurance, and vitality.

In looking at the amazing history of how Afro-Americans have been able to endure and proliferate in the alien New World, we must never underestimate the role of respectability and women. It was not just as "Mammy" that black women persisted in asserting their self-respect. The "Mammy" role grew in importance because of the manipulation by which respect might be negotiated even in the enslavement situation. The record on this is clear. Henry Breen's statement about St. Lucian blacks from the perspective of the plantation owner in 1844 is characteristic of plantation literature on this issue: "in the Negro's ear, . . . to be deemed *insolent* is the lowest depth of degradation, [but] to be held *respectable* is the highest step in the ladder of social distinctions. From Marigot to Maborya, from Cape Maynard to the Mole-à-chiques, respectability is the aim and end of every pursuit."[68]

Respectability never provides the only set of possible actions, but it does set out alternatives, which must be borne in mind in making any assessment of the systems and dramatizations of black culture. Though "acting respectable" means filling a role of woman and especially of Momma as demanded by the social structure, the more one looks at the negotiations the more one sees that the role is also *played* in most situations, and often joyously.[69]

☐ *Notes* ∎

1. Abraham Miller, "On the Road: Hitchhiking on the Highway," *Society* 10, no. 5 (1973), 16.

2. "On Face Work," *Psychiatry: Journal for the Study of Interpersonal Processes* 18 (1955), 213. Cf. "The concept of 'naming'" in Kenneth Burke, *The Philosophy of Literary Form* (New York, 1957), 1 ff., where he argues the importance of strategy and situation.

3. Ibid., 213.

4. Ibid., 215.

5. Ibid., 217.

6. I take the term from Lee Rainwater, *Behind Ghetto Walls* (Chicago, 1970), 284, where he mainly discusses male strategies and routines for giving testimony with regard to maturity in one's sex role.

7. The term as used here comes from the work of Marion B. Scott and Sanford M. Lyman. See their "Accounts," *American Sociological Review* 33 (1968), 46–62, where they define the term as "a linguistic device employed whenever an action is subjected to valuative inquiry . . . they prevent conflicts from arising by verbally bridging the gap between action and expectation" (p. 46). Michael Moerman, in his "Analysis of Lue Conversation: Providing Accounts, Finding Breaches, and Taking Sides," in David Sudnow, *Studies in Social Interaction* (New York, 1972), 75–119, utilizes the term in the sense of *accounts of,* but not *account for.*

8. Alan Dundes's conception of "folk ideas" in "Folk Ideas as Units of Worldview," in *Toward New Perspectives in Folklore,* ed.

Américo Paredes and Richard Bauman (Austin, Texas, 1972), 93–103, is similar to what is meant by presentation genres here.

9. That is, communities in which cultural patterns originating in gardening cultures are maintained in the more complex and technologically oriented, sophisticated, urban social environment.

10. Ulf Hannerz, *Soulside* (New York, 1969), 94.

11. For example, see Rainwater; Joyce A. Ladner, *Tomorrow's Tomorrow: The Black Woman* (New York, 1972); see also Camille Jeffers, *Living Poor* (Ann Arbor, 1967).

12. G.W.F. Hegel, *The Phenomenology of Mind,* trans. Sir Jas. Baillie (New York, 1964), 163–164. Cf. Robert Farris Thompson, *African Art in Motion* (Los Angeles, 1974), 7–8, where he utilizes the concept to illustrate how a rhythmic beat can be suspended and maintained simultaneously as a means of aesthetic elevation.

13. Cf. Thompson, *African Art,* 7.

14. Barbara Pyle, "Madame Queens," unpublished manuscript, 1972. Jeffers has one informant-friend whom she calls a "dowager queen," who demonstrates a similar personality. For one of the many fictional accounts of such a type, see Ernest J. Gaines, *The Autobiography of Miss Jane Pittman* (New York, 1971).

15. For a scene in which the two are distinguished, see Rainwater, *Behind Ghetto Walls,* 212.

16. J. Mason Brewer, *Aunt Dicy Tales* (privately printed, 1956).

17. Katherine L. Morgan, "Caddy Buffers: Legends of a Middle Class Negro Family in Philadelphia," *Keystone Folklore Quarterly* II (1966), 67–88.

18. See my *Positively Black* (Englewood Cliffs, New Jersey, 1970) and *Deep Down in the Jungle* (Chicago, 1970), for texts.

19. Hannerz, *Soulside,* 97. He discusses this range of argument extensively, 95–102. For similarly stereotypical account and testimony behavior from men, see *Positively Black,* 109, 112.

20. Carlye Ladner and Ossie Guffy, *Ossie: The Autobiography of a Black Woman* (New York, 1972), 3. See also Jeffers, *Living Poor,* 35.

21. *Soulside,* 97; see also Jeffers, *Living Poor,* 35, 50, where she notes the recurrence of this theme in women's talk.

22. *Soulside,* 99.

23. Maya Angelou, *I Know Why the Caged Bird Sings,* (New York, 1971), 176.

24. Beverly Stoeltje, "Bow-Legged Bastard: A Manner of Speaking," in *Folklore Annual of the University Folklore Association* 4–5, ed. Tom Ireland, Joanne Krauss, Beverly Stoeltje, Frances Terry (Austin, Texas, 1972–1973), 174. See the similar argument pursued by a Mississippi country informant in George Mitchell's *Blow My Blues Away* (Baton Rouge, 1971), 23.

25. See my "Black Talking on the Streets," in *Explorations in the Ethnography of Speaking,* ed. Richard Bauman and Joel Sherzer (Cambridge and New York, 1974), 534.

26. Herbert Gans, *The Urban Villagers* (New York, 1962).

27. Peter Wilson, "Reputation and Respectability: Suggestions for Caribbean Ethnology," *Man* 4 (1969), 70–84. See also my "Black Talking on the Streets"; *Positively Black;* and "Joking: The Training of the Man of Words in Talking Broad," in *Rappin' and Stylin' Out,* ed. Thomas Kochman (Champaign-Urbana, Illinois, 1972).

28. Rainwater, *Behind Ghetto Walls*, 21.

29. Ibid., 22.

30. Ibid., 29. Italics in the original. For a similar routine from a woman, see Jeffers, *Living Poor,* 43.

31. Carol Stack, "Parenthood and Personal Kinship Networks among Blacks on Aid," unpublished manuscript.

32. *Behind Ghetto Walls*, 205.

33. Louise Meriwether, *My Daddy Was a Numbers Runner* (New York, 1969), 28.

34. Zora Neale Hurston, *Their Eyes Were Watching God* (New York, 1969), 39.

35. Virginia Heyer Young, "Family and Childhood in a Southern Negro Community," *American Anthropologist* 72 (1970), 282. For data that argue somewhat in the same direction, but are not read in this manner, see *Living Poor,* 60 ff. Her remarks on "independence training" at this stage are apposite, if sometimes inconsistent.

36. Young, "Family and Childhood," 286. Young's observations of parent-child interactions are paralleled in many regards in Martha Coonfield Ward, *Them Children: A Study in Language Learning* (New York, 1971), 36–38, 71–73.

37. Ward, *Them Children,* 72–73.

38. Maya Angelou describes this behavior ideal in her reminiscences of her childhood in Stamps, Arkansas, in *I Know Why,* 22–23.

39. See, for instance, the brief discussion in *Living Poor,* 65, 67.

40. *Them Children,* 68.

41. See *Living Poor,* 64, and Ladner, *Tomorrow's Tomorrow,* 60 ff., for descriptions of this role and the social situation in which it operates. See especially "The Case of Kin" in *Tomorrow's Tomorrow,* 65–67.

42. Wilham H. Friedland and Dorothy Nelkin, *Migrant* (New York, 1972), 124–125.

43. See Wilson "Reputation and Respectability"; *Soulside,* and Elliot Liebow, *Tally's Corner* (Boston, 1967), *passim.*

44. See Jeffers's description in *Living Poor* 37–41) of the Queene family problems arising from a husband's buying a car and running around in it.

45. Ladner, *Tomorrow's Tomorrow,* 180.

46. Ibid., 182. Unfortunately, for our present purposes, Ladner's data are derived from highly directed interviews; thus we are given little information on what these strategies are and how they operate.

47. Alston Anderson, *Lover Man* (New York, 1959).

48. Joe L. Dillard, *Black English* (New York, 1972).

49. Hurston, *Their Eyes,* 37–38, and *Jonah's Gourd Vine* (Philadelphia, 1934), 70–72. The latter has commentary on how not to make such speeches.

50. Newbell Niles Puckett, *Folk Beliefs of the Southern Negro* (Chapel Hill, North Carolina, 1926), 29–30.

51. Hurston, *Their Eyes,* 58–59.

52. Ibid., 60. See also Hurston, *Mules and Men* (Philadelphia, 1935), 90–91.

53. Hurston, *Their Eyes,* 68–69.

54. Mitchell-Kernan, *Language Behavior in a Black Urban Community,* Monographs of the Language Behavior Laboratory, University of California, Berkeley, No. 2 (February, 1971), 106–107.

55. Stoeltje's informant makes such a distinction though on somewhat different grounds ("Bow-Legged Bastard," 164 ff). For a discussion of the range of street-talking types, see my "Black Talking on the Streets."

56. Angelou, *I Know Why,* 174–176.

57. See especially Toni Cade Bambara's short stories, collected in *Gorilla, My Love* (New York, 1972).

58. Mitchell-Kernan, *Language Behavior,* 180.

59. *Gorilla, My Love,* 144–159.

60. *Soulside,* 96.

61. Ibid.

62. Ibid.

63. Hylan Lewis, *Blackways of Kent* (New Haven, 1964), 104.

64. See, for instance, the remarks in *Living Poor,* 69, concerning how children are dressed; also the discussion in Anne Moody's *Coming of Age in Mississippi* (New York, 1968), 69 ff., on how the specter of being bad-mouthed by a Madam Queen operated in gaining converts to a local church in a small-town situation.

65. For examples of both these last two strategies, see the opening of Hurston, *Their Eyes.*

66. In a sense, this is the theme of such diverse works as Hurston's *Their Eyes* and Lorraine Hansberry's *Raisin in the Sun,* both of which survey some of the possibilities of achieving and maintaining respect, at different places and in different historical times.

67. Hurston, *Their Eyes,* 3.

68. Henry J. Breen, *A History of St. Lucia* (London, 1844), 200–201.

69. Some of these ideas were embodied in earlier papers: "A True and Exact Survey of Talking Black," read at the Conference on the Ethnography of Communication, Austin, Texas, April 21–23, 1972, sponsored by the Social Science Research Council's Committee on Sociolinguistics, and "Toward a Black Rhetoric," prepared for the Conference on Black Communications, University of Pittsburgh, Pittsburgh, Pennsylvania, November, 1972, sponsored by the American Speech Communications Association. I wrote the present paper while on a grant from the Center of Urban Ethnography. I am indebted to my wife, Barbara, for her suggestions for revision and to many of my students, especially Barbara Pyle, Minta Tidwell, Beverly Stoeltje, Danielle Roemer, and Claire Farrer for their commentary.

106

A Selection of Blues and Spirituals

Black Snake Moan

Ummmmh oh
         ain't got no mama now
Ummmmh oh
         ain't got no mama now
She told me late last night
                  you don't need no mama no how

Mmmmmm mmmm
            black snake crawling in my room
Mmmmmm mmmm
            black snake crawling in my room
And some pretty mama
                 better come and get this black
                 snake soon

Ummmmh uh
         that must have been a bed bug
                    baby, a chinch can't bite that
                    hard
Ummmmh uh
         that must have been a bed bug
                    honey, a chinch can't bite
                    that hard

Blind Lemon Jefferson, "Black Snake Moan," Okeh Record 8455. Others from Sterling A. Brown, Arthur P. Davis, and Ulysses Lee, eds., *The Negro Caravan* (1941; reprint, New York: Arno Press, 1969); Roland Hayes, *My Songs* (Boston: Atlantic Monthly Press, 1948); and James Weldon Johnson, ed., *The Book of American Negro Spirituals* (New York: Viking, 1925).

Asked my sugar for fifty cent
                              she said, Lemon, ain't a dime
                              in the yard

Mmmmama that's all right
                              mama that's all right for you
Mmmmama that's all right
                              mama that's all right for you
Mama that's all right
                              most any old way you do

Mmmmmm mmmm
                              what's that matter now
Mmmmmm mmmm
                              honey, what's the matter now
Sugar, what's the matter:
                              don't like no black snake no how

Mmmmmm mmmm
                              wonder where is my black snake gone
Mmmmmm mmmm
                              wonder where is the black snake gone
Black snake, mama, done
                              run my darling home

Deep River

Deep river, my home is over Jordan,
Deep river, Lord; I want to cross over into camp ground.

O, don't you want to go to that gospel feast,
That promised land, where all is peace?

Deep river, my home is over Jordan,
Deep river, Lord; I want to cross over into camp ground.

Walk into heaven and take my seat, and cast my crown at
    Jesus feet,
Lord, I want to cross over into camp ground.

Deep river, my home is over Jordan,
Deep river, Lord; I want to cross over into camp ground.

108

Stan' Still Jordan

Stan' still Jordan,
Stan' still Jordan,
Stan' still Jordan,
Lord, I can't stan' still.

I got a mother in heaven,
I got a mother in heaven,
I got a mother in heaven,
Lord, I can't stan' still.

Stan' still Jordan,
Stan' still Jordan
Stan' still Jordan,
Lord, I can't stan' still.

When I get up in glory,
When I get up in glory,
When I get up in glory,
Lord, I can't stan' still.

Stan' still Jordan,
Stan' still Jordan,
Stan' still Jordan,
Lord, I can't stan' still.

Jordan river,
Jordan river,
Jordan river,
is chilly and cold

It will chill-a my body,
It will chill-a my body,
It will chill-a my body,
but not my soul.

Stan' still Jordan,
Stan' still Jordan,
Stan' still Jordan,
Lord, I can't stan' still.

O, Wasn't Dat a Wide River?

O, wasn't dat a wide river,
dat river of Jordan,
Lord, wide river!
Dere's one mo' river to cross.

O, wasn't dat a wide river,
dat river of Jordan,
Lord, wide river!
Dere's one mo' river to cross.

O, de river of Jordan is so wide,
One mo' river to cross.
I don't know how to get on de other side;
One mo' river to cross.

Satan am nothin' but a snake in de grass,
One mo' river to cross.
If you ain't mighty careful, he will hol' you fas';
One mo' river to cross.

O, wasn't dat a wide river,
dat river of Jordan,
Lord, wide river!
Dere's one mo' river to cross.

Give-a Way, Jordan

Give-a way Jordan,
Give-a way Jordan, Lord,
Give-a way Jordan,
I mus' go for to see my Lord.

Give-a way Jordan,
Give-a way Jordan, Lord,
Give-a way Jordan,
I mus' go for to see my Lord.

Nebuchadnezzar sat on his royal seat.
I mus' go for to see my Lord.
He saw the three Hebrew chillun boun' hands an' feet.
I mus' go for to see my Lord.

110

Give-a way Jordan,
Give-a way Jordan, Lord,
Give-a way Jordan,
I mus' go for to see my Lord.

Roll, Jordan, Roll

Roll Jordan, roll,
Roll Jordan, roll
I wanter go to heav'n when I die,
To hear ol' Jordan roll.

O, {brethren}
    {sisteren}.
Roll Jordan, roll
Roll Jordan, roll
I wanter go to heav'n when I die,
To hear ol' Jordan roll.

O brothers you oughter been dere,
Yes my Lord
A sittin' up in de kingdom,
To hear ol' Jordan roll

Sing it ovah,
Roll Jordan, roll
Roll Jordan, roll,
I wanter go to heav'n when I die,
To hear ol' Jordan roll.

Genesis 1 – 3

In the beginning God created the heaven and the earth.

2 And the earth was without form, and void; and darkness *was* upon the face of the deep. And the Spirit of God moved upon the face of the waters.

3 ¶ And God said, Let there be light: and there was light.

4 And God saw the light, that *it was* good: and God divided the light from the darkness.

5 And God called the light Day, and the darkness he called Night. And the evening and the morning were the first day.

6 ¶ And God said, Let there be a firmament in the midst of the waters, and let it divide the waters from the waters.

7 And God made the firmament, and divided the waters which *were* under the firmament from the waters which *were* above the firmament: and it was so.

8 And God called the firmament Heaven. And the evening and the morning were the second day.

9 ¶ And God said, Let the waters under the heaven be gathered together unto one place, and let the dry *land* appear: and it was so.

10 And God called the dry *land* Earth; and the gathering together of the waters called he Seas: and God saw that *it was* good.

11 And God said, Let the earth bring forth grass, the herb yielding seed, *and* the fruit tree yielding fruit after his kind, whose seed *is* in itself, upon the earth: and it was so.

12 And the earth brought forth grass, *and* herb yielding seed after his kind, and the tree yielding fruit, whose seed *was* in itself, after his kind: and God saw that *it was* good.

13 And the evening and the morning were the third day.

14 ¶ And God said, Let there be lights in the firmament of the heaven to divide the day from the night; and let them be for signs, and for seasons, and for days, and years:

15 And let them be for lights in the firmament of the heaven to give light upon the earth: and it was so.

16 And God made two great lights; the greater light to rule the day, and the lesser light to rule the night: *he made* the stars also.

17 And God set them in the firmament of the heaven to give light upon the earth.

18 And to rule over the day and over the night, and to divide the light from the darkness: and God saw that *it was* good.

19 And the evening and the morning were the fourth day.

20 And God said, let the waters bring forth abundantly the moving creature that hath life, and fowl *that* may fly above the earth in the open firmament of heaven.

21 And God created great whales, and every living creature that moveth, which the waters brought forth abundantly, after their kind, and every winged fowl after his kind: and God saw that *it was* good.

22 And God blessed them, saying, Be fruitful, and multiply, and fill the waters in the seas, and let fowl multiply in the earth.

23 And the evening and the morning were the fifth day.

24 ¶ And God said, Let the earth bring forth the living creature after his kind, cattle, and creeping things, and beast of the earth after his kind: and it was so.

25 And God made the beast of the earth after his kind, and cattle after their kind, and every thing that creepeth upon the earth after his kind: and God saw that *it was* good.

26 ¶ And God said, let us make man in our image, after our likeness: and let them have dominion over the fish of the sea, and over the fowl of the air, and over the cattle, and over all the earth, and over every creeping thing that creepeth upon the earth.

27 So God created man in his *own* image, in the image of God created he him; male and female created he them.

28 And God blessed them, and God said unto them, Be fruitful, and multiply, and replenish the earth, and subdue it: and have dominion over the fish of the sea, and over the fowl of the air, and over every living thing that moveth upon the earth.

29 ¶ And God said, Behold, I have given you every herb bearing seed, which *is* upon the face of all the earth, and every tree,

in the the which *is* the fruit of a tree yielding seed; to you it shall be for meat.

30 And to every beast of the earth, and to every fowl of the air, and to every thing that creepeth upon the earth, wherein *there is* life, *I have given* every green herb for meat: and it was so.

31 And God saw every thing that he had made, and, behold, *it was* very good. And the evening and the morning were the sixth day.

Chapter 2

Thus the heavens and the earth were finished, and all the host of them.

2 And on the seventh day God ended his work which he had made; and he rested on the seventh day from all his work which he had made.

3 And God blessed the seventh day, and sanctified it: because that in it he had rested from all his work which God created and made.

4 ¶ These *are* the generations of the heavens and of the earth when they were created, in the day that the LORD God made the earth and the heavens,

5 And every plant of the field before it was in the earth and every herb of the field before it grew: for the LORD God had not caused it to rain upon the earth, and *there was* not a man to till the ground.

6 But there went up a mist from the earth, and watered the whole face of the ground.

7 And the LORD God formed man *of* the dust of the ground, and breathed into his nostrils the breath of life; and man became a living soul.

8 ¶ And the LORD God planted a garden eastward in Eden; and there he put the man whom he had formed.

9 And out of the ground made the LORD God to grow every tree that is pleasant to the sight, and good for food; the tree of life also in the midst of the garden, and the tree of knowledge of good and evil.

10 And a river went out of Eden to water the garden; and from thence it was parted, and became into four heads.

11 The name of the first *is* Pison: that *is* it which compasseth the whole land of Havilah, where *there is* gold;

12 And the gold of that land *is* good: there *is* bdellium and the onyx stone.

13 And the name of the second river *is* Gihon: the same *is* it that compasseth the whole land of Ethiopia.

14 And the name of the third river *is* Hiddekel: that *is* it which goeth toward the east of Assyria. And the fourth river *is* Euphrates.

15 And the LORD God took the man, and put him into the garden of Eden to dress it and to keep it.

16 And the LORD God commanded the man, saying, Of every tree of the garden thou mayest freely eat:

17 But of the tree of the knowledge of good and evil, thou shalt not eat of it: for in the day that thou eatest thereof thou shalt surely die.

18 ¶ And the LORD God said, *It is* not good that the man should be alone; I will make him an help meet for him.

19 And out of the ground the LORD God formed every beast of the field, and every fowl of the air; and brought *them* unto Adam to see what he would call them: and whatsoever Adam called every living creature, that *was* the name thereof.

20 And Adam gave names to all cattle, and to the fowl of the air, and to every beast of the field; but for Adam there was not found an help meet for him.

21 And the LORD God caused a deep sleep to fall upon Adam, and he slept: and he took one of his ribs, and closed up the flesh instead thereof;

22 And the rib, which the LORD God had taken from man, made he a woman, and brought her unto the man.

23 And Adam said, This *is* now bone of my bones, and flesh of my flesh: she shall be called Woman, because she was taken out of Man.

24 Therefore shall a man leave his father and his mother, and shall cleave unto his wife: and they shall be one flesh.

25 And they were both naked, the man and his wife, and were not ashamed.

Chapter 3

Now the serpent was more subtil than any beast of the field which the LORD God had made. And he said unto the woman, Yea, hath God said, Ye shall not eat of every tree of the garden?

2 And the woman said unto the serpent, We may eat of the fruit of the trees of the garden:

3 But of the fruit of the tree which *is* in the midst of the garden, God hath said, Ye shall not eat of it, neither shall ye touch it, lest ye die.

4 And the serpent said unto the woman, Ye shall not surely die:

5 For God doth know that in the day ye eat thereof, then your eyes shall be opened, and ye shall be as gods, knowing good and evil.

6 And when the woman saw that the tree *was* good for food, and that it *was* pleasant to the eyes, and a tree to be desired to make *one* wise, she took of the fruit thereof, and did eat, and gave also unto her husband with her; and he did eat.

7 And the eyes of them both were opened, and they knew that they *were* naked; and they sewed fig leaves together, and made themselves aprons.

8 And they heard the voice of the LORD God walking in the garden in the cool of the day: and Adam and his wife hid themselves from the presence of the LORD God amongst the trees of the garden.

9 And the LORD God called unto Adam, and said unto him, Where *art* thou?

10 And he said, I heard thy voice in the garden, and I was afraid, because I *was* naked; and I hid myself.

11 And he said, Who told thee that thou *wast* naked? Hast thou eaten of the tree, whereof I commanded thee that thou shouldest not eat?

12 And the man said, The woman whom thou gavest *to be* with me, she gave me of the tree, and I did eat.

13 And the LORD God said unto the woman, What *is* this *that* thou has done? And the woman said, The serpent beguiled me, and I did eat.

14 And the LORD God said unto the serpent, Because thou

hast done this, thou *art* cursed above all cattle, and above every beast of the field; upon thy belly shalt thou go, and dust shalt thou eat all the days of thy life:

15 And I will put enmity between thee and the woman, and between thy seed and her seed; it shall bruise thy head, and thou shalt bruise his heel.

16 Unto the woman he said, I will greatly multiply thy sorrow and thy conception; in sorrow thou shalt bring forth children; and thy desire *shall be* to thy husband, and he shall rule over thee.

17 And unto Adam he said, Because thou hast hearkened unto the voice of thy wife, and hast eaten of the tree, of which I commanded thee, saying, Thou shalt not eat of it: cursed *is* the ground for thy sake; in sorrow shalt thou eat *of* it all the days of thy life;

18 Thorns also and thistles shall it bring forth to thee; and thou shalt eat the herb of the field;

19 In the sweat of thy face shalt thou eat bread, till thou return unto the ground; for out of it wast thou taken: for dust thou *art,* and unto dust shalt thou return.

20 And Adam called his wife's name Eve; because she was the mother of all living.

21 Unto Adam also and to his wife did the LORD God make coats of skins, and clothed them.

22 ¶ And the LORD God said, Behold, the man is become as one of us, to know good and evil: and now, lest he put forth his hand, and take also of the tree of life, and eat, and live for ever:

23 Therefore the LORD God sent him forth from the garden of Eden, to till the ground from whence he was taken.

24 So he drove out the man; and he placed at the east of the garden of Eden Cherubims, and a flaming sword which turned every way, to keep the way of the tree of life.

118

Zora Neale Hurston and the Speakerly Text

Our house stood within a few rods of the Chesapeake Bay, whose broad bosom was ever white with sails from every quarter of the habitable globe. Those beautiful vessels, robed in purest white, so delightful to the eye of freemen, were to me so many shrouded ghosts, to terrify and torment me with thoughts of my wretched condition. I have often, in the deep stillness of a summer's Sabbath, stood all alone upon the lofty banks of that noble bay, and traced, with saddened heart and tearful eye, the countless number of sails moving off to the mighty ocean. The sight of these always affected me powerfully. My thoughts would compel utterance; and there, with no audience but the Almighty, I would pour out my soul's complaint, in my rude way, with an apostrophe to the moving multitude of ships:— "You are loosed from your moorings, and are free; I am fast in my chains, and am a slave! You move merrily before the gentle gale, and I sadly before the bloody whip! You are freedom's swift-winged angels, that fly around the world; I am confined in bands of iron! O that I were free!"
FREDERICK DOUGLASS, 1845

Ships at a distance have every man's wish on board. For some they come in with the tide. For others they sail forever on the horizon, never out of sight, never landing until the Watcher turns his eyes away in resignation, his dreams mocked to death by Time. That is the life of men. Now, women forget all those things they don't want to remember, and remember everything they don't want to forget. The dream is the truth. Then they act and do things accordingly.
ZORA NEALE HURSTON, 1937

119

The eighteenth-century revisions of the trope of the Talking Book that I traced in Chapter 4 and its displacement into tropes of freedom and literacy in the slave narratives published after 1815 help us to understand the remarkable degree to which the quest to register a public black voice in Western letters preoccupied the Afro-American tradition's first century. Writing could be no mean thing in the life of the slave. What was at stake for the earliest black authors was nothing less than the implicit testimony to their humanity, a common humanity which they sought to demonstrate through the very writing of a text of an ex-slave's life. In one sense, not even legal manumission was of more importance to the slave community's status in Western culture than was the negation of the image of the black as an absence. To redress their image as a negation of all that was white and Western, black authors published as if their collective fate depended on how their texts would be received. It is as difficult to judge how effective this tacitly political gesture was as it is to judge how the negative image of the black in Western culture was affected by the publication of black texts. It seems apparent, however, that the abolition of slavery did not diminish the force of this impulse to write the race fully into the human community. Rather, the liberation of the slave community and the slow but steady growth of a black middle class between Reconstruction (1865–1876) and the sudden ending of the New Negro Renaissance (circa 1930) only seem to have made this impulse even more intense than it had been in antebellum America. Perhaps this was the case because, once slavery was abolished, racism assumed vastly more subtle forms. If slavery had been an immoral institution, it had also been a large, fixed target; once abolished, the target of racism splintered into hundreds of fragments, all of which seemed to be moving in as many directions. Just as the ex-slaves wrote to end slavery, so too did free black authors write to redress the myriad forms that the fluid mask of racism assumed between the end of the Civil War and the end of the Jazz Age.

    If the writings of black people retained their implicitly

Excerpted from the chapter "Zora Hurston and the Speakerly Text," in *The Signifying Monkey: A Theory of Afro-American Literary Criticism* (New York: Oxford University Press, 1989).

political import after the war and especially after the sudden death of Reconstruction, then it should not surprise us that the search for a voice in black letters became a matter of grave concern among the black literati. This concern, as we might expect, led to remarkably polemical debates over the precise register which an "authentic" black voice would, or could, assume. It is also clear that postbellum black authors continued to read and revise the central figures they received from the fragments of tradition that somehow survived the latter nineteenth century's onslaught of de facto and de jure segregation. Zora Neale Hurston's revision of Frederick Douglass's apostrophe, to the ships (the epigraphs to this chapter) is only one example of many such instances of a black textual grounding through revision.

Hurston underscores her revision of Douglass's canonical text by using two chiasmuses in her opening paragraphs.[1] The subject of the second paragraph of *Their Eyes Were Watching God* (women) reverses the subject of the first (men) and figures the nature of their respective desire in opposite terms. A man's desire becomes reified onto a disappearing ship, and he is transformed from a human being into "a Watcher," his desire personified onto an object, beyond his grasp or control, external to himself. Nanny, significantly, uses this "male" figure—"Ah could see uh big ship at a distance" (p. 35)—as does Tea Cake, whose use reverses Douglass's by indicating Tea Cake's claim of control of his fate and ability to satisfy Janie's desire: "Can't no ole man stop me from gittin' no ship for yuh if dat's whut you want. Ah'd git dat ship out from under him so slick til he'd be walkin' de water lak ole Peter befo' he knowed it" (p. 154).

A woman, by contrast, represents desire metaphorically, rather than metonymically, by controlling the process of memory, an active subjective process figured in the pun on (re) membering, as in the process of narration which Janie will share with her friend, Phoeby, and which we shall "overhear." For a woman, "The dream is the truth"; the truth is her dream. Janie, as we shall see, is thought to be (and is maintained) "inarticulate" by her first two husbands but is a master of metaphorical narration; Joe Starks, her most oppressive husband, by contrast, is a master of metonym, an opposition which Janie must navigate her selves through to achieve self-knowledge. The first sentence ("Now, women forget all those things they don't want to remember, and remember everything they don't want to forget") is itself a chiasmus (women/remember//remember/forget), similar in structure to Douglass's famous chiasmas, "You have seen how a man became a slave, you will see how a slave became a man." Indeed, Douglass's major contribution to the slave's narrative was to make chiasmus the central trope of slave narration, in which a slave-object writes himself or herself into a human-subject through the act of writing. The overarching rhetorical strategy of the slave narratives written after 1845 can be represented as a chiasmus, as repetition and reversal. Hurston, in these enigmatic opening paragraphs, Signifies upon Douglass through formal revision.

This sort of formal revision is one mode of tacit commentary about the shape and status of received tradition. A more explicit mode was the literary criticism published by blacks as a response to specific black texts which, despite great difficulties, somehow managed to be published. While this subject demands a full-length study, I can summarize its salient aspects here. The debate about the register of the black voice assumed two poles. By the end of the Civil War, the first pole of the debate, the value of the representation, of the reality imitated in the text, had been firmly established. Black authors wrote almost exclusively about their social and political condition as black people living in a society in which race was, at best, problematical. By the turn of the century, a second and more subtle pole of the debate had become predominant, and that pole turned upon precisely how an authentic black voice should be represented in print. The proper manner and matter of representation of a black printed voice are not truly separable, of course; these poles of concern could merge, and often did, as in the heated issue of the import of Paul Laurence Dunbar's late-nineteenth-century dialect poetry. To understand more fully just how curious were Zora Neale Hurston's rhetorical strategies of revision in *Their Eyes Were Watching God* (1937) and just how engaged in debate these strategies were with the Afro-American tradition, it is useful to summarize the nineteenth-century arguments about representation.

We gain some understanding of this concern over representation by examining *The Anglo-African Magazine*, published in New York by Thomas Hamilton between January 1859 and March 1860. Hamilton, in his introductory "Apology" to the first number, argues what for his generation was self-evident: "[black people], in order to assert and maintain their rank as men among men, must speak for themselves; no outside tongue, however gifted with eloquence, can tell their story." Blacks must "speak for themselves," Hamilton writes, to counter the racist "endeavor to write down the negro as something less than a man."[2] In the second number, W. J. Wilson, in a poem entitled "The Coming Man," defines the presence of the text to be that which separates "the undefinable present," "the dim misty past," and "the unknown future":

> I am resolved. 'Tis more than half my task;
> 'Twas the great need of all my passed existence.
> The glooms that have so long shrouded me,
> Recede as vapor from the new presence,
> And the light-gleam—it must be life
> So brightens and spreads its rays before,
> That I read my Mission as 'twere a book.[3]

Wilson's figure of life as a text to be read, of the race's life as embodied in the book, Frances E. W. Harper elaborated upon in a letter to the editor later that same year. In this letter, we have recorded one of the first challenges to what was then, and has remained, the preoccupation of Afro-American male writers: the great and terrible subject of white racism. "If our talents are to be recognized," Frances Harper writes,

> we must write less of issues that are particular and more of feelings that are general. We are blessed with hearts and brains that compass more than ourselves in our present plight. . . . We must look to the future which, God willing, will be better than the present or the past, and delve into the heart of the world.[4]

Consider the sheer audacity of this black woman, perhaps our first truly professional writer, who could so freely advocate this position in the great crisis year of 1859, which witnessed both John Brown's aborted raid on the Harper's Ferry arsenal and the U.S. Supreme Court's decision to uphold the constitutionality of the Fugitive Slave Act of 1850. Harper, in this statement about representation and in her poems and fictions, demanded that black writers embrace as their subjects "feelings that are general," feelings such as love and sex, birth and death. The debate over the content of black literature had begun, then, as articulated by a black woman writer.

Whereas Harper expressed concern for a new content or "signifier," a content that was at once black, self-contained, and humanly general, the other pole of the debate about representation concerned itself with the exact form that the signifier should take. This concern over what I am calling the signifier occupied, in several ways and for various reasons, the center of black aesthetic theory roughly between the publication of Paul Laurence Dunbar's *Lyrics of Lowly Life* in 1895 and at least the publication in 1937 of Zora Neale Hurston's *Their Eyes Were Watching God*. This debate, curiously enough, returns us in the broadest sense to the point of departure of this chapter, namely the absence and presence of the black voice in the text, that which caused Gronniosaw so much consternation and perplexity. It is not surprising that Dunbar's widely noted presence should engender, in part, the turn of critical attention to matters of language and voice, since it is he who stands, unquestionably, as the most accomplished black dialect poet, and the most successful black poet before Langston Hughes. Nor is it surprising that Hurston's lyrical text should demarcate an ending of this debate, since Hurston's very rhetorical strategy, her invention of what I have chosen to call the speakerly text, seems designed to mediate between, for fiction, what Sterling A. Brown's representation of the black voice mediated between for black poetic diction: namely, a profoundly lyrical, densely metaphorical, quasi-musical, privileged black oral tradition on the one hand, and a received but not yet fully appropriated standard English literary tradition on the other hand. The quandary for the writer was to find a third term, a bold and novel signifier, informed by these two related yet distinct literary languages. This is what Hurston tried to do in *Their Eyes*.

Critics widely heralded Dunbar's black poetic diction, and poets, white and black, widely imitated it. It is difficult to understand the millennarian tones of Dunbar's critical reception. The urgent calls for a black "redeemer-poet," so common

124

in the black newspapers and periodicals published between 1827 and 1919, by the late 1880s were being echoed by white critics. One anonymous white woman critic, for example, who signed herself only as "A Lady from Philadelphia," wrote in *Lippincott's Monthly Magazine* in 1886 that "The Coming American Novelist" would be "of African origin."[5] This great author would be one "With us" but "not of us," one who "has suffered everything a poet, a dramatist, a novelist need suffer before he comes to have his lips anointed." "When one comes to consider the subject," this critic concludes, "there is no improbability to it." After all, she continues, the African "has given us the only national music we have ever had," a corpus of art "distinctive in musical history." He is, moreover, "a natural story-teller,"[6] uniquely able to fabricate what she calls "acts of the imagination," discourses in which no "morality is involved."

> [Why] should not this man, who has suffered so much, who is so easy to amuse, so full of his own resources, and who is yet undeveloped, why should he not some day soon tell a story that shall interest, amuse us, stir our hearts, and make a new epoch in our literature?[7]

Then, in a remarkable reversal, the writer makes an even bolder claim:

> Yet farther: I have used the generic masculine pronoun because it is convenient; but Fate keeps revenges in store. It was a woman who, taking the wrongs of the African as her theme, wrote the novel that awakened the world to their reality, and why should not the coming novelist be a woman as well as an African? She—the woman of that race—has some claims on Fate which are not yet paid up.

It is difficult to discern which of this critic's two claims is the bolder: that the great American writer would be black or that she would be a black woman. It is not difficult, however, to summarize the energizing effect on our literary tradition which this critic's prediction was to have. Even as late as 1899, W. S. Scarborough would still cite this *Lippincott's* essay to urge black writers to redeem "the race."[8]

W.H.A. Moore, writing about "A Void in Our Literature" in 1890, called for the appearance of a great black poet whose presence would stand as "an indication of the character of [the Afro-American's] development on those lines which determine the capacity of a people." "The Afro-American," he continues,

> has not given to English literature a good poet. No one of his kind has, up to this day, lent influence to the literature of his time, save Phillis Wheatley. It is not to be expected that he would. And yet every fragment, every whispering of his be-nighted muse is scanned with eager and curious interest in the hope that here may be found the gathered breathings of a true singer.[9]

"The keynote," Moore concludes, "has not yet been struck." To find a poetic diction which reflects "the inner workings of the subject which it seeks to portray," Moore argues, "is the mission of the race." Moore's essay is merely typical of many others published between 1865 and 1930. For example, in 1893, H. T. Johnson, editor of the *Recorder,* outlined the need for race authors to express racial aspirations. Five years later, H. T. Kealing wrote of the unique contributions that only Negro authors could make. The literature of any people, he said, had an indigenous quality, "the product of the national peculiarities and race idiosyncrasies that no alien could duplicate." He called upon the Negro author not to imitate whites, as had been the case hitherto, but to reach "down to the original and unexplored depths of his own being where lies unused the material that is to provide him a place among the great writers." Similarly, Scarborough, speaking at the Hampton Negro Conference in 1899, called for something higher than the false dialect types depicted by white authors; even Chestnutt's and Dunbar's short stories had not gone far enough in portraying the higher aspirations of the race. Only the Negro author could portray the Negro best—his "loves and hates, his hopes and fears, his ambitions, his whole life, in such a way that the world will weep and laugh . . . forgetting completely that the hero and heroine are God's bronze image, but knowing only that they are men and women with joys and sorrows that belong to the whole human family." In the discussion that followed Scarborough's paper, it was agreed that the types portrayed in "vaudeville" were false. Lucy Laney, principal of the Haines Norman and Industrial Institute, prefigured a major interest of the 1920s when she spoke of the material for short stories to be found in the rural South and called upon Negro writers to go down to the sea islands of Georgia and South Carolina "where they could study the Negro in his original purity," with a culture and a voice "close to the African." [10]

Into this black milieu wrote Paul Lawrence Dunbar. Perhaps because we tend to read Dunbar backwards, as it were, through the poetry of Sterling A. Brown and the early Langston Hughes, and through the often unfortunate poetic efforts of Dunbar's less talented imitators, we tend to forget how startling was Dunbar's use of black dialect as the basis of a poetic diction. After all, by 1895, dialect had come to connote black innate mental inferiority, the linguistic sign both of human bondage (as origin) and of the continued failure of "improvability" or "progress," two turn-of-the-century key-words. Dialect signified both "black difference" and that the figure of the black in literature existed primarily as object, not subject; and even sympathetic characterizations of the black, such as Uncle Remus by Joel Chandler Harris, were far more related to a racist textual tradition that stemmed from minstrelsy, the plantation novel, and vaudeville than to representations of spoken language. As Scarborough summarized the matter:

> Both northern and southern writers have presented Negro nature, Negro dialect, Negro thought, as they conceived it, too often, alas, as evolved out of their own consciousness. Too often the dialect has been inconsistent, the types presented, mere composite photographs as it were, or uncouth specimens served up so as the humorous side of the literary setting might be properly balanced. [11]

This received literary tradition of plantation and vaudeville art, Scarborough concluded, demanded "realism" to refute the twin gross stereotypes of characterization and the representation of black speech.

For Dunbar to draw upon dialect as the medium through which to posit this mode of realism suggests both a certain bold-ness as well as a certain opportunism, two qualities that helped to inform Dunbar's mixed results, which we know so well, he lamented to his death. Dunbar, nevertheless, Signified upon the received white racist textual tradition and posited in its stead a black poetic diction which his more gifted literary heirs would, in their turn, Signify upon, with often pathetic results. What Sterling A. Brown would realize in the language of his poetry, Zora Neale Hurston would realize in the language of her fiction. For, after Dunbar, the two separate poles of the debate over black mimetic principles, over the shape of the signifier and the nature of the signified, could no longer be thought of independently. Dunbar's primary rhetorical gesture, as Scar-borough concluded in 1899, had been to do just that:

> And here we pause to see what [Dunbar and Chestnutt] have added to our literature, what new artistic value they have dis-covered. [Both] have followed closely the "suffering side," the portrayal of the old fashioned Negro of "befo' de wah,"—the Negro that [Thomas Nelson] Page and [Joel Chandler] Harris and others have given a permanent place in literature. But they have done one thing more; they have presented the facts of Negro life with a thread running through both warp and woof that shows not only humour and pathos, humility, self-sacrifice, courtesy and loyalty, but something at times of the higher aims, ambition, desires, hopes, and aspiration of the race—but by no means as fully and to as great an extent as we had hoped they would do.[12]

How the black writer represented, and what he or she repre-sented, were now indissolubly linked in black aesthetic theory.

In the curious manner by which one generation's par-enthetical concerns come to form the central questions of a subsequent generation's critical debate, Scarborough's judge-ment that Dunbar's representations of the folk "befo' de wah" were potentially capable of encompassing more than "humour and pathos" became the linchpin of James Weldon Johnson's attack on dialect as a poetic diction. I have sketched the de-

128

bate over dialect elsewhere.[13] Suffice it to say here that that great American realist, William Dean Howells, in 1896, thought that Dunbar's dialect verse was a representation of reality, a "portrait . . . undeniably like." The political import of this artistic achievement, Howells maintained, was unassailable: "A race which has reached this effect in any of its members can no longer be held wholly uncivilized; and intellectually Mr. Dunbar makes a stronger claim for the negro than the negro has yet done."[14] By the 1920s, however, dialect was thought to be a literary trap.

A careful study of the aesthetic theories of the New Negro Renaissance suggests strongly that the issue of dialect as an inappropriate literary language seems to have been raised in order for a second poetic diction to be posited in its place. Indeed, we can with some justification set as boundaries of this literary movement James Weldon Johnson's critiques of dialect, which he published in his separate "Prefaces" to the first and second editions of *The Book of American Negro Poetry,* printed in 1923 and 1931, respectively, but also Johnson's "Introduction" to the first edition of Sterling A. Brown's *Southern Road,* printed in 1932.

In his "Preface," Johnson had defined the urgent task of the new black writer to be the "break away from, not Negro dialect itself, but the limitations of Negro dialect imposed by the fixing effects of long convention." And what were these limitations? Said Johnson, "it is an instrument with but two full stops, humor and pathos," repeating and reversing Scarborough's terms. Nine years later, in his second "Preface," Johnson could assert assuredly that "the passing of traditional dialect as a medium for Negro poets is complete." Just one year later, however, Brown's poetry forced Johnson to admit that, although Brown "began writing just after Negro poets had generally discarded conventionalized dialect, with its minstrel traditions of Negro life," he has "infused his [dialect] poetry with genuine characteristic flavor by adopting as his medium the common, racy living speech of the Negro in certain phases of *real* life." Brown's achievement, Johnson acknowledges, is that he has turned to "folk poetry" as a source of a poetic diction, "deepened its meanings and multiplied its implications. . . . In a word, he has taken this raw material and worked it into original and authentic power." Brown's poetry, then, in a remarkably tangible sense, marks the end of the New Negro Renaissance as well as the resolution, for black poetic diction, of a long debate over its mimetic principles.[15]

Brown's achievement in poetry, however, had no counterpart in fiction. True, Jean Tommer's *Cane* can be thought of as a fictional antecedent of Brown's poetic diction, both of whose works inform the structure of *Their Eyes Were Watching God*. Yet Toomer's use of the privileged oral voice, and especially its poignant silences, is not without its ironies, since Toomer employs the black oral voice in his text both as a counterpoint to that standard English voice of his succession of narrators but also as evidence of the modernist claim that there had existed no privileged, romantic movement of unified consciousness, especially or not even in the cane fields of a rural Georgia echoing its own swan song. Existence, in the world of *Cane,* is bifurcated, fundamentally opposed, as represented by all sorts of binary oppositions, among these standard English and black speech, as well as black and white, male and female, South and North, textual desire and sensual consummation. Even in that fiction's long, final section, called "Kabnis," in which the place of the narrator becomes that of stage directions in a tragedy, the presence of the oral voice retains its primarily antiphonal function, as in the following exchange among Halsey, Layman, and Kabnis:

> Halsey (in a mock religious tone): Amen t that, brother Layman. Amen (turning to Kabnis, half playful, yet somehow dead in earnest). An Mr. Kabnis, kindly remember youre in th land of cotton—hell of a land. Th white folks get the boll; th niggers get th stalk. An dont you dare touch th boll, or even look at it. They'll swing y sho. (Laughs)
>
> Kabnis: But they wouldnt touch a gentleman—fellows, men like us three here—
>
> Layman: Nigger's a nigger down this away, Professor. An only two dividins: good an bad. An even they aint permanent categories. They sometimes mixes um up when it comes t lynchin. I've seen um do it.[16]

Toomer's representation of black spoken language, even in this instance, stands essentially as an element of plot and of theme.

Rather than as a self-contained element of literary structure, the oral voice in *Cane* is a motivated sign of duality, of opposition, which Toomer thematizes in each section of his fiction, and specifically in this passage:

> Kabnis: . . . An besides, he aint my past. My ancestors were Southern blue-bloods—
> Lewis: And black.
> Kabnis: Aint much difference between blue an black.
> Lewis: Enough to draw a denial from you. Cant hold them, can you? Master; slave. Soil; and the overarching heavens. Dusk; dawn. They fight and bastardize you. The sun tint of your cheeks, flame of the great season's multi-colored leaves, tarnished, burned. Split, shredded: easily burned. No use . . .
> His gaze shifts to Stella. Stella's face draws back, her breasts come towards him.
> Stella: I aint got nothin f y, mister. Taint no use t look at me.
> (p. 217–218)

It would not be until Zora Neale Hurston began to publish novels that Toomer's rhetorical innovation would be extended in black fiction, although the line between Toomer's lyricism and Brown's regionalism is a direct one. Indeed, although Toomer received enthusiastic praise for *Cane,* this praise remained vague and ill defined. Du Bois, for instance, saw the import of the book as its subject matter, which he defined to be male-female sexual relations, which, he protested, were notably absent from the corpus of black fiction. There is not much truly consummated or untroubled sex in *Cane* either, but at least for Du Bois the text treated its possibility. For Du Bois, this stood as *Cane*'s significant breakthrough.

By 1923, when Toomer published *Cane,* the concern over the nature and function of representation, of what we might profitably think of as the ideology of mimesis, had focused on one aesthetic issue, which Du Bois would call "How Shall the Negro Be Portrayed?" and which we can, boldly I admit, think of as "What to do with the folk?" Despite scores of essays, exchanges, and debates over this problematic of representation, however, by 1929 not only had Toomer's innovations apparently been forgotten, but ironclad "Instructions for Contributors" had been widely circulated among black writers in the "Illustrated Feature Section" of the Negro press. Since these help us to begin to understand the major place of *Their Eyes Were Watching God* in the history of black rhetorical strategies, let me reprint these instructions, written by George S. Schuyler, in full:

> Every manuscript submitted must be written in each-sentence-a-paragraph style.
>
> Stories must be full of human interest. Short, simple words. No attempt to parade erudition to the bewilderment of the reader. No colloquialisms such as "nigger," "darkey," "coon," etc. Plenty of dialogue, and language that is realistic.
>
> We will not accept any stories that are depressing, saddening, or gloomy. Our people have enough troubles without reading about any. We want them to be interested, cheered, and buoyed up; comforted, gladdened, and made to laugh.
>
> Nothing that casts the least reflection on contemporary moral or sex standards will be allowed. Keep away from the erotic! Contributions must be clean and wholesome.
>
> Everything must be written in that intimate manner that wins the reader's confidence at once and makes him or her feel that what is written is being spoken exclusively to that particular reader.
>
> No attempt should be made to be obviously artistic. Be artistic, of course, but "put it over" on the reader so he or she will be unaware of it.
>
> Stories must be swiftly moving, gripping the interest and sweeping on to a climax. The heroine should always be beautiful and desirable, sincere and virtuous. The hero should be of the he-man type, but not stiff, stereotyped, or vulgar. The villain should obviously be a villain and of the deepest-dyed variety: crafty, unscrupulous, suave, and resourceful. Above all, however, these characters must live and breathe, and be just ordinary folks such as the reader has met. The heroine should be of the brown-skin type.
>
> All matter should deal exclusively with Negro life. Nothing will be permitted that is likely to engender ill feelings between

blacks and whites. The color problem is bad enough without adding any fuel to the fire.[17]

It is precisely these strictures, widely circulated in those very journals in which black authors could most readily publish, which, along with the extended controversy over black oral forms, enable us to begin to understand the black milieu against which Hurston would define herself as a writer of fiction. Here we can only recall, with some irony, W. S. Scarborough's 1899 plea for a great black novelist:

> We are tired of vaudeville, of minstrelsy and of the Negro's pre-eminence in those lines. We want something higher, something more inspiring than that. We turn to the Negro for it. Shall we have it? The black novelist is like the white novelist, in too many instances swayed by the almighty dollar. . . . Like Esau he is ready to sell his birthright for a mess of pottage.
>
> Let the Negro writer of fiction make of his pen and brain all-compelling forces to treat of that which he well knows, best knows, and give it to the world with all the imaginative power possible, with all the magic touch of an artist. Let him portray the Negro's loves and hates, his hopes and fears, his ambitions, his whole life, in such a way that the world will weep and laugh over the pages, finding the touch that makes all nature kin, forgetting completely that hero and heroine are God's bronze images, but knowing only that they are men and women with joys and sorrows that belong alike to the whole human family. Such is the novelist that the race desires. Who is he that will do it? Who is he that can do it?[18]

He that could do it, it seems, turned out to be a she, Zora Neale Hurston.

 # Notes ■

1. Hurston's revision of Douglass's apostrophe was suggested to me by Kimberly W. Benston. On chiasmus in *Their Eyes*, see Ephi Paul, "Mah Tongue Is in Mah Friend's Mouf," unpublished essay, pp. 10–12.

2. Thomas Hamilton, "Apology," *The Anglo-African Magazine* 1, no. 1 (January 1859): 1.

3. W. J. Wilson, "The Coming Man," *The Anglo-African Magazine* 1, no. 2 (February 1859): 58.

4. Frances E. W. Harper, letter to Thomas Hamilton, dated 1861.

5. A Lady from Philadelphia, "The Coming American Novelist," *Lippincott's Monthly Magazine* 37 (April 1886): 440–443.

6. Ibid., p. 441.

7. Ibid., p. 443.

8. Ibid. On Scarborough's citation, see note 11 below.

9. W. H. A. Moore, "A Void in Our Literature," *New York Age* 3 (July 5, 1890): 3.

10. *Recorder,* August 1, 1893; *A.M.E. Church Review* 15 (October 1898): 629–630. On Scarborough, see note 11 below. For an excellent discussion of these positions, see August Meier, *Negro Thought in America, 1880–1915: Racial Ideologies in the Age of Booker T. Washington* (Ann Arbor: University of Michigan Press, 1969), pp. 265–266.

11. W. S. Scarborough, "The Negro in Fiction as Portrayer and Portrayed," *Hampton Negro Conference* (Hampton, Virginia: Hampton Institute, 1899), pp. 65–66.

12. Ibid., p. 67.

13. See "Dis and Dat: Dialect and the Descent," in Henry Louis Gates, Jr., *Figures in Black* (New York: Oxford University Press, 1986), pp. 167–195.

14. Ibid., p. 22.

15. Johnson's 1922 comments are found in his "Preface" to Brown's *Southern Road,* reprinted in *The Collected Poems of Sterling A. Brown* (New York: Harper & Row, 1980), pp. 16–17.

16. Jean Toomer, *Cane* (1923; reprint, New York: Harper & Row, 1969), pp. 171–172.

17. George Schuyler, "Instructions for Contributors," reprinted in Eugene Gordon, "Negro Fictionist in America," *The Saturday Evening Quill* (April 1929): 20.

18. Scarborough, "The Negro in Fiction," p. 67.

The Gilded Six-Bits

It was a Negro yard around a Negro house in a Negro settlement that looked to the payroll of the G and G Fertilizer works for its support.

But there was something happy about the place. The front yard was parted in the middle by a sidewalk from gate to doorstep, a sidewalk edged on either side by quart bottles driven neck down to the ground on a slant. A mess of homey flowers planted without a plan but blooming cheerily from their helterskelter places. The fence and house were whitewashed. The porch and steps scrubbed white.

The front door stood open to the sunshine so that the floor of the front room could finish drying after its weekly scouring. It was Saturday. Everything clean from the front gate to the privy house. Yard raked so that the strokes of the rake would make a pattern. Fresh newspaper cut in fancy-edge on the kitchen shelves.

Missie May was bathing herself in the galvanized washtub in the bedroom. Her dark-brown skin glistened under the soapsuds that skittered down from her wash rag. Her stiff young breasts thrust forward aggressively like broad-based cones with the tips lacquered in black.

She heard men's voices in the distance and glanced at the dollar clock on the dresser.

"Humph! Ah'm way behind time t'day! Joe gointer be heah 'fore Ah git mah clothes on if Ah don't make haste."

She grabbed the clean meal sack at hand and dried herself hurriedly and began to dress. But before she could tie her slippers, there came the ring of singing metal on wood. Nine times.

Missie May grinned with delight. She had not seen the big tall man come stealing in the gate and creep up the walk grinning happily at the joyful mischief he was about to commit. But she knew that it was her husband throwing silver dollars in the door for her to pick up and pile beside her plate at dinner. It was this way every Saturday afternoon. The nine dollars hurled into the open door, he scurried to a hiding place behind the cape jasmine bush and waited.

Missie May promptly appeared at the door in mock alarm.

"Who dat chunkin' money in mah do'way?" she demanded. No answer from the yard. She leaped off the porch and began to search the shrubbery. She peeped under the porch and hung over the gate to look up and down the road. While she did this, the man behind the jasmine darted to the chinaberry tree. She spied him and gave chase.

"Nobody ain't gointer be chunkin' money at me and Ah not do'em nothin'," she shouted in mock anger. He ran around the house with Missie May at his heels. She overtook him at the kitchen door. He ran inside but could not close it after him before she crowded in and locked with him in a rough and tumble. For several minutes the two were a furious mass of male and female energy. Shouting, laughing, twisting, turning, and Joe trying, but not too hard, to get away.

"Missie May, take yo' hand out mah pocket!" Joe shouted out between laughs.

"Ah ain't, Joe, not lessen you gwine gimme whateve' it is good you got in yo' pocket. Turn it go Jo, do Ah'll tear yo' clothes."

"Go on tear 'em. You de one dat pushes de needles round heah. Move yo' hand Missie May."

"Lemme git dat paper sack out yo' pocket. Ah bet its candy kisses."

"Tain't. Move yo' hand. Woman ain't got no business in a man's clothes nohow. Go 'way."

Missie May gouged way down and gave an upward jerk and triumphed.

"Unhhunh! Ah got it. It 'tis so candy kisses. Ah knowed you had somethin' for me in yo' clothes. Now Ah got to see whut's in every pocket you got."

Joe smiled indulgently and let his wife go through all of

136

his pockets and take out the things that he had hidden there for her to find. She bore off the chewing gum, the cake of sweet soap, the pocket handkerchief as if she has wrested them from him, as if they had not been bought for the sake of this friendly battle.

"Whew! dat play-fight done got me all warmed up," Joe exclaimed. "Got me some water in de kittle?"

"Yo' water is on de fire and yo' clean things is cross de bed. Hurry up and wash yo'self and git changed so we kin eat. Ah'm hongry." As Missie said this, she bore the steaming kettle into the bedroom.

"You ain't hongry, sugar," Joe contradicted her. "Youse jes's little empty. Ah'm de one whut's hongry. Ah could eat up camp meetin', back off 'ssociation, and drink Jurdan dry. Have it on de table when Ah git out de tub."

"Don't you mess wid mah business, man. You git in yo' clothes. Ah'm a real wife, not no dress and breath. Ah might not look lak one, but if you burn me, you won't git a thing but wife ashes."

Joe splashed in the bedroom and Missie May fanned around in the kitchen. A fresh red and white checked cloth on the table. Big pitcher of buttermilk beaded with pale drops of butter from the churn. Hot fried mullet, crackling bread, ham hocks atop a mound of string beans and new potatoes, and perched on the window-sill a pone of spicy potato pudding.

Very little talk during the meal but that little consisted of banter that pretended to deny affection but in reality flaunted it. Like when Missie May reached for a second helping of the tater pone. Joe snatched it out of her reach. After Missis May had made two or three unsuccessful grabs at the pan, she begged, "Aw, Joe gimme some mo' dat tater pone."

"Nope, sweetenin' is for us men-folks. Y'all pritty li'l frail eels don't need nothin' lak dis. You too sweet already."

"Please, Joe."

"Naw, naw. Ah don't want you to git no sweeter than whut you is already. We goin' down de road al li'l piece t'night so you go put on yo' Sunday-go-to-meetin' things."

Missie May looked at her husband to see if he was playing some prank. "Sho' nuff, Joe?"

"Yeah. We goin' to de ice cream parlor."

"Where de ice cream parlor at, Joe?"

"A new man done come heah from Chicago and he done got a place and took and opened it up for a ice cream parlor, and bein' as it's real swell, Ah wants you to be one de first ladies to walk in dere and have some set down."

"Do Jesus, Ah ain't knowed nothin' 'bout it. Who de man done it?"

"Mister Otis D. Slemmons, of spots and places—Memphis, Chicago, Jacksonville, Philadelphia and so on."

"Dat heavy-set man wid his mouth full of gold teethes?"

"Yeah. Where did you see 'im at?"

"Ah went down to de sto' tuh git a box of lye and Ah seen 'im standin' on de corner talkin' to some of de mens, and Ah come on back and went to scrubbin' de floor, and he passed and tipped his hat whilst Ah was scourin' de steps. Ah thought never Ah seen *him* befo'."

Joe smiled pleasantly. "Yeah, he's up to date. He got de finest clothes Ah ever seen on a colored man's back."

"Aw, he don't look no better in his clothes than you do in yourn. He got a puzzlegut on 'im and he so chuckle-headed, he got a pone behind his neck."

Joe looked down at his own abdomen and said wistfully, "Wisht Ah had a build on me lak he got. He ain't puzzle-gutted, honey. He jes' got a corperation. Dat make 'm look lak a rich white man. All rich mens is got some belly on 'em."

"Ah seen de pitchers of Henry Ford and he's a spare-built man and Rockefeller look lak he ain't got but one gut. But Ford and Rockefeller and dis Slemmons and all de rest kin be as many-gutted as dey please, ah'm satisfied wid you jes' lak you is, baby. God took pattern after a pine tree and built you noble. Youse a pritty still man, and if Ah knowed any way to make you mo' pritty still Ah'd take and do it."

Joe reached over gently and toyed with Missie May's ear. "You jes' say dat cause you love me, but Ah know Ah can't hold no light to Otis D. Slemmons. Ah ain't never been nowhere and Ah ain't got nothin' but you."

"How you know dat, Joe."

"He tole us so hisself."

"Dat don't make it so. His mouf is cut cross-ways, ain't it? Well, he kin lie jes' lak anybody els."

138

"Good Lawd, Missie! You womens sho' is hard to sense into things. He's got a five-dollar gold piece for a stick-pin and he got a ten-dollar gold piece on his watch chain and his mouf is jes' crammed full of gold teethes. Sho' wisht it wuz mine. And whut make it so cool, he got money 'cumulated. And womens give it all to 'im."

"Ah don't see whut de womens see on 'im. Ah wouldn't give 'im a wind if de sherff wuz after 'im."

"Well, he tole us how de white womens in Chicago give 'im all dat gold money. So he don't 'low nobody to touch it at all. Not even put dey finger on it. Dey tole 'im not to. You kin make 'miration at it, but don't tetch it."

"Whyn't he stay up dere where dey so crazy 'bout 'im?"

"Ah reckon dey done made 'im vast-rich and he wants to travel some. He say dey wouldn't leave 'im hit a lick of work. He got mo' lady people crazy 'bout him than he kin shake a stick at."

"Joe, Ah hates to see you so dumb. Dat stray nigger jes' tell y'all anything and y'all b'lieve it."

"Go 'head on now, honey and put on yo' clothes. He talkin' 'bout his pretty womens—Ah want 'im to see *mine*."

Missie May went off to dress and Joe spent the time trying to make his stomach punch out like Slemmons' middle. He tried the rolling swagger of the stranger, but found that his tall bone-and-muscle stride fitted ill with it. He just had time to drop back into his seat before Missie May came in dressed to go.

On the way home that night Joe was exultant. "Didn't Ah say old Otis was swell? Can't he talk Chicago talk? Wuzn't dat funny whut he said when great big fat ole Ida Armstrong come in? He asted me, "'Who is dat broad wid de forty shake?' Dat's a new word. Us always thought forty was a set of figgers but he showed us where it means a whole heap of things. Sometimes he don't say forty, he jes' say thirty-eight and two and dat mean de same thing. Know whut he tole me when Ah was payin' for our ice cream? He say, 'Ah have to hand it to you, Joe. Dat wife of yours is jes' thirty-eight and two. Yessuh, she's forte!' Ain't he killin'?"

"He'll do in case of a rush. But he sho' is got uh heap uh gold on 'im. Dat's de first time Ah ever seed gold money. It lookted good on him sho' nuff, but it'd look a whole heap better on you."

"Who, me? Missie May was youse crazy! Where would a po' man lak me git gold money from?"

Missie May was silent for a minute, then she said, "Us might find some goin' long de road some time. Us could."

"Who would be losin' gold money 'round heah? We ain't even seen none dese white folks wearin' no gold money on dey watch chain. You must be figgeren' Mister Packard or Mister Cadillac goin' pass through heah . . ."

"You don't know whut been lost 'round heah. Maybe somebody way back in memorial times lost they gold money and went on off and it ain't never been found. And then if we wuz to find it, you could wear some 'thout havin' no gang of womens lak dat Slemmons say he got."

Joe laughed and hugged her. "Don't be so wishful 'bout me. Ah'm satisfied de way Ah is. So long as Ah be yo' husband, ah don't keer 'bout nothin' else. Ah'd ruther all de other womens in de world to be dead than for you to have de toothache. Less we got to bed and git our night rest."

It was Saturday night once more before Joe could parade his wife in Slemmons' ice cream parlor again. He worked the night shift and Saturday was his only night off. Every other evening around six o'clock he left home, and dying dawn saw him hustling home around the lake where the challenging sun flung a flaming sword from east to west across the trembling water.

That was the best part of life—going home to Missie May. Their whitewashed house, the mock battle on Saturday, the dinner and ice cream parlor afterwards, church on Sunday nights when Missie outdressed any woman in town—all, everything was right.

One night around eleven the acid ran out at the G and G. The foreman knocked off the crew and let the steam die down. As Joe rounded the lake on his way home, a lean moon rode the lake in a silver boat. If anybody had asked Joe about the moon on the lake, he would have said he hadn't paid it any attention. But he saw it with his feelings. It made him yearn painfully for Missie. Creation obsessed him. He thought about children. They had been married for more than a year now.

140

They had money put away. They ought to be making little feet for shoes. A little boy child would be about right.

He saw a dim light in the bedroom and decided to come in through the kitchen door. He could wash the fertilizer dust off himself before presenting himself to Missie May. It would be nice for her not to know that he was there until he slipped into his place in bed and hugged her back. She always liked that.

He eased the kitchen door open slowly and silently, but when he went to set his dinner bucket on the table he bumped it into a pile of dishes, and something crashed to the floor. He heard his wife gasp in fright and hurried to reassure her.

"Iss me, honey Don't get skeered."

There was a quick, large movement in the bedroom. A rustle, a thud, and a stealthy silence. The light went out.

What? Robbers? Murderers? Some varmint attacking his helpless wife, perhaps. He struck a match, threw himself on guard and stepped over the door-sill into the bedroom.

The great belt on the wheel of Time slipped and eternity stood still. By the match light he could see the man's legs fighting with his breeches in his frantic desire to get them on. He had both chance and time to kill the intruder in his helpless condition—half-in and half-out of his pants—but he was too weak to take action. The shapeless enemies of humanity that live in the hours of Time had waylaid Joe. He was assaulted in his weakness. Like Samson awakening after his haircut. So he just opened his mouth and laughed.

The match went out and he struck another and lit the lamp. A howling wind raced across his heart, but underneath its fury he heard his wife sobbing and Slemmons pleading for his life. Offering to buy it with all that he had. "Please, suh, don't kill me. Sixty-two dollars at de sto' gold money."

Joe just stood. Slemmons looked at the window, but it was screened. Joe stood out like a rough-backed mountain between him and the door. Barring him from escape, from sunrise, from life.

He considered a surprise attack upon the big clown that stood there laughing like a chessy cat. But before his fist could travel an inch, Joe's own rushed out to crush him like a battering ram. Then Joe stood over him.

"Git into yo' damn rags, Slemmons, and dat quick."

Slemmons scrambled to his feet and into his vest and coat. As he grabbed his hat, Joe's fury overrode his intentions and he grabbed at Slemmons with his left hand and struck at him with his right. The right landed. The left grazed the front of his vest. Slemmons was knocked a somersault into the kitchen and fled through the open door. Joe found himself alone with Missie May, with the golden watch charm clutched in his left fist. A short bit of broken chain dangled between his fingers.

Missie May was sobbing. Wails of weeping without words. Joe stood, and after awhile she found out that he had something in his hand. And then he stood and felt without thinking and without seeing with his natural eyes. Missie May kept on crying and Joe kept on feeling so much and not knowing what to do with all his feelings, he put Slemmons' watch charm in his pants pocket and took a good laugh and went to bed.

"Missie May, whut you crying for?"

"Cause Ah love you so hard and Ah know you don't love *me* no mo'."

Joe sank his face into the pillow for a spell then he said huskily, "You don't know de feelings of dat yet, Missie May."

"Oh Joe, honey, he said he wuz gointer gimme dat gold money and he jes' kept on after me—"

Joe was very still and silent for a long time. Then he said, "Well, don't cry no mo', Missie May. Ah got you' gold piece for you."

The hours went past on their rusty ankles. Joe still and quiet on one bed-rail and Missie May wrung dry of sobs on the other. Finally the sun's tide crept upon the shore of night and drowned all its hours. Missie May with her face stiff and streaked towards the window saw the dawn come into her yard. It was day. Nothing more. Joe wouldn't be coming home as usual. No need to fling open the front door and sweep off the porch, making it nice for Joe. Never no more breakfast to cook; no more washing and starching of Joe's jumper-jackets and pants. No more nothing. So why get up?

With this strange man in her bed, she felt embarrassed to get up and dress. She decided to wait till he had dressed and gone. Then she would get up, dress quickly and be gone forever beyond reach of Joe's looks and laughs. But he never moved. Red light turned to yellow, then white.

From beyond the no'man's land between them came a voice. A strange voice that yesterday had been Joe's.

"Missie May, ain't you gonna fix me no breakfus'?"

She sprang out of bed. "Yeah, Joe. Ah didn't reckon you wuz hongry."

No need to die today. Joe needed her for a few more minutes anyhow.

Soon there was a roaring fire in the cook stove. Water bucket full and two chickens killed. Joe loved fried chicken and rice. She didn't deserve a thing and good Joe was letting her cook him some breakfast. She rushed hot biscuits to the table as Joe took his seat.

He ate with his eyes on his plate. No laughter, no banter.

"Missie May, you ain't eatin' yo' breakfus'."

"Ah don't choose none, Ah thank yuh."

His coffee cup was empty. She sprang to refill it. When she turned from the stove and bent to set the cup beside Joe's plate, she saw the yellow coin on the table between them.

She slumped into her seat and wept into her arms.

Presently Joe said calmly, "Missie May, you cry too much. Don't look back lak Lot's wife and turn to salt."

The sun, the hero of every day, the impersonal old man that beams as brightly on death as on birth, came up every morning and raced across the blue dome and dipped into the sea of fire every evening. Water ran down hill and birds nested.

Missie knew why she didn't leave Joe. She couldn't. She loved him too much. But she couldn't understand why Joe didn't leave her. He was polite, even kind at times, but aloof.

There were no more Saturday romps. No ringing silver dollars to stack beside her plate. No pockets to rifle. In fact the yellow coin in his trousers was like a monster hiding in the cave of his pockets to destroy her.

She often wondered if he still had it, but nothing could have induced her to ask nor yet to explore his pockets to see for herself. Its shadow was in the house whether or no.

One night Joe came home around midnight and complained of pains in the back. He asked Missie to rub him down with liniment. It had been three months since Missie had touched his body and it all seemed strange. But she rubbed him. Grateful for the chance. Before morning, youth triumphed and Missie exulted. But the next day, as she joyfully made up their bed, beneath her pillow she found the piece of money with the bit of chain attached.

Alone to herself, she looked at the thing with loathing, but look she must. She took it into her hands with trembling and saw first thing that it was no gold piece. It was a gilded half-dollar. Then she knew why Slemmons had forbidden anyone to touch his gold. He trusted village eyes at a distance not to recognize his stick-pin as a gilded quarter, and his watch charm as a four-bit piece.

She was glad at first that Joe had left it there. Perhaps he was through with her punishment. They were man and wife again. Then another thought came clawing at her. He had come home to buy from her as if she were any woman in the long house. Fifty cents for her love. As if to say that he could pay as well as Slemmons. She slid the coin into his Sunday pants pocket and dressed herself and left his house.

Halfway between her house and the quarters she met her husband's mother, and after a short talk she turned and went back home. If she had not the substance of marriage, she had the outside show. Joe must leave *her*. She let him see she didn't want his old gold four-bits too.

She saw no more of the coin for some time though she knew that Joe could not help finding it in his pocket. But his health kept poor, and he came home at least every ten days to be rubbed.

The sun swept around the horizon, trailing its robes of weeks and days. One morning as Joe came in from work, he found Missie May chopping wood. Without a word he took the ax and chopped a huge pile before he stopped.

"You ain't got no business choppin' wood, and you know it."

"How come? Ah been choppin' it for de last longest."

"Ah ain't blind. You makin' feet for shoes."

"Won't you be glad to have a li'l baby chile, Joe?"

"You know dat 'thout astin' me."

"Iss gointer be a boy chile and de very spit of you."

"You reckon, Missie May?"

"Who else could it look lak?"

Joe said nothing, but he thrust his hand deep into his pocket and fingered something there.

It was almost six months later Missie May took to bed and Joe went and got his mother to come wait on the house.

Missie May delivered a fine boy. Her travail was over when Joe came in from work one morning. His mother and the old women were drinking great bowls of coffee around the fire in the kitchen.

The minute Joe came into the room his mother called him aside.

"How did Missie May make out?" he asked quickly.

"Who, dat gal? She strong as a ox. She gointer have plenty mo'. We done fixed her wid de sugar and lard to sweeten her for de nex' one."

Joe stood silent awhile.

"You ain't ast 'bout de baby, Joe. You oughter be mighty proud cause he sho' is de spittin' image of yuh, son. Dat's yourn all right, if you never git another one, dat un is yourn. And you know Ah'm mighty proud too, son, cause Ah never thought well of you marryin' Missie May cause her ma used tuh fan her foot 'round right smart and Ah been mighty skeered dat Missie May wuz gointer git misput on her road."

Joe said nothing. He fooled around the house till late in the day then just before he went to work, he went and stood at the foot of the bed and asked his wife how she felt. He did this every day during the week.

On Saturday he went to Orlando to make his market. It had been a long time since he had done that.

Meat and lard, meal and flour, soap and starch. Cans of corn and tomatoes. All the staples. He fooled around town for awhile and bought bananas and apples. Way after while he went around to the candy store.

"Hellow, Joe," the clerk greeted him. "Ain't seen you in a long time."

"Nope, Ah ain't been heah. Been 'round spots and places."

"Want some of them molasses kisses you always buy?"

"Yessuh." He threw the gilded half-dollar on the counter. "Will dat spend?"

"Whut is it, Joe? Well, I'll be doggone! A gold-plated four-bit piece. Where'd you git it, Joe?"

"Offen a stray nigger dat come through Eatonville. He had it on his watch chain for a charm—goin' 'round making out iss gold money. Ha ha! He had a quarter on his tie pin and it wuz all golded up too. Tryin' to fool people. Makin' out he so rich and everything. Ha! Ha! Tryin' to tole off folkses wives from home."

"How did you git it, Joe? Did he fool you, too?"

"Who, me? Naw suh! He ain't fooled me none. Know whut Ah done? He come 'round me wid his smart talk. Ah hauled off and knocked 'im down and took his old four-bits 'way from 'im. Gointer buy my wife some good ole 'lasses kisses wid it. Gimme fifty center worth of dem candy kisses."

"Fifty cents buys a mightly lot of candy kisses, Joe. Why don't you split it up and take some chocolate bars, too. They eat good, too."

"Yessuh, dey do, but Ah wants all dat in kisses. Ah got a li'l boy chile home now. Tain't a week old yet, but he kin suck a sugar tit and maybe eat one them kisses hisself."

Joe got his candy and left the store. The clerk turned to the next customer. "Wisht I could be like these darkies. Laughin' all the time. Nothin' worries 'em."

Back in Eatonville, Joe reached his own front door. There was the ring of singing metal on wood. Fifteen times. Missie May couldn't run to the door, but she crept there as quickly as she could.

"Joe Banks, Ah hear you chunkin' money in mah do'way. You wait till Ah got mah strength back and Ah'm gointer fix you for dat."

Critical Essays

⬚ ROBERT E. HEMENWAY ■

From *Zora Neale Hurston:*
A Literary Biography

Fire!!'s "Sweat" is a story remarkably complex at both narrative and symbolic levels, yet so subtly done that one at first senses only the fairly simple narrative line. The account of a Christian woman learning how to hate in spite of herself, a story of marital cruelty and the oppression of marital relationships, an allegory of good and evil, it concentrates on folk character rather than on folk environment.

The story is about Delia, a washwoman, and her husband, Sykes. Sykes hates his wife, beats her, and openly courts another woman. He finds excuses to prey on Delia's obsessive fear of snakes; as the story opens, he throws his snake-like bull whip into the room to scare her. Sykes feels emasculated because his wife has earned much of their income by washing white people's clothes. This is a peril for unemployed black men, and Sykes sees the clothes as a constant challenge to his manhood, a recurring symbol of his inadequacy. Although he has told Delia "time and again to keep them white folks' clothes outa dis house," she has for fifteen years taken in washing in order that they both may survive. The result has been the loss of the love of her husband, and "sweat, sweat, sweat! Work and sweat, cry and sweat, pray and sweat!" Praying brings her the most solace, and her religious faith is connected, in Sykes's mind, to her work and its emasculating effects. In a speech logically irrational, but emotionally lucid with frustration, Sykes tries to hurt Delia: "You ain't nothing but a hypocrite. One of them Amen-corner Christians—sing, whoop, and shout, and then come home and wash white folks clothes on the Sabbath."

From *Zora Neale Hurston: A Literary Biography* (Urbana: University of Illinois Press, 1977).

Searching for a characteristic that Delia can do nothing to change, Sykes finally decides that the thing he dislikes most about her is her gauntness: "Gawd! how ah hates skinny wimmen." His paramour, on the other hand, is quite the opposite: "Lawdy, you sho is got one portly shape on you." Hurston's favorite Eatonville businessman, Joe Clarke, understands Sykes's behavior with all the wisdom of a village philosopher:

> There's plenty men dat takes a wife lak dey do a joint uh sugar cane. It's round, juicy an sweet when dey gits. But dey squeeze an' grind, squeeze an' grind an' wring tell dey wring every drop uh pleasure dats in 'em out. When dey's satisfied dat dey is wrung dry, dey treats em jes lak dey do a cane-chew. Dey throws 'em away. Dey knows whut dey is doin' while dey is at it, an' hates theirselves fuh it but they keeps on hangin' after huh tell she's empty. Den dey hates huh fuh being' a cane-chew an' in de way.

Sykes eventually tries to drive Delia from her own house by penning a rattlesnake near the back door. Then he attempts murder by moving the snake to the clothes hamper, hoping it will kill her when she reaches in to begin sorting the week's clothes. Delia escapes, however, and the released rattler kills Sykes as he returns to look for her body. Delia could have saved him, or at least comforted him in his dying moments, and we begin to understand how high Delia's "spiritual earthworks" of Old Testament vengeance have been built against Sykes. As she tells him, "Ah hates you, Sykes. . . . Ah hates you tuh de same degree dat Ah useter love yuh. Ah done took and took till mah belly is full up tuh mah neck. . . . Ah hates yuh lak uh suck-egg dog."

But this makes the story Delia's tragedy, too, for she does not warn him about the loose snake, or help him when bitten; and when Sykes dies at her feet with "his horribly swollen neck and his one open eye shining with hope," a burden is not lifted but newly imposed. Delia ends the story with great pity for Sykes, since his dying glance focused on the clothes tubs that have destroyed him. Even though her husband has attempted murder, her burden of knowledge becomes two-fold: the awareness that his evil provided the means for her to fulfill a wish for his death, and the recognition that in his dying seconds Sykes learned that the immensity of her hate precluded assistance— "She waited in the growing heat while inside she knew the cold river was creeping up to extinguish that eye which must know by now that she knew."

"Sweat" also illustrates a characteristic of Hurston's best fiction: a complex imagistic structure, with Freudian overtones, that reinforces the thematic statement of the story. "Sweat" depends heavily on traditional Christian symbolism, the snake being referred to once as "Ol Satan," another time as "Ol Scratch." The serpent is identified with Sykes's evil ways, and throughout the story the imagery associated with the man evokes sinuosity. The very first scene has Sykes throwing his bull whip at Delia: "Just then something long, round, limp and black fell upon her shoulder and slithered to the floor beside her." The action is important because Delia is deathly afraid of snakes, even having "a fit over a earthworm or a string," and Sykes cruelly exploits the fear. In the context of Delia's unremitting faith, the snake comes to represent the evil that lives inside despite her Christianity, a force she knows and is afraid of, but which Sykes's cruelty will not permit her to overcome. Sykes himself becomes a kind of devil, whose demonic desires eventually lead to a struggle for Delia's life *and* soul, even though he does not quite understand the dramatic part he plays. The pity Delia can feel for Sykes as he dies in sight of the clothes—"A surge of pity too strong to support bore her away from that eye that must, could not, fail to see the tubs"—redeems her from her hate. Circumstances also cause Sykes to die knowing of her wish for his destruction. She ends the story holding to a chinaberry tree, a rigid, linear symbol that provides rootedness in a world of slithering sinuosity. Such contrasting imagery adds tension to Delia's struggle with herself and her husband—the evil both inside and out. The phallic resonates in this imagery, and the imagistic tension illustrates how Hurston's best writing assumes meaning at a variety of levels. Delia is frightened of Sykes not only because of his cruelty; he also represents male sexuality ominous in its desire.

"Sweat" contains little identifiable folklore. There are no references to conjure or hoodoo, and neither plot nor characterization depends on traditional behavior. Delia and Sykes are particularized by their love turned to hate, and their tragedy has little to do with forces outside themselves. The communal morality of Eatonville informs the story's movement—the men on Joe Clarke's store porch disapprove of Sykes and consider what punitive action the community should take toward him—but "Sweat" depends much less on the Eatonville scene than on the interplay between the two principals.

"Sweat" serves to illustrate why Hurston's fellow artists could become so exasperated with her seeming lack of literary commitment. When she depended less directly on the folklore of Eatonville and presented the folk characters in a drama of human motives, the result was superior art. But when she borrowed straightforwardly from the beliefs and customs of her village without integrating them into a literary design, the result was a "Spunk" or an "Eatonville Anthology"—interesting, but not overpowerful fiction. The difference is between the scrupulous reportage appropriate to anthropological description and the unprincipled selectivity characterizing esthetic construction. The reporter describes as much as she can of the event. The artist uses the event for her own selfish purposes. When Locke and James Weldon Johnson argued for a conscious art based on folk sources, they were advocating a disciplined irresponsibility to the folk idiom; Hurston had to reconcile licensed irresponsibility with her knowledge of the original source.

Breaking out of the Conventions of Dialect

Minstrelsy and Early Literary Dialect

The history of African American fiction, along with poetry, reveals a tension between oral and literary forms. In his book *Neo-African Literature,* Janheinz Jahn speaks of "Afro-American folklore making its breakthrough to literature" in the works of Paul Laurence Dunbar and Charles Waddell Chesnutt; but he also refers to Dunbar as a "black nigger minstrel." [1] This points to a dual problem in African American literary history. First, African American folklore existed in viable and complex literary forms, and African American writers, certainly from the turn-of-the-century, made deliberate artistic use of these forms in their literary creations. Second, the distortions—human and linguistic—of minstrelsy also existed as literary models in the language and character of the three stock characters: the interlocutor, Mr. Bones, and Mr. Tambo. The interlocutor was usually white and spoke in formal, standard, "intelligent" and serious language (the beginning of the "straight man" in American comedy), while Mr. Bones and Mr. Tambo spoke in dialect and their subject matter was limited to clownish discourse. [2] Hence not only was there tension between the "pure" oral and literary models as complex forms, but the uses of oral tradition and "black speech" were further complicated by the intrusion of the "artistic models" (and one may say this) of the minstrel show, and its reduction of the artistic possibilities of the African American oral tradition—speech and folklore—through distortion and caricature. It is curious that American comedic

From *Liberating Voices: Oral Tradition in African American Literature* (Cambridge, Mass.: Harvard University Press, 1991).

153

teams still continue this pattern, which is also the precedent for the American musical comedy. Even the first American talking movie, the 1927 *Jazz Singer,* was without question in the minstrel tradition.

Minstrelsy, then, contributed to the ambivalence of the early African American writers toward "the dialect" and fastened their attitudes toward this language as distortion, compounding, molding, and securing apparent distortions of character and the relationship between language and character. Because audiences were used to hearing "dialect" only in comic contexts, even the writers who used the dialect for other purposes or with different intentions were often accused, as Richard Wright accused Zora Neale Hurston, of "perpetuating the minstrel tradition,"[3] although Hurston's meticulous rendering of dialect was necessary for the serious purpose of authentic representation of the speech of her characters, while it also contributed to broadening the range of dialect in literature.

Paul Laurence Dunbar's short story "The Lynching of Jube Benson" brings together all of the early problems of dialect and demonstrates early attempts at breaking through folklore into literature. James Weldon Johnson, an African American writer whose own works, such as *God's Trombones: Seven Negro Sermons in Verse* (1927), showed efforts to resolve the tensions of literary dialect, clarifies the problems in his introduction to *The Book of American Negro Poetry* (1931):

> Almost all poetry in the conventionalized dialect is either based upon the minstrel traditions of Negro life, traditions that had but slight relation—often no relation at all—to actual Negro life, or is permeated with artificial sentiment. It is now realized both by the poets and by their public that as an instrument for poetry the dialect has only two main stops, humor and pathos.
>
> That this is not a shortcoming inherent in the dialect as dialect is demonstrated by the wide compass it displays in its use in the folk creations. The limitation is due to conventions that have been fixed upon the dialect and the conformity to them by individual writers. Negro dialect poetry had its origin in the minstrel traditions, and a persisting pattern was set. When the individual writer attempted to get away from that

154

pattern, the fixed conventions allowed him only to slip over into a slough of sentimentality.[4]

Elsewhere in the introduction, Johnson suggests that if African American writers had been the first to "fix" their dialect as literature, perhaps these conventions of distortion and caricature for the benefit of outsiders could have been superseded. He cites Robert Burns's use of the Scottish dialect as an example of what might have been done. Readers of the poetry of Burns apprehend its elegance, variety of subjects, and range of humanity; it is not the language solely of burlesque or pathos, though even Burns was once "hailed by the literati of Edinburgh as an instance of the natural genius . . . whose poems were the *spontaneous overflow* of his *native feelings*" (my italics).[5] Of course, this accusation of artlessness, as observed in the work of the Canadian Margaret Laurence, continues to be the bane of writers writing outside of standard literary conventions despite the "intelligence and sensibility" their efforts bring to or cull from their indigenous speech and their "deliberate craft." But "the Scottish oral tradition of folklore and folk song, and the highly developed Scottish literary tradition" were jointly parts of Burns's artistic heritage. Perhaps it is this sense of security in both a literary and oral tradition that provided Burns's "sure fix" on intricate poetry in Scottish dialect. But, for the slaves in America, literacy was a criminal act. Not only were they denied legal access to the literary heritage of the West, but they suffered a loss of clear continuity with the African oral literatures, as an aesthetic alternative in a "highly developed African oral tradition" (Finnegan) that included ritual dramas and great epics. The only outlet for their visions, concerns, and struggles in the New World were the oral forms developed here: the blues, spirituals, worksongs. Later African American writers drew upon these forms to insure a new connection with tradition, but they did not hold the same currency or status in a literary culture that had been alien and denied to their ancestors.

Social history, as well then, compounded the problems of the early African American writers who incorporated African American dialect and folklore into their literatures. The two to be considered here are Paul Laurence Dunbar and Zora Neale Hurston; the first a turn-of-the-century writer and the second a representative of the Harlem Renaissance period. The questions that may be raised in reviewing the works of these writers are: How does one use in literature a dialect that has already been codified into burlesque? How does one employ the language in order to return it to the elasticity, viability, and indeed complexity, "intelligence and sensibility," that it often has when not divorced from the oral modes and folk creators?

Paul Laurence Dunbar

Paul Laurence Dunbar's "The Lynching of Jube Benson" illustrates the codification of literary dialect in turn-of-the-century African American fiction, and the links between dialect, perspective, character, and audience.

In the beginning of the story three white men are seated with Gordon Fairfax in his library, and Dunbar uses not only Dr. Melville's viewpoint but indirection to initiate the story. First, through the dialogue of the four, Dunbar sets up the popular feeling of the time of Jim Crow codes and legislation at home, and encroachments abroad in the Pacific and Caribbean extending the convolvulus of white supremacy—a time when lynchings were advertised in newspapers under "amusements." In the conversation, Gay rather callously says, "I would like to see a real lynching." And if a real lynching were to come his way, Fairfax admits, "I should not avoid it." "I should," Dr. Melville speaks up "from the depths of his chair, where he had been puffing in moody silence"; and thus begins "The Lynching of Jube Benson."

This restriction of perspective to Dr. Melville's viewpoint and the use of him as the storyteller is of course related to the audience of this turn-of-the-century fiction. Addressed to white readers, it admonishes them to change their social attitudes and put an end to lynching. Similarly, the nineteenth-century slave narrators addressed such audiences to change them to abolitionist sentiments. As in most literature in that tradition of protest, it is a fellow white man who argues and authenticates the case of Jube and who comes to consciousness and realization, thus giving the lynching story its authenticity.

156

But there are problems. Jube Benson remains essentially invisible. Revealed solely in a frame-story told by Dr. Melville, he must be seen only through the stereotypes and clichéd metaphors of Melville. The "perfect Cerberus," he is "black but gentle." And as Melville describes Jube, he reveals more of himself than he does of Jube Benson. In addition, the descriptions of Jube allow for dramatic ironies, for instance, when Melville recognizes his "false education" yet persists in being circumscribed by it. "I saw his black face glooming there in the half light, and I could only think of him as a monster. It's tradition. At first I was told that the black man would catch me, and when I got over that, they taught me that the devil was black, and when I recovered from the sickness of that belief, here were Jube and his fellows with faces of menacing blackness. There was only one conclusion: This black man stood for all the powers of evil, the result of whose machinations had been gathering in my mind from childhood up. But this has nothing to do with what happened."[6] Dr. Melville recognizes but ironically continues to be guided by this false education in his symbolic, linguistic, and metaphorical systems. Dunbar compounds the irony, for what happens—the false judgment and its consequence, the lynching of Jube Benson—has everything to do with these machinations.

Dr. Melville is in love with Jube's mistress, Ann. When she is sick Jube takes care of her: "He was a fellow whom everybody trusted—an apparently steady-going, grinning sort, as we used to call him . . . faithful servitor." Jube not only nurses Annie when she falls victim to the typhoid outbreak, but he also nurses the doctor "as if I were a sick kitten and he my mother . . . a black but gentle demon" he sees in his delirium, a "chimerical vision."

These appreciations notwithstanding, when Annie was attacked and murdered by a white fellow masked with soot on his face to resemble a black, and before dying she exclaimed, "that black," Jube is the first to be suspected. The "black rascal" identification, psychosexual myths, and "the diabolical reason of his slyness" insure the white mob's ability to see Jube only as a "human tiger" and judge him guilty of the crime without evidence or trial. The white men pursue Jube—"he gave a scream like an animal's"; they lynched him.

Later, when Jube's brother Ben and another black man come up with the real culprit, his face "blackened to imitate a Negro's," it is too late. Jube's brother Ben accuses fiercely, "you he'ped murder my brothah, you dat was his frien'; go 'way, go 'way! I'll take him home myse'f."

It is Dr. Melville, however, who delivers the final judgment for the story, calling himself and the others in the mob "blood guilty" and telling the "gentlemen" gathered in Gordon Fairfax's library that that was his last lynching.

Because everything is seen from the perspective of Dr. Melville and much of Jube's dialect is contained within this framed story, we may surmise that many of the restrictions and conventions of literary dialect, like the metaphorical restrictions on Jube's humanity, could be ascribed equally to Melville and to the author's concern with the truth and consistency of the narrator's personality. Whether or not this is true, Dunbar's use of dialect in the story clinches the problems in the turn-of-the-century use of the conventions of literary dialect.

First, the emotional range, as James Weldon Johnson argues, is restricted to pathos. We do not rise above pathos to the tragic potential of the story, and are only allowed to glimpse its possibility near the conclusion, when Jube's brother and another black man briefly enter the scene and brother Ben gives his strong accusation. But Dr. Melville's rendering of Jube's language, gestures, and mannerisms has elements of minstrel parody, though Melville doesn't recognize this in what he considers his affective and serious rendering of Jube and genuine sentiment. In his article on Booker T. Washington's *Up From Slavery,* Robert Stepto noted a "real life" example of this kind of description: James Creelman's *New York World* account of Washington's Atlanta address.

> The most offensive passage occurs when Creelman attempts to add a little sentiment and "color" to his story: "A ragged ebony giant, squatted on the floor in one of the aisles, watched the orator with burning eyes and tremulous face until the supreme burst of applause came, and then the tears ran down his face. Most of the Negroes in the audience were crying, perhaps without knowing just why." We needn't labor over Creel-

man's opinion of the Negroes in the audience, or strain to mine his attitude toward (or anxiety over) the responses of the white women: "The fairest women of Georgia stood up and cheered. . . . It was as if the orator [Washington] had bewitched them." Of Washington, Creelman writes that he is a "Negro Moses," a "tall tawny Negro" with "heavy jaws, and strong, determined mouth, with big white teeth, piercing eyes . . . bronzed neck . . . muscular right arm . . . clenched brown fist . . . big feet . . . and dusky hand."[7]

As in Melville's account of Jube, the language is more apt to tell us about the teller's psychology and attitudes than to give an accurate portraiture.

The second problem concerning dialect in Dunbar's story is that the transcription techniques depend on easy mutilations of spelling and grammar, as well as the use of "eye dialect"—unnecessary orthographic changes such as "tuk" for "took," "a laffin" for "laughing." Such words do not depend on pronunciation for their changes but add to the visual distortion, increasing the sense of the language as humorous or pathetic aberration.

Finally, literary formulas are used in the place of heard speech. However, again, the character of Dr. Melville accounts for much of the formula in his retelling of Jube's language. Since everyone's rehearing is somehow distorted by imagination, memory, or judgment, and compounded with his "false education," Dr. Melville does not surprise us here. Nevertheless, the problems of literary dialect delineated by James Weldon Johnson are finely illuminated by this story: the restricted emotional range, and the limited range of subject matter, experience, and perception.

Although it is not clear in "The Lynching of Jube Benson" how much of the conventions of dialect are due to persona/perspective/audience or world view, it is important to reiterate and clarify that the limitations of literary dialect are not just limitations of language and not just a literary or artistic dilemma, but that language is inseparable from our comprehension and sense of character. Because of the restrictions on the emotional experiential ranges, as well as the distractions brought about by transcription techniques, a fully realized complex character is impossible. But let us suppose Jube's brother Ben had told the story. Would the range of emotions have been extended beyond pathos and parody? What other aspects of Jube's character, hidden to Melville, might have been revealed? Would a broader range and context of subjects and concerns have entered the story? Would African American characters have been moved from the background to the foreground in dramatic scenes? Even if the "eye dialect" and other transcription devices shared by all the writers of the turn-of-the-century had been used, could the dialect have been made to do more and had more to do? How might it have been stretched? These questions lead us again to the problem of audience, and it was taken for granted at the time that the audience with the "broader perspective" was always white, and the significant relationships were always interracial ones of unambiguous conflict and dangerous confrontation. Only later, when the folklore tradition gained more of its own authority in literature, did it become possible to answer such questions and to have character, audience, point of view and language gain more elasticity.

Zora Neale Hurston

Zora Neale Hurston's short story "The Gilded Six-Bits" (1933) takes us out of the conventional restrictions observed in the literary dialect of Paul Laurence Dunbar. This transformation is partly due to the shift in perspective—inside rather than outside the black community—and the storyteller does not share Dunbar's double-conscious concern with an exclusive, white audience. Because her theme is not part of the protest literature tradition as such, Hurston can be concerned with the relationship between a man and woman in a Negro settlement. She can expand the range beyond humor and pathos to a crisis-of-love story; there can be development and recognition, dilemma and resolution, delineated personality. George Kent has called this a "simple story." In an interview with Roseann P. Bell in *Sturdy Black Bridges: Visions of Black Women in Literature* he says "That one (the story) suggests that really simple people could suddenly resolve all problems by suddenly forgiving each

160

other very easily . . . I . . . recall that incident being very tediously resolved. I don't recall a really imposing short story by her."[8]

Although the story is about simple people whose relationship seems to be apparently simply resolved, in view of the dialect tradition and particularly those problems manifest in Dunbar's turn-of-the-century story, Hurston's simple short story might be reviewed in a more complex light. Its shift in perspective (what Ellison would term "restoring of perspective"), its lack of preoccupation with audience, its sense that Southern rural black speech as dialect may contain any emotion in literature add degrees of complexity not easily acknowledged or perceived in a cursory reading. And although there is humor certainly in places, as in all of Hurston's work, it is the spontaneous good humor of fully realized characters in interaction, not the one-dimensional minstrel humor. We laugh along *with* the characters in their happy moments; we go down into the depths with them during the crisis of love, we come out with them. We are brought beyond humor and pathos.

The focus of the whole story is on relationships, interpersonal conflict, and conflict of values. There are some elements of sophistication in the story—particularly in the many reversals. But the question for Hurston—and this perhaps accounts for George Kent's reaction—is how to write of ordinary people without making the writer's concerns and the story itself seem ordinary, even trivial. The subject of Dunbar's story is perhaps a more "significant event"[9] in sociohistorical reality, nevertheless in rendering that significance his African American characters remain in the background in physical presence and psychological reality. In contrast, Hurston's characters are pulled to the foreground in both these respects. Like most literary transitions, this one doesn't appear to be of great note these days. Contemporary African American writers automatically pull their African American characters to the foreground, and notwithstanding certain persistent (nay, recalcitrant) white critics who may still be asking black writers whether they write about "black people or human beings," consider the African American character's perspective "the broader perspective" and the significant one. However, it was an important transition and should be read as an initial link between a literary technique—

viewpoint—and its broader humanistic implications in the depiction of black humanity in literature.

We first meet Missie May and Joe in a ritual scene they enact every Saturday morning, when Joe throws nine silver dollars in the door "for her to pick up and pile beside her plate at dinner." He also brings her candy kisses. The beginning is full of happiness, "joyful mischief," "mock anger," and the "play fight."

Otis Slemmons, introduced shortly after this playful scene, becomes the center of a conflict of values (this, the subject of much of Hurston's fiction, should be considered a worthy subject, even what E. M. Forster would call a noble one). We learn Otis is from Chicago and "spots and places." In the initial dialogue between the husband and wife we see what things interest the couple about him: he has been places, he has gold teeth, he wears "up to date" clothes, his "puzzlegutted" build makes him "look like a rich white man," he has the attention of many women (including white ones up North), and he has gold pieces. These are the things that Joe notices and talks about. Initially, Missie May seems to have no material concerns, and her love for Joe is uppermost; she loves him as he is. Joe, however, feels he "can't hold no light to Otis D. Slemmons" because he "ain't never been nowhere" and "ain't got nothing but you."

At first Missie May is not taken in by Otis and what he represents. But in a reversal, the next time we hear the husband and wife talking together, after they have returned from seeing Otis Slemmons at the local ice-cream parlor, Joe is expressing Missie May's earlier values and she is expressing his. We see then all the things Missie May wants for Joe. There is some blending of values because she wants these things for him "because she loves him," but nevertheless she wants them. Joe's response now is: "Joe laughed and hugged her, 'Don't be so wishful 'bout me. Ah'm satisfied de way Ah is. So long as Ah be yo' husband, Ah don't keer 'bout nothin' else.'"

However, to get the things she wants—the gilded six-bits which the gold coins turn out to be—Missie May betrays Joe with Otis Slemmons. Joe comes home early from work and finds them together. There is a fine handling of emotional reactions here. Joe sees them and "opens his mouth and laughs."

Because this is not the expected response—it seems to contradict the occasion—it deepens our sense of the emotion which, like "a howling wind raced through his heart," and he "kept on feeling so much." He fights Slemmons, drives him away, and the crisis of love begins. There is no more laughter or banter.

George Kent calls the resolution easy. I think that it appears easy because here Hurston handles all the emotional reversals and complications in narrative summary rather than active dramatic scenes. One reads over them quickly and so it seems that they are done quickly, but really there are subtle and difficult changes. Once Joe makes love to Missie May, then leaves a piece of Slemmon's "gold" "with the bit of chain attached" under her pillow. She discovers then it was no gold piece. "It was a gilded half dollar." After the love making she had thought "they were man and wife again. Then another thought came clawing at her. He had come home to buy from her as if she were any woman in the long house. Fifty cents for her love." She dresses and leaves the house, but she encounters her husband's mother, and so as not to "admit defeat to that woman" she returns home. Joe discovers she is pregnant and when she has the child he knows it is his (his mother even confirms that the baby looks like him—so it must be his!) and they reconcile. The story is perhaps resolved too simply at that point, the "baby chile" a kind of deus ex machina; nevertheless Hurston's handling of their complications and reversals of emotion before that point is superb, and certainly adds more shadings of emotions than were easily revealed in earlier dialect stories. The dialect itself is more complex and shows more literary sophistication. The links with the interior of characters, the processes of emotional transformation, as well as the foreground presentation carry it away from the "simple story" though it deals with ordinary folks.

Yet this story challenges by containing everything that was considered not the stuff of important fiction—it is regional, it focuses on the relationship between a black man and woman, and it does not make interracial conflict its reason for being. The problem of the "stuff of important fiction" of course transcends racial lines. The white American woman writer Mary Gordon speaks of "bad specters" that she must work to banish. "Let us pretend these specters are two men, two famous poets, saying, 'Your experience is an embarrassment; your experience is insignificant.' . . . it was all right for the young men I knew, according to my specters, to write about the hymens they had broken, the diner waitresses they had seduced. Those experiences were significant. But we were not to write about our broken hearts, about the married men we loved disastrously, about our mothers or our children. Men could write about their fears of dying by exposure in the forest; we could not write about our fears of being suffocated in the kitchen. Our desire to write about these experiences only revealed our shallowness." [10] Most female writers—black and white—have experienced this from male critics. Black writers—male and female—have experienced it from (white) male critics—and ironically—given Gordon's remarks—from (white) female critics. For writers dominated by others' literary standards of "significant events"—national, sexual, racial—the problem is not only finding one's voice but of trusting it when one does find it; then finding the voice or voices that one most values—avoiding destructions of the creative spirit and discovering how one can best, as George Kent would term it, "assert one's existence" and the existences of all one's characters. Kent himself feels that black women writers fail to explore real depth—"Often, the problem is that you don't get a deep enough definition of all the things that the woman encounters which are her responses to power . . . I would say that Black women writers that I've read don't seem to get much into subtle possibilities . . . I don't see much possibility, and I'm not sure that there is always depth." Yet, unlike most critics, Kent acknowledges that "It might be that male thing you were talking about." [11] It could be "elliptical details" in the work for which a male critic would need more "analytical commentary." [12] Conversely, as the Wife of Bath might put it, "if wommen hadde juged stories," had had the dominant voices in the "juggementz"—well, Gordon's comments suggest the direction.

But regardless of the subtleties—"subtle possibilities" (of society, history, gender?)—that critics confuse with aesthetics, for Hurston, dialect as regional vernacular can do and contain anything: subject, experience, emotion, revelation. Two biographical reasons for this new attitude and sense of possibility in character and dialect might be that Hurston was born in the first incorporated all-black town of Eatonville, Florida, and she was a folklorist with an exact as well as creative ear. In her foreword to the University of Illinois Press edition of *Their Eyes Were Watching God,* Sherley Anne Williams speaks of her "command": "She had at her command a large store of stories, songs, incidents, idiomatic phrases, and metaphors; her ear for speech rhythms must have been remarkable. Most importantly, she had the literary intelligence and developed the literary skill to convey the power and beauty of this heard speech and lived experience on the printed page . . . In the speech of her characters, black voices—whether rural or urban, northern or southern—come alive. Her fidelity to diction, metaphor, and syntax—whether in direct quotations or in paraphrases of characters' thoughts—rings, even across forty years, with an arching familiarity that is a testament to Hurston's skill and to the durability of black speech."

In "The Gilded Six-Bits" one sees the folklorist in the metaphors, images, descriptions in the dialogue: "He ain't puzzlegutted, honey"; "God took pattern after a pine tree and built you noble"; "You can make 'miration at it, but don't tetch it"; "Ah reckon dey done made him vast-rich." Certainly there is a difference between the metaphors here and those in Dr. Melville's descriptive evaluation of Jube or James Creelman's of Booker T. Washington; here there is individuality, range, and elegance.

Oral tradition enters, complements, and complicates character, in the use of storytelling or reported scenes to reinforce the dramatic ones. After Missie and Joe see Otis at the ice-cream parlor, Joe retells the encounter on the way back:

> On the way home that night Joe was exultant. "Didn't Ah say ole Otis was swell? Cain't he talk Chicago talk? Wuzn't dat funny whut he said when great big fat ole Ida Armstrong come in? He asted me, 'Who is dat broad wid de forte shake?' Dat's a new word. Us always thought forty was a set of figgers but he showed us where it means a whole heap of things. Sometimes he don't say forty, he jes' say thirty-eight and two, and dat mean de same thing. Know whut he told me when Ah wuz payin' for

our ice cream? He say, 'Ah have to hand it to you, Joe. Dat wife of yours is jes' thirty-eight and two. Yessuh, she's forte!" Ain't he killin'?"

Joe's description of the scene is important. Hurston does not take us to the ice-cream parlor directly and dramatically; she skips the scene and lets Joe's storytelling serve as a flashback. Joe does the telling and the story advances through the characters' reactions to the moment. The psychology of relationships is explored as complicating reversals and confusions of value give way to renewed and stronger affection.

Besides the use of dialect in the storytelling dialogue, Hurston also moves the folk expressions into the narrative, while in most early fiction, and certainly the turn-of-the-century fiction of both Dunbar and Chesnutt, it was confined to dialogue: "Way after while," "make his market," "mess of honey flowers." Here the syntax, lexicon, and expressive techniques of oral tradition break through to the narrative and alter it; this enlarges the scope of dialect to the modes of exposition. It is possible for this extensible language to tell a story too.

Hurston breaks new ground here. The novelist John Wideman speaks of this important evolution: "From the point of view of American literature then, the fact of black speech (and the oral roots of a distinct literary tradition—ultimately the tradition itself) existed only when it was properly 'framed,' within works which had status in the dominant literary system. For black speech the frame was the means of entering the literate culture and the frame also defined the purposes or ends for which black speech could be employed."[13] Hurston, in her use of dialect, was one of the first to initiate this breaking out of the frame, an important step for writers committed to such linguistic explorations in fiction.

In "The Gilded Six-Bits" the dialect acquires more functions and is used in a story of greater complexity of character, greater thematic range and literary sophistication. Though the people themselves are "simple" in the sense of ordinary folks, their emotional range extends beyond the sentimental or comic. Because Hurston gives the dialect a fuller value and use, she moves a step further toward a fuller exploration of black personalities in fiction. But not until Hurston's novel *Their Eyes Were*

166

Watching God did language, thought, experience, emotion, and imagination break through and add to the text like an apical bud increasing the length of the stem, or to use Hurston's own image, a peartree bud coming to flower. Hurston actualizes the possibility of what dialect might do when moved beyond the literary conventions and allowed more of the magic and flexibility of authentic folk creation.

☐ *Notes* ■

1. Janheinz Jahn, *Neo-African Literature: A History of Black Writing* (New York: Grove Press, 1969), pp. 149–151.

2. Camille Yarbrough, "Black Dance in America," *The Black Collegian*, April/May 1981, pp. 20–21. See also Robert C. Toll, *On With the Show* (New York: Oxford University Press, 1976), Chap. 4.

3. Robert Hemenway, *Zora Neale Hurston: A Literary Biography* (Urbana: University of Illinois Press, 1977), p. 241. See also Wright's review of *Their Eyes Were Watching God* in *New Masses,* October 5, 1937.

4. James Weldon Johnson, *The Book of American Negro Poetry* (New York: Harcourt, Brace and World, 1959), p. 4.

5. M. H. Abrams, ed., *The Norton Anthology of English Literature,* 4th ed., Vol. 2 (New York: Norton, 1979), p. 89.

6. Paul Laurence Dunbar, "The Lynching of Rube Benson," *American Negro Short Stories,* ed. John Henrik Clarke (New York: Hill and Wang, 1966), pp. 1–8. All quotations are taken from this anthology.

7. Robert B. Stepto, *From Behind the Veil: A Study of Afro-American Narrative* (Urbana: University of Illinois Press, 1979), pp. 43–44.

8. Roseann P. Bell, Bettye J. Parker, and Beverly Guy-Sheftall, editors, *Sturdy Black Bridges: Visions of Black Women in Literature* (New York: Anchor, 1979), p. 225.

9. W. E. Abraham, *The Mind of Africa* (Chicago: University of Chicago Press, 1962), p. 11. Abraham speaks of historical events which "derive their significance from the culture in which they find themselves." His discussion may also raise questions regarding the significance of events in literature and "evaluation of facts and events."

10. Mary Gordon, "The Parable of the Cave or: In Praise of Water Colors," in *The Writer On Her Work,* ed. Janet Sternburg (New York: W. W. Norton, 1980), pp. 28–29.

11. *Sturdy Black Bridges,* pp. 226, 228–229.

12. Lloyd W. Brown, *Women Writers in Black Africa* (Westport, Connecticut: Greenwood Press, 1981), p. 140.

13. John Wideman, "Frame and Dialect: The Evolution of the Black Voice," in *American Poetry Review,* September/October 1976, pp. 34–37.

The Artist in the Kitchen: The Economics of Creativity in Hurston's "Sweat"

Zora Neale Hurston's short story "Sweat" (1926) presents a radical transformation of an oppressed black domestic worker who attempts to envision her work as a work of art. The story is remarkable in Hurston's body of work for its harsh, unrelenting indictment of the economic and personal degradation of marriage in a racist and sexist society.

To accomplish this, "Sweat" functions at one level as a documentary of the economic situation of Eatonville in the early decades of the twentieth century. Hurston uses a naturalistic narrator to comment on the roles of Delia and Sykes Jones as workers as well as marriage partners, but ultimately the story veers away from naturalistic fiction and becomes a modernist rumination on Delia as an artist figure. The story's coherence of theme and structure makes it one of Hurston's most powerful pieces of fiction.

Preserved not only as a place but as an idea of a place, Eatonville, Florida, retains the atmosphere of which Hurston wrote. As putatively the oldest town in the United States incorporated by blacks, Eatonville possesses understandable pride in its unique history. When Hurston writes of Eatonville in "How It Feels To Be Colored Me," she implies that her childhood place was idyllic because "it is exclusively a colored town" ([1928] 1979, 152), one in which the young Zora was happily unaware of the restrictions that race conferred elsewhere. However, this gloss of nostalgia can be read simultaneously

From *Zora in Florida,* ed. Steve Glassman and Kathryn Lee Seidel (Gainesville: University Presses of Florida, 1991).

with "Sweat," published only two years earlier. Although Hurston's biographer, Robert Hemenway, writes perceptively that "Sweat" is a personal story without identifiable local folklore (73), in the story Hurston reveals the somber and multifaced variations of life in Eatonville in the first part of this century.

Economically Eatonville in "Sweat" exists as a twin, a double with its neighbor, the town of Winter Park. Far from being identical, the twin towns are configured like Siamese twins, joined as they are by economic necessity. Winter Park is an all-white, wealthy town that caters to rich northerners from New England who journey south each fall to "winter" in Florida—"snowbirds," as the natives call them. Winter Park then as now boasts brick streets, huge oaks, landscaped lakes, and large, spacious houses. To clean these houses, tend these gardens, cook the meals, and watch the children of Winter Park, residents of Eatonville made a daily exodus across the railroad tracks on which Amtrak now runs to work as domestics. This pattern has been described in detail by sociologist John Dollard whose study *Caste and Class in a Southern Town* (1937) remains the classic contemporaneous account of a small segregated town in the 1920s and 1930s, approximately the time in which the action of "Sweat" occurs. What is unique about Eatonville and Winter Park is that they are not one town divided in two but two towns. Eatonville's self-governance, its pride in its historic traditions, and its social mores were thus able to develop far more autonomously than those in the many towns of which Dollard wrote where the black community had to struggle to develop a sense of independent identity.

In "Sweat" we see the results of this economic situation. On Saturdays the men of the town congregate on the porch of the general store chewing sugarcane and discussing the lamentable marriage of Delia and Sykes Jones. Although these men may be employed during the week, Sykes is not. Some working people mentioned besides Joe Clarke, the store owner, are the woman who runs a rooming house where Bertha, Sykes's mistress, stays, the minister of the church Delia attends, and the people who organize dances that Sykes frequents. Work as farm laborers on land owned by whites is probably available, but it pays very little and is seasonal. Jacqueline Jones points out that in 1900, not long before the time of the story, 50 to 70 percent of adult black women were employed full time as compared to only 20 percent of men (113). A black man might be unemployed 50 percent of the time (124). One reason that unemployed men congregated at the local general store was not merely out of idleness, as whites alleged, nor out of a desire to create oral narratives, as we Hurston critics would like to imagine, but there they could be "visible to potential employers," as Jones asserts (125).

There is not enough work for the men as it is, but the townspeople discuss Sykes's particular aversion to what work is available. Old man Anderson reports that Sykes was always "ovahbearin' . . . but since dat white w'eman from up north done teached 'im how to run a automobile, he done got too biggety to live-an' we oughter kill 'im." The identity of this woman and her exact role in Sykes's life is not referred to again, but if she was a Winter Park woman, then perhaps Sykes worked for a time as a driver for residents there. All the more ironic, then, his comment to Delia in which he berates her for doing white people's laundry: "ah done tole you time and again to keep them white folks' clothes outa this house." The comment suggests that Sykes does not work out of protest against the economic system of Eatonville in which blacks are dependent on whites for their livelihood. Has he chosen to be unemployed to resist the system? Within the story, this reading is fragile at best. The townspeople point out that Sykes has used and abused Delia; he has "squeezed" her dry, like a piece of sugarcane. They report that she was in her youth a pert, lively, and pretty girl, but that marriage to a man like Sykes has worn her out.

In fact, Delia's work is their only source of income. In the early days of their marriage Sykes was employed, but he "took his wages to Orlando," the large city about ten miles from Eatonville, where he spent every penny. At some point Sykes stopped working and began to rely entirely on Delia for income. As she says, "Mah tub full of suds is filled yo belly with vittles more times than yo hands is filled it. Mah sweat is done paid for this house." Delia's sense of ownership is that of the traditional work ethic; if one works hard, one can buy a house and support a family. That Delia is the breadwinner, however, is a role reversal but not ostensibly a liberation; her sweat has brought her some meager material rewards but has enraged her husband.

171

Although she may at one time have considered stopping work so that Sykes might be impelled to "feel like man again" and become a worker once more, at the time of the story that possibility is long past. Sykes wants her to stop working so she can be dainty, not sweaty, fat, not thin. Moreover, he wants to oust her from the house so that he and his girlfriend can live there. Robert Hemenway perceptively notes that Sykes's exaggerated reliance on phallic objects—bullwhips and snakes in particular—is an overcompensation for his "emasculated" condition as a dependent of his wife (71). Sykes's brutality is a chosen compensation because he does not participate in the work of the community. He chooses instead to become the town's womanizer and bully who spends his earnings when he has them; he lives for the moment and for himself.

Houston A. Baker's ideological analysis of *Their Eyes Were Watching God* emphasizes what he calls the "economics of slavery" in Hurston's works (57). This term refers to the historical use of human beings for profit, a potent theme he identifies in African-American authors from Linda Brent and Frederick Douglas to Hurston. In this context, one can point out that Delia's work, difficult as it is, is productive; it allows her to sustain herself (and Sykes) and to become a landowner, a rare situation for blacks, as John Dollard points out. With her house she possesses not only a piece of property, but she also gains the right to declare herself as a person, not a piece of property. Because Sykes has not shared in the labor that results in the purchase of this property, he remains in a dependent state. He is rebellious against Delia whom he feels controls him by denying him the house he feels ought to be his; his only reason for this assertion is that he is a man and Delia is his wife.

Thus, the economics of slavery in "Sweat" becomes a meditation on marriage as an institution that perpetuates the possession of women for profit. Indeed, Sykes is the slaveholder here; he does not work, he is sustained by the harsh physical labor of a black woman, he relies on the work of another person to obtain his own pleasure (in this case buying presents for his mistress Bertha). He regards Delia's property and her body as his possessions to be disposed of as he pleases. Sykes's brutal beatings of Delia and his insulting remarks about her appearance are the tools with which he perpetuates her subordination to him for the sixteen years of their marriage.

Sykes has been transformed during his marriage, or perhaps because of it, from contributor to the family economy to the chief recipient of its benefits. Delia is a producer of goods (she grows food) and a provider of services (cooks, cleans); she also works at a service activity that brings in cash. Sykes responds by becoming a consumer. He uses her to buy the goods and services he desires (Bertha's favors, liquor, dances, etc.) rather than using this income to contribute to the family. Because he is a consumer only, he cannot become an owner of real estate, for he has a cash-flow problem. As a result, to use Walter Benn Michael's terminology, Sykes determines to possess the owner, to regard her body and her property as his possessions (56–57). Like the Simon Legrees of abolitionist fiction, Sykes proves his ownership by the brutality he shows toward Delia. His hatred of her rests not on a feeling of inferiority because she owns the house; rather, he hates her because as one of his consumable goods, she ought to be desirable, not sweaty; compliant, not resisting. He prefers Bertha because her fatness suggests an overly fed commodity; like a cow, she has been opulently and extravagantly fed beyond her needs. Sykes desires the large and the luxurious commodity; he does not want what he needs.

Given this hopeless set of economic forces, the story does not sink into a trough of despair, largely because of Hurston's choice of its narrative point of view. While generally Hurston is associated with the lyrical, oral structure of *Their Eyes Were Watching God* (1937), the narrative strategy of "Sweat" is a sophisticated amalgam of the naturalistic narrator and narrative voice that Henry Louis Gates identifies in *Their Eyes Were Watching God* as that of "speakerly text." Gates defines such a text as incorporating oral tradition, indirect discourse, and a transcendent, lyrical voice that is "primarily . . . oriented toward imitating one of the numerous forms of oral narration to be found in classical Afro-American vernacular literature" (181). Gates points out further that in oral tradition the speaker tells the story to a listener who is part of the teller's group; thus, in *Their Eyes Were Watching God*, Janie tells her tale to her friend, Phoeby, with the result that the first-person narrative is subtly shaped by the implied and the explicit dialogue. This type of novel is sharply defined in Alice Walker's *The Color Purple* (1982), in which the epistolary frame embodies the dialogic, oral tradition to which Gates refers. Gates contrasts this narrative mode with that of Richard Wright's *Native Son* (1940). In that work the third-person narrator is a removed authoritative, third commentor who possesses the knowledge of the larger context but does not permit characters to develop self-knowledge. Hurston's speakerly text exists to permit the main character, Janie, to search for self-knowledge, indeed for self, in a way that focuses on central themes but does not rely on the architectural plot scaffolding that characterizes Wright's fiction.

It is important to recognize that the narrative mode of "Sweat" is more similar to that of *Native Son* than *Their Eyes Were Watching God*. In "Sweat" the third-person narrator speaks in past tense about the events in the lives of Delia and Sykes. The narrator's voice is one of an educated observer who has complete knowledge of the sociology of the town of Eatonville, its place as a poor, all-black town in central Florida, and the litany of troubles in Delia's fifteen-year-long marriage. This narrator is, in short, the narrator of naturalism, who sees Delia's life as a short, brutish thing because of the nature of marriage within an economic miasma of poverty and powerlessness. At first glance, the story conforms to Donald Pizer's definition of naturalistic fiction as that which "unites detailed documentation of the more sensationalistic aspects of experience with heavily ideological [often allegorical] themes, the burden of these themes being the demonstration that man is circumscribed" (xi). Not only has Delia's life been a stream of "her tears, her sweat, her blood," as the narrator despairingly reports, but her marriage to a womanizer and wife-beater becomes worse when he also adds attempted murder to the list of forces that literally threaten her. This narrative mode allows Hurston a wider context for Delia's misery, the context of the economics of a central Florida community composed of black women who work as domestics in elite, white Winter Park. Hurston's narrator is especially effective when speaking of the setting itself, the long, hot central Florida August that both par-

174

allels and contributes to the climax of the story. The narrator gives shape to the natural cycles that influence Delia and Sykes, as in this passage that forms a transition to the story's climax: "The heat streamed down like a million hot arrows . . . grass withered, leaves browned, snakes went blind . . . and man and dogs went mad." But the perils of choosing an omniscient naturalistic narrator sometimes results in heavy-handed didacticism: "Delia's workworn knees crawled over the earth in Gethsemane and up the rocks of Calvary many, many times."

Because Hurston's narrator in "Sweat" has many features of the naturalistic narrator, the question arises as to whether this story itself is naturalistic. Donald Pizer points out that the 1930s was a time when naturalistic fiction such as *The Grapes of Wrath* offered at least partial solutions to the problems besetting the protagonist. One of the remarkable aspects of "Sweat" is Hurston's variation and escape from the naturalistic narrator. In the classic rhetoric of naturalism, characters are often curiously untouched by self-insight, as Pizer points out (6–7). In Theodore Dreiser's *Sister Carrie* (1900), for example, Carrie's victimization is unchallenged by anything more than a vague film of discontent that she feels now and then. Delia does fall from a state of relative success only to become brutalized, but she then begins the treacherous journey to self-knowledge and then self-esteem, the very journey that Janie makes in *Their Eyes Were Watching God*. Delia's marriage is far worse than any of Janie's; her economic situation is more impoverished. She does not have a friend like Phoeby or a grandmother to provide support, information, sympathy, and love. Yet Delia does change and grow in spite of her circumstances and her narrator. How does Delia (and Hurston) escape the narrator?

Hurston moves beyond the naturalistic narrator by employing a Henry Louis Gatesian dual focus; she uses the townspeople as a chorus who comment orally on the characters of Delia and Sykes. From them we learn of Delia's former beauty, of Sykes's early infatuation with her, of his difficult and brutal personality. We also learn that the town does not condone this behavior at all, but considers it an anomaly at best that their town should have produced a Sykes. Hurston sets up a dialogue between the narrator and the townspeople, the result of which is a double focus upon central characters. Unlike a Greek chorus, the townspeople are not omniscient; they are, on the contrary, interested in maintaining peace and harmony. They praise Delia's work, regarding her weekly delivery schedule with respect: "hot or col', rain or shine, jes ez reg'lar ez de weeks roll roun' Delia carries em an' fetches 'em on Sat'day." Delia's work has become a predictable ritual for the town. Their reaction clarifies the attitude toward work: Work is admirable; the fact that Delia works on a Saturday and is as predictable as the seasons establishes her as worthy of their respect.

It is her work and her own attitude toward it that ultimately allow Delia to become a person who possesses self-esteem, pride, and the ability to create an ordered and harmonious existence. Delia has created her small world; she has lovingly planted trees and flowers in the garden around her house; her home and garden are "lovely, lovely" to her, as the narrator explains. For all her woes, Delia takes joy in her tidy house, her garden, and her work. These images establish the archetypal undertone of the story, that of the Edenic place. Hurston presents Delia's portion of Eden/Eatonville as a female-created place, ordered and beautiful because of the efforts of a woman.

Among Delia's efforts, and the central focus of the story, is her work. Although the stereotype of the mammy is all too pervasive as a symbol of black women's work, Jacqueline Jones points out that the most frequent job for black women in the early twentieth century was not as a full-time domestic in the household of whites. For over 50 percent of working black women, "washing and ironing clothes provided an opportunity to work without the interference of whites, and with the help of their own children, at home" (125). Mothers generally were reluctant to leave their own young children and to tolerate the all too frequent humiliation by their white women employers. Being a "washerwoman" was as arduous a task as being a field hand, and thus was of lower status and lower pay than that of a maid or cook within a household—but it did offer a measure of independence.

Jones found that the typical laundry woman collected clothes on Monday, boiled them in a large pot, scrubbed them, "rinsed, starched, wrung out, hung up, and ironed" often in the hot days of summer. Starch and soap she paid out of the one or two dollars a week she received. She delivered the clothes on Saturday and collected the next week's if she was lucky; otherwise she had to return on Monday (125–126). This pattern matches Delia's, but her work assumes an importance beyond sociological accuracy.

Delia's work acts as a metaphor for the work of the human creator, that is, the artist. Susan Gubar describes metaphors for the female artist in her essay "'The Blank Page' and the Issues of Female Creativity." She comments that "many women experience their own bodies as the only available medium for their art. . . . Within the life of domesticity, the body is the only accessible medium for self expression" (296). When we apply these statements to Delia, the sweat of her body, which has laundered, cooked, and scrubbed, is the corporal medium of her art. Her basket of pristine laundry stands as the artistic object created by her body. Her creation exists surrounded by home and garden, a miniature Eden made by a woman.

The laundry is a brilliant and evocative symbol in the story. It is, of course, white, pure white, the narrator reports; its whiteness and purity connote Delia's innate goodness as opposed to the evil darkness of Sykes's snake. The whiteness also indicates that her created object is indeed a blank page waiting for inscription; however, the appropriate inscriber, Delia, must of necessity keep her canvas blank; only Sykes writes upon it with the dirt of his boots and eventually the male object, the snake/penis, that symbolizes his desire to be the controller of the objects Delia's body has created.

The laundry has been created by the sweat and blood of her body; it rests quiet and serene like a tabula rasa, awaiting purposeful fulfillment. Nestled snugly in a basket, the laundry is an object Delia protects and to which she devotes her time, her attention, and her body. The laundry thus functions as a cherished child, the child of their own that Sykes and Delia do not have. One can only speculate that Delia's hard-muscled thinness coupled with the stress of the work itself and the cruelty of her husband have rendered her physically infertile. How much more pregnant, then, the potential fruitfulness of the laundry, the object of Delia's devotion, the object of Sykes's hatred. Had the laundry been literally a child, the story would devolve into a naturalistic tale on child abuse. But Hurston establishes herself as a writer, *the* Afro-American writer of her time and among the greatest in our century, by transcending such a cul-de-sac.

In *Invisible Man,* written twenty-four years after "Sweat," Ralph Ellison's nameless narrator, himself a blank page, ruminates on the qualities of whiteness and blackness in the brilliant section in the paint factory. The whiteness of the paint, considered so desirable, so good, so pure by white customers, results from the minute drops of blackness carefully, artistically added by the black paint makers. Ellison's scene is prefigured in "Sweat." Hurston takes the discourse on whiteness suggested by the laundry far beyond the stereotype that white is right and black is invisible. One could line up the side of the good in the story with Delia, the laundry, and whiteness opposed to Sykes, the snake, and blackness, but this easy dichotomy would overlook Hurston's ultimate accomplishment. The laundry created by Delia does not belong to her. The laundry, her creation, belongs to the white people of Winter Park, her patrons, who will be the ultimate inscribers of it; they will turn the laundry into clothes. Delia has prepared the perfect canvas for her patrons, but she is not able to participate in the use, evaluation, or assignment of worth to the creation. Like Hurston as an artist, Delia depends ultimately on the white patron for recognition. As Hurston was in the late 1920s the companion of Fannie Hurst, a white patron indeed, the story shades into a troubling comment on Hurston's relationship with her employer as a restriction on her art. Delia does not own her art. If the laundry represents a baby, then the baby is not Delia's; it is a white person's baby whom Delia tends so carefully. She is its mammy, creating the child but not owning it. But again, Hurston avoids the simple sociological statement of making the object of Delia's sweat an actual child.

In keeping with the Edenic imagery is the serpent in Delia's house, her husband. Sykes is not an Adam at all; his potential as a mate has been supplanted by the bullwhip he carries, which is the satanic object associated with a snake as it "slithers to the floor" when he threatens to strike Delia with it, as Robert Hemenway has noted (71). Sykes attempts to destroy everything Delia has created. He begins by complaining that she should "keep them white folks' clothes outa dis house," and purposely kicks the neatly folded stack of white laundry into a dirty, disordered heap. His demand is irrational on a literal level because these clothes are their only source of money. In an ironic way, however, Sykes is reflecting a lingering Adamic need to establish his home as terrain in which he too has power. He owns nothing of his own; the house legally belongs to Delia. His protest against a white-controlled labor system embodies a somber problem for black men, but Sykes's anger and frustration cannot be directed toward the white perpetrators of his situation because he lacks the power to change the status quo. Instead he passes his days with careless pursuits and becomes increasingly violent with Delia. Her response to his violence has been excruciatingly passive, but when Sykes criticizes her work, he is not only protesting against his own economic condition. He has intuitively violated the one object, the laundry, that Delia values above all others.

Sykes's attack on the laundry brings about Delia's first assertion against him in fifteen years of marriage. When she grabs a heavy iron skillet from the stove, she is threatening her husband with a female object used for creation, in this case a cooking pot. Sykes responds by threatening her with the object of male creativity and violence with which he is most familiar, the bullwhip. The choices of these objects reveal that to Hurston, male creativity (the whip) exists only to injure and destroy; female creativity (the pot) *can* be used destructively but is intended primarily to be positive, that is, to cook and create a meal. Thus, women can use their creative power to defend themselves against the destruction that is the only intended use of male power.

The scene acts as a foreshadowing of the couple's climactic confrontation when Sykes brings home in a crate the satanic object of destruction, a snake. He leaves the snake in the kitchen for several days; Delia is terrified and terrorized by the snake, but she repeats her assertive stance by ordering her husband to remove it. Sykes responds by criticizing Delia's appearance. This apparent non sequitur reveals Sykes's attempt to control Delia by reminding her of the role he expects her to play, that of wife/sex object, prettied up and passive for the husband's use. Sykes criticizes her thin, hard-muscled body; he prefers fat women with flaccid bodies. Delia is strong because she works hard, another Sojourner Truth in her ability to work like a man. But as a representative of patriarchal masculinity, Sykes cannot prize Delia for what she is; he expects her to make herself, her body, into the image he prefers.

In the climax of the story Delia picks up the basket of white laundry and sees the snake in it. She drops the basket, runs outside in terror, and huddles in a gully beside a creek; Sykes returns home to the darkened house, picks up the snake's cage, and discards it. In this way the reader realizes that Sykes knew the snake was no longer in the cage; thus, it was Sykes who had placed it in the basket in order to murder Delia. When he goes inside to verify her death, he cannot see the snake in the dark house. Delia must decide whether to call out to warn her husband. If she does, he will live another day to take her life. She can save his life or she can save her own. In placing the snake in the laundry, Sykes has violated Delia's creation; he has disordered her house and finally actually intends to take her life. Delia chooses not to call out; the snake strikes, and Delia is permitted the gruesome revenge of seeing Sykes die before her eyes.

Delia's decision involves not only saving her life but preserving her vision of reality; her alternative choice would be to save her oppressor and thereby perpetuate not only her bondage to him but also to the corrupt, diseased vision of life he represents. As a female artist figure, Delia represents the power of the female artist who must adopt strategies that directly and violently bring change and allow her art to thrive. The debased condition of Sykes and of their marriage, even though it is in part a product of the economic disenfranchisement of black men, is not salvageable in this desperate story. Delia's choice implies that the oppressors of the woman worker/artist must be eliminated because they are evil, that the oppressors will bring about their own destruction. The tension for the black woman of creating art in a milieu controlled absolutely by whites remains unresolved. Hurston's story suggests that women artists must be free to create art and to contribute to a harmonious, ordered world. The issue of the need for a world that suits both men and women remains to be addressed, a task Hurston takes up in her later writing, especially in *Their Eyes Were Watching*

God (1937). The issue of the situation of the black female artist remained her lifelong subject.

⬜ *Works Cited* ■

Baker, Houston A., Jr. *Blues, Ideology, and Afro-American Literature.* Chicago: University of Chicago Press, 1984.

Dollard, John. *Caste and Class in a Southern Town.* 1937. Reprint. New York: Doubleday, 1957.

Dreiser, Theodore. *Sister Carrie.* New York: Doubleday, Page, 1900.

Ellison, Ralph. *Invisible Man.* New York: Random House, 1952.

Gates, Henry Louis. *The Signifying Monkey: A Theory of Afro-American Literary Criticism.* New York: Oxford University Press, 1988.

Gubar, Susan. "'The Blank Page' and Issues of Female Creativity." In *The New Feminist Criticism: Essays on Women, Literature, and Theory,* edited by Elaine Showalter. New York: Pantheon, 1985.

Hemenway, Robert E. *Zora Neale Hurston: A Literary Biography.* Urbana: University of Illinois Press, 1977.

Hurston, Zora Neale. "How It Feels To Be Colored Me" (1928). Reprinted in *I Love Myself . . . ,* 152–155. Old Westbury, NY: The Feminist Press, 1979.

——— "Sweat," 1926. Reprinted in *I Love Myself When I Am Laughing . . .* Old Westbury, New York: The Feminist Press, 1979.

——— *Their Eyes Were Watching God.* Philadelphia: J. B. Lippincott, 1937. Reprint. Urbana: University of Illinois Press, 1978.

Jones, Jacqueline. *Labor of Love, Labor of Sorrow: Black Women, Work, and the Family from Slavery to the Present.* New York: Basic Books, 1985.

Michaels, Walter Benn. *The Gold Standard and the Logic of Naturalism: American Literature at the Turn of the Century.* Berkeley: University of California Press, 1987.

Pizer, Donald. *Twentieth Century American Literary Naturalism.* Carbondale: Southern Illinois University Press, 1982.

Walker, Alice. *The Color Purple.* New York: Washington Square Press, 1982.

Wright, Richard. *Native Son.* New York: Harper, 1940.

From *Jump at the Sun:* Zora Neale Hurston's Cosmic Comedy

Hurston's comic gifts, simmering in "Muttsy," came to a boil with *Fire!!* the magazine issued by the "New Negro" group in 1926. "Sweat," the more gripping of her two contributions, details the grim story of hardworking Delia Jones and her no-good, philandering husband, also a devotee of practical jokes. Hurston cleverly turns this aspect of her villain into a structural device, for the entire story turns on the idea of jokes and joking. She begins with one of Sykes's cruel jokes: he throws his "long, round, limp and black" bullwhip around Delia's shoulders as she sorts the wash she must do for white folk in order to support herself. Sykes's prank, motivated by Delia's abnormal fear of snakes, begins the sexual imagery that makes the story more complex. Is Delia's fear of the explicitly phallic nature of the snakes a sign of her innate fear of sex or, more likely, a fear that has been beaten into her? What has caused Sykes to seek the beds of other women? The story raises but never really answers these questions, yet suggests Sykes cannot stand his wife's supporting them by washing the soiled sheets, towels, and undergarments of white folks. Lillie Howard thinks that "whether [Delia] needs Sykes at all is questionable and perhaps he senses this and looks elsewhere for someone who does need him." [1] On the other hand, Delia reflects that she "had brought love to the union and he had brought a longing after the flesh." Only two months into the marriage he beats her. Why? [2]

From *Jump at the Sun: Zora Neale Hurston's Classic Comedy* (Urbana: University of Illinois Press, 1994).

In any case, Sykes's laughter at his wife and her fears fill the story; he continually slaps his leg and doubles over with merriment at the expense of the "big fool" he married fifteen years ago. Clearly, his insults deflect attention away from the "big fool" he knows he appears to be in the community, as he has never held a steady job himself and depends on Delia for his livelihood. Hurston in this story seems to be developing gender-specific forms of humor, which will be extremely important in *Jonah, Their Eyes,* and *Seraph.*

We may thus notice a difference in the rhetoric employed here. Delia too, although grimly serious in her defiance of Sykes, uses the deadly comic signifying language of female rivalry; referring to her husband's mistress, she states, "'That ole snaggle-toothed black woman you runnin' with aint comin' heah to pile up on *mah* sweat and blood. You aint paid for nothin' on this place, and Ah'm gointer stay right heah till Ah'm toted out foot foremost.'" Later, alone, Delia takes comfort in folk wisdom: "'Oh well, whatever goes over the Devil's back, is got to come under his belly. Sometime or ruther, Sykes, like everybody else, is gointer reap his sowing.'"

The appearance of the communal comic chorus in the personages of the loiterers on Joe Clarke's porch constitutes another significant development in Hurston's craft. When Delia passes by with her pony cart delivering clothes, they render the community's sense of pity for her and contempt toward Sykes, especially regarding his new mistress: "'How Syke kin stommuck dat big black greasy Mogul he's layin' roun' wid, gits me. Ah swear dat eight-rock couldn't kiss a sardine can Ah done throwed out de back do' 'way las' yeah.'" The men's humor rises a notch as they wryly observe that Sykes has always preferred heavy lovers over the thin Delia. Hurston signifies here on jokes in the black community about some men's preference for hefty women. A classic blues expression goes: "Big fat momma wid de meat shakin' on huh bones / Evah time she wiggles, skinny woman los' huh home."[3] The last line should particularly intrigue readers of "Sweat," for Sykes's plot is designed not so much to kill Delia but to secure her property.

Significantly, all of the men on the porch continually chew cane, but they do not throw the knots as usual, which creates a foundation for the extended natural metaphor that

Clarke, their leader, uses to summarize the inversion of the story they are actually helping us to read.

> "Taint no law on earth dat kin make a man behave decent if it aint in 'im. There's plenty men dat takes a wife lak dey do a joint uh sugar-cane. It's round, juicy an' sweet when dey gits it. But dey squeeze an' grind, squeeze an' grind an' wring tell dey wring every drop uh pleasure dat's in 'em out. When dey's satisfied dat dey is wrung dry, dey treats 'em jes lak dey do a cane-chew. Dey throws 'em away. Dey knows whut dey is doin' while dey is at it, an' hates theirselves fuh it but they keeps on hangin' after huh tell she's empty. Den dey hates huh fuh bein' a cane-chew an' in de way."

This casually brilliant rendering of a tragic truth provides a double irony for readers who know all of Hurston's work, for this same Joe Clarke emerges as a wife-beater himself in "The Eatonville Anthology" and becomes the model for Jody Starks in *Their Eyes,* who treats Janie like a mule he owns. Furthermore, the liquid squeezed out, the receptacle discarded, mirrors the title figuration of a woman's sweat and her weary body.

   Normally comic expressions can be used to deadly effect as well. In the heat of August's "Dog Days!" the "maddog" Sykes plays his ultimate and cruelest joke to drive Delia from the house that he has promised to Bertha. He keeps a caged rattlesnake on the porch, knowing Delia fears even earthworms. When she asks him to kill the rattler, he replies with a comically coined word and devastating irony: "Doan ast me tuh do nothin' fuh yuh. Goin' roun' tryin' tuh be so damn asterperious. Naw, Ah aint gonna kill it. Ah think uh damn sight mo' uh him dan you! Dat's a nice snake an' anybody doan lak 'im kin jes' hit de grit.'" When Delia's fury overflows into courage, she tells Sykes, "'Ah hates yuh lak uh suck-egg dog,'" and, of course, the imagery seems right, for Sykes's gender is usually associated with dogs, and a "suck-egg" dog would be a predator of women, egg bearers. Hurston would later use the egg and snake symbolism to characterize the couple in *Jonah.*

   When Sykes replies with insults about her looks, she replies in kind, joining a verbal duel that finally silences him: "'Yo' ole black hide don't look lak nothin' tuh me, but uh passle uh wrinkled up rubber, wid yo' big ole yeahs flappin' on each side lak uh paih uh buzzard wings. Don't think Ah'm gointuh be run 'way fum mah house neither. Ah'm goin' tuh de white folks bout *you,* mah young man; de very nex' time you lay yo' han's on me. Mah cup is done run ovah.'" Delia here effectively "caps" Joe by verbally emasculating him, in a doubled way. The "wrinkled rubber" seems obvious enough, but the buzzard reference varies her refrain that he is not man enough to support her; he just preys on her. This speech has much in common with Janie's silencing of Joe in the great scene in *Their Eyes,* but our pleasure in "Sweat" at Sykes's punishment is compromised by the ambiguity of our response throughout the story. Certainly, we feel for Delia, but the emasculation of the black man by a racist, capitalist society is on Hurston's mind here too, and Delia's threat to bring the white folks, whose laundry she washes, down on Joe, partially mitigates our natural inclinations to champion Delia; so does her tendency to taunt Joe about the fact that she brings home the bacon. Delia's Christian righteousness, evident in the scene when she returns from a "Love Feast" at church, also seems challenged by her failure to seek help for Sykes after he has been bitten by the snake at the end of the story and by her deliberate showing herself to him so he will know she knows what he attempted and that there is no hope for him.

This climax occurs when Joe, trapped in the dark bedroom with the snake he left in Delia's basket, jumps in terror onto the bed, where he thinks he'll be safe; the snake, of course, lies coiled there. In Tennessee Williams's *Cat on a Hot Tin Roof,* Big Mama, advising her daughter-in-law, Maggie, pats the bed she is sitting on and tells her that all the big problems in marriages can ultimately be traced *here;* Hurston, at least in this story, would seem to agree. The final joke on Sykes is that his obsession with male, phallic power, and the way he misuses it in his marriage, finally kills him, in a doubly figurative and dreadfully comic way.

What made this story special? For one thing, it was written after Hurston had been collecting black folklore for several years in the South and returned to live in Eatonville. When writing this story, she seemed to have learned how intertwined comedy and tragedy were in folk culture and also how the comic was embedded in the cosmic. These relationships are always manifest in her best work, like "The Gilded Six-Bits."

The story concerns a young married couple, Missie May and Joe Banks, who create a clean, sunny, happy home out of ordinary ingredients: "Yard raked so that the strokes of the rake would make a pattern. Fresh newspaper cut in fancy edge on the kitchen shelves." Although Hurston did not choose to emphasize it, the patterned dirt yard and the bottles stuck along the walk are African survivalisms, the latter connected with providing lodging places for the spirits of the ancestors, a type of communal art form that has been described and analyzed by Robert Farris Thompson, Robert L. Hall, and others. The creativity of these expressions, the only thing emphasized in the story itself, nevertheless has little to do with the white world and suggests a self-sufficiency and authenticity that seems vital to racial health in Hurston's fiction. The first line's repetitions emphasize this: "It was a Negro yard around a Negro house in a Negro settlement," and even though the inhabitants are dependent on the fertilizer factory where Joe works, "there was something happy about the place."

Why? Because the Bankses keep their relationship fresh and lively through elaborate games, jokes, and rituals. Each payday Joe hides and throws money through the doorway; Missie May pretends to be mad and gives chase, which results in a comic tumble. They speak in hyperbolic but culturally specific terms to express ordinary facts: "'Ah could eat up camp meetin', back off 'ssociation, and drink Jurdan dry.'" Hurston describes their dinner lovingly and deliciously, in an effort to portray the healthy satisfaction of appetite that the marriage represents: "Very little talk . . . but that consisted of banter that pretended to deny affection but in reality flaunted it." This is a wonderful example of communication by indirection and humor, one that foreshadows the marriage of Janie and Tea Cake.

The twin themes of sexuality and cleanliness are merged in the opening interior image, as we voyeuristically watch Missie May bathe herself and admire her black beauty. The theme of washing becomes metaphysical after her adultery, when she knows better than to think that she can wash herself clean like a cat, with its tongue, although this phrase won't be used until *Jonah*. Missie May learns that expiation must be earned through deeds, not talk.

The tragicomedy stage becomes set for her adultery when Joe mentions the proprietor of the new ice-cream store, Mr. Otis D. Slemmons, a pompous imposter just arrived from the North who apparently has many gold teeth and plenty of money. Missie May expresses her contempt through folksy food imagery: "'Aw, he don't look no better in his clothes than you do in yourn. He got a puzzlegut on 'im and he so chuckle-headed, he got a pone behind his neck. . . . His mouf is cut cross-ways, ain't it? Well, he kin lie jes' lak anybody else. . . . A wouldn't give 'im a wink if de sheriff wuz after 'im.'" The passage indicates Missie May discerns more than the reader might think, also demonstrated by the way she "talks that talk," in signifying judgment. Appropriately, and ironically, she bases her "reading" of Slemmons on a glimpse she caught of him when she was purchasing a box of *lye*.

Hurston creates a little physical comedy too; while Missie May dresses, Joe, who admires Slemmons's "puzzle-gut" as a sign of prosperity, tries to make his "stomach punch out like Slemmons' middle. He tried the rolling swagger of the stranger, but found that his tall bone-and-muscle stride fitted ill with it."[4]

Later we find that Joe admires Slemmons for his verbal ability as well; he quotes him as saying, "'Who is dat broad wid de forte shake?'" Hurston creates broad humor here, for as in "Muttsy," a broad with a "forty" shake would be a prostitute who charged forty dollars a night. Ma Turner in that story, her husband tells Pinkie rather proudly, and thus pathetically, was once called "Forty-dollars-Kate": "'She didn't lose no time wid dem dat didn't have it.'" Pinkie, however, like Joe here, naively doesn't understand, and comic innocence in both stories gets underlined by reader-author irony, especially when Joe tells Missie that Slemmons found her to be "'jes' thirty-eight and two. Yessuh, she's forte!'" Joe's remark of appreciation, however, ironically predicts Slemmons's ultimate effect: "'Ain't he killin'?'"

Hurston then transforms the story with tragicomic irony. Slemmons succeeds in seducing Missie May one night while

188

her husband toils at the G. and G. fertilizer plant. Joe unexpectedly comes home; it seems the acid supply at the fertilizer plant has run out, but an abundance of acidic marital bitterness awaits him at home. Although he always carefully washes himself before joining Missie May at table and later in the bed, she has brought defilement to the bed and the marriage. We readers know, however (and surely Joe does too, eventually) that he had much to do with it in his oft-expressed yearning for money and power.

In the dramatic scene of discovery, Joe strikes a match and strides into the bedroom; he thus ironically puts to the lie his earlier assertion, "'Ah can't hold no light to Otis D. Slemmons.'" Joe's stunned reaction to what he sees? He laughs before punching his rival out and grabbing his gold watch chain. Although a callous reader might feel Joe laughs at the undeniably funny image Hurston paints of the lumbering Slemmons "fighting with his breeches in his frantic desire to get them on" or Hurston's sexual innuendo as she describes "the intruder in his helpless condition—half in and half out of his pants," we know Joe cannot be amused. In black culture, laughing does not necessarily occur as a response to a joke or something funny; it can mean a strong point has been made.[5] Pearl Stone has the same reaction when Janie walks back into town in *Their Eyes*.[6]

Hurston balances the tragicomedy, however, with the cosmic in a beautiful expression she had taken from an African American sermon: "The great belt on the wheel of Time slipped and eternity stood still." This moment, however, for all its pain, proves liberating, for Joe and Missie May understand now how wrong they were to yearn for the gold Slemmons represented. The link between historical slavery and the ideology of consumerism emerges clearly in the piece of broken chain Joe has grabbed along with the gilded coin.

Joe's laugh, however, is a last one in more ways than one; although the marriage continues, the absence of laughter and banter reflects its changed state. After a long period of abstinence, Joe returns to Missie May's bed and leaves her the gold watch chain and its attached coin, which she discovers to be a gilded half dollar, thereby laying bare the extended joke of Slemmons's imposture. Further, in its doubling of the whore's traditional "two-bits," it offers her wages for sleeping with both men. Insulted, she leaves, she thinks forever, but in a stereotypical scene, she meets her mother-in-law, speaks briefly, and returns. "Never would she admit defeat to that woman who prayed for it nightly"—another example of Hurston's interest in depicting the various ironies of female rivalry.

Months later, when Missie delivers a son that is "'de spittin' image'"of Joe, everyone, including the reader, breathes a sigh of relief, especially Joe's formerly suspicious mother, who confesses her previous doubts in a rush of folk-warmed euphemisms: "'And you know Ah'm mighty proud son, cause Ah never thought well of you marryin' Missie May cause her ma used tuh fan her foot round right smart and Ah been mighty skeered dat Missie May wuz gointer git misput on her road.'" All of this richly metaphorical language lends a great deal of humor and interest to the story, yet never intrudes as it sometimes does in the more sprawling pages of *Jonah;* moreover, although Hurston creates the impression of a natural spontaneity, the metaphors actually work in a system of reference. For example, the rather refined "road" euphemism used by Joe's mother had been employed by Missie earlier, when she speculated to Joe that they might discover some gold, like Slemmons's: "'Us might find some gon' long de road some time,'" for indeed, her misbehavior in the "road" with Slemmons obtains the gold. Similarly, the real breakdown at the fertilizer plant works beautifully to set up the cosmic slippage of a belt at God's "factory," which seemingly "deals in shit" on occasion too, obviously on the command of the Cosmic Joker.

The various levels of the comic in the final pages once again conceal the cosmic. Joe's forgiveness floods forth after the birth of his son. As he buys a load of candy kisses with Slemmons's gilded coin, transforming a token of shame and stain into a staple of love and nourishment, he furnishes the story's key symbol, which expresses the magical ability of charity, love, and forgiveness to render the polluted pure and testifies to the way deeds, not words, can indeed "wash" away sin. Hurston plays the scene for laughs at first, however. Joe boasts about the way he outsmarted Slemmons to the callous white clerk, leaving out, of course, the real details. The clerk remarks to his next customer, a white, "'Wisht I could be like these darkies. Laughin' all the time. Nothin' worries 'em,'" signaling his failure to read Joe as a human, but rather as a type, little suspecting the pain that underlies Joe's brave laughter.

This harks back to another misreading. In a startling move, Hurston takes us into Slemmons's mind just after Joe laughs when discovering him and Missie May: "He considered a surprise attack upon the big clown that stood there laughing like a chessy cat." His link with the clerk is unmistakable. Slemmons, who represents the corruption of folk values by a sojourn in the materialistic North, has lost his ability to truly "see" his own people, as he has acquired the con artist's values.

The story ends when Joe resumes the ritual of throwing money on the porch, accompanied by Missie May's game reply: "'Joe Banks, Ah hear you chinkin' money in mah do'way. You wait till Ah got mah strength back and Ah'm gointer fix you for dat.'" The barometer of laughter thus signals the return of joy, and therefore health, to the marriage, one presumably stronger because of the testing it has received.

After reading this story, Lippincott called on Hurston for a novel, and she responded by writing a remarkable book, *Jonah's Gourd Vine,* which, like this beautiful and funny story, would center on the concept of marriage. The belts of time seem to have worked exceedingly well at this point for Hurston, for as "The Gilded Six-Bits" testifies, she had reached a new maturity in both her form and content, and she had never been closer to an understanding of the way humor provided, as the spiritual says, the "wheel within the wheel" of folk culture, an always spinning mechanism that would never fail her.

☐ Notes ■

1. Lillie P. Howard, *Zora Neale Hurston* (Boston: Twayne, 1980), 260–262.

2. The theme of love that sours shortly after marriage was the subject of Lizzie Miles's popular twenties blues song about a washerwoman who supports her philandering husband:

I hate a man like you, don't like the things you do,
When I met you, I thought you was right,
You married me and stayed out the first night.

. . . .

Walkin' around with a switch and a rod, shooting' dice,
always playing cards,
While I bring a pan from the white folks' yard.

. . . .

Eatin' and drinkin', sittin' at the inn,
Grinnin' in my face and winkin' at my friends.
When my back is turned you're like a rooster at a hen,
Oh, I hate a man like you.

Cited in Daphne D. Harrison, *Black Pearls: Blues Queens of the 1920s* (New Brunswick, New Jersey: Rutgers University Press, 1988), p. 87.

3. Langston Hughes and Arna Bontemps, eds., *The Book of Negro Folklore* (New York: Dodd, Mead, 1958), p. 384.

4. The 1990 New York Stage production of the story in *Mule Bone* made very effective physical comedy from this moment.

5. Geneva Smitherman, *Talkin' and Testifyin': The Language of Black America* (Boston: Houghton Mifflin, 1977), p. 106.

6. This connection of laughter to revenge is even more interesting when linked to Africa. The Yoruba god Ogun is the powerful god of fire, hunting, war, and iron, but he is also the god of laughter and debauchery. His laugh, however, can be terrible, for he is also the god of revenge, and a Yoruba *ijala* (a hunting poem) warns, "Ogun's laughter is no joke." See Kofi Awoonor, *The Breast of the Earth: A Survey of the History, Culture, and Literature of Africa South of the Sahara* (Garden City, N.Y.: Doubleday Anchor, 1975), p. 94.

"I Love the Way Janie Crawford Left Her Husbands": Zora Neale Hurston's Emergent Female Hero

In the past few years of teaching Zora Neale Hurston's *Their Eyes Were Watching God,*[1] I have become increasingly disturbed by this text, particularly by two problematic relationships I see in the novel: women's relationship to the community and women's relationship to language. *Their Eyes* has often been described as a novel about a woman in a folk community, but it might be more accurately described as a novel about a woman outside of the folk community. And while feminists have been eager to seize upon this text as an expression of female power, I think it is a novel that represents women's exclusion from power, particularly from the power of oral speech. Most contemporary critics contend that Janie is the articulate voice in the tradition, that the novel celebrates a woman coming to self-discovery and that this self-discovery leads her ultimately to a meaningful participation in black folk traditions.[2] Perhaps. But before bestowing the title of "articulate hero" on Janie, we should look to Hurston's first novel, *Jonah's Gourd Vine,* to its main character, Reverend John Pearson, and to the power that Hurston is able to confer on a male folk hero.[3]

From the beginning of his life, John Pearson's relationship to the community is as assured as Janie's is problematic. Living in a small Alabama town and then in Eatonville, where Janie also migrates, he discovers his preaching voice early and

---

From *Invented Lives* (Garden City, N.Y.: Doubleday/Anchor, 1988).

193

is encouraged to use it. His ability to control and manipulate the folk language is a source of power within the community. Even his relationships with women help him to connect to his community, leading him to literacy and to speech while Janie's relationships with men deprive her of community and of her voice. John's friendship with Hambo, his closest friend, is much more dynamic than Janie and Pheoby's because Hurston makes the male friendship a deeper and more complex one, and because the community acknowledges and comments on the men's friendship. In his Introduction to *Jonah's Gourd Vine,* Larry Neal describes John Pearson's exalted function in the folk community:

> John Pearson, as Zora notes in her letter to [James Weldon] Johnson is a poet. That is to say, one who manipulates words in order to convey to others the mystery of that Unknowable force which we call God. And he is more; he is the intelligence of the community, the bearer of its traditions and highest possibilities.[4]

One could hardly make such an unequivocal claim for Janie's heroic posture in *Their Eyes*. Singled out for her extraordinary, anglicized beauty, Janie cannot "get but so close to them [the people in Eatonville] in spirit." Her friendship with Pheoby, occurring apart from the community, encapsulates Janie and Pheoby in a private dyad that insulates Janie from the jealousy of other women. Like the other women in the town, she is barred from participation in the culture's oral tradition. When the voice of the black oral tradition is summoned in *Their Eyes,* it is not used to represent the collective black community, but to invoke and valorize the voice of the black *male* community.[5]

As critic Margaret Homans points out, our attentiveness to the possibility that women are excluded categorically from the language of the dominant discourse should help us to be aware of the inadequacy of language, its inability to represent female experience, its tendency not only to silence women but to make women complicitous in that silence.[6] Part of Janie's dilemma in *Their Eyes* is that she is both subject and object—both hero and heroine—and Hurston, apparently could not retrieve her from that paradoxical position except in the frame story, where she is talking to her friend and equal, Pheoby Watson. As object in that text, Janie is often passive when she should be active, deprived of speech when she should be in command of language, made powerless by her three husbands and by Hurston's narrative strategies. I would like to focus on several passages in *Jonah's Gourd Vine* and in *Their Eyes* to show how Janie is trapped in her status as object, as passive female, and to contrast the freedom John Pearson has as subject to aspire to an heroic posture in his community.

In both *Their Eyes* and in *Jonah's Gourd Vine* sexuality is established in the early lives of Janie and John as a symbol of their growing maturity. The symbol of Janie's emerging sexuality is the blossoming pear tree being pollinated by the dust-bearing bee. Early in the text, when Janie is about fifteen, Hurston presents her stretched out on her back beneath a pear tree, observing the activity of the bees:

> She saw a dust-bearing bee sink into the sanctum of a bloom; the thousand sister-calyxes arch to meet the love embrace and the ecstatic shiver of the tree from root to tiniest branch creaming in every blossom and frothing with delight. So this was marriage! She had been summoned to behold a revelation. Then Janie felt a pain remorseless sweet that left her limp and languid. (24)

She leaves this scene of the pear tree looking for "an answer seeking her" and finds that answer in the person of Johnny Taylor who, in her rapturous state, looks like a golden glorious being. Janie's first sexual encounter is observed by her grandmother and she is summarily punished.[7] To introduce such a sexual scene at the age when Janie is about to enter adulthood, to turn it into romantic fantasy, and to make it end in punishment certainly limits the possibility of any growth resulting from that experience.

John's sexual encounters are never observed by any adult and thus he is spared the humiliation and the punishment Janie endures for her adolescent experimentation. In an early scene when he is playing a game called "Hide the Switch" with the girl in the quarters where he works, he is the active pursuer, and, in contrast to Janie's romantic fantasies, John's experience of sexuality is earthy and energetic and confirms his sense of power:

> When he was "it" he managed to catch every girl in the quarters. The other boys were less successful but girls were screaming under John's lash behind the cowpen and under sweetgum trees around the spring until the moon rose. John never forgot that night. Even the strong odor of their sweaty bodies was lovely to remember. He went in to bed when all of the girls had been called in by their folks. He could have romped till morning. (41)

A recurring symbol Hurston uses to represent John's sexuality is the train, which he sees for the first time after he meets Lucy, the woman destined to become his first wife. A country boy, John is at first terrified by the "panting monster," but he is also mesmerized by this threatening machine whose sides "seemed to expand and contract like a fiery-lunged monster." It looks frightening, but it is also "uh pretty thing" and it has as many destinations as John in his philandering will have. As a symbol of male sexuality, the train suggests power, dynamism, and mobility.[8]

Janie's image of herself as a blossom waiting to be pollinated by a bee transforms her figuratively and literally into the space in which men's action may occur.[9] She waits for an answer and the answer appears in the form of two men, both of whom direct Janie's life and the action of the plot. Janie at least resists her first husband, Logan, but once Jody takes her to Eatonville, he controls her life as well as the narrative. He buys the land, builds the town, makes Janie tie up her hair, and prescribes her relationship with the rest of the town. We know that Hurston means for Janie to free herself from male domination, but Hurston's language, as much as Jody's behavior, signifies Janie's status as an object. Janie's arrival in Eatonville is described through the eyes and speech of the men on the front porch. Jody joins the men, but Janie is seen "through the bedroom window getting settled." Not only are Janie and the other women barred from participation in the ceremonies and rituals of the community, but they become the objects of the sessions on the porch, included in the men's tale-telling as the butt of their jokes, or their flattery, or their scorn. The experience of having one's body become an object to be looked at is considered so demeaning that when it happens to a man, it figuratively transforms him into a woman. When Janie launches her most devastating attack on Jody in front of all the men in the store, she tells him not to talk about her looking old because "When you pull down yo' britches you look lah de change uh life." Since the "change of life" ordinarily refers to a woman's menopause, Janie is signifying that Jody, like a woman, is subject to the humiliation of exposure. Now that he is the object of the gaze, Jody realizes that other men will "look" on him with pity: "Janie had robbed him of his illusion of irresistible maleness that all men cherish" (123).

Eventually Janie does speak, and, interestingly, her first speech, on behalf of women, is a commentary on the limitations of a male-dominated society:

> Sometimes God gits familiar wid us womenfolks too and talks His inside business. He told me how surprised He was 'bout y'all turning out so smart after Him makin' yuh different; and how surprised y'all is goin' tuh be if you ever find out you don't know half as much 'bout us as you think you do. (117)

Speech does not lead Janie to power, however, but to self-division and to further acquiescence in her status as object. As her marriage to Jody deteriorates she begins to observe herself: "One day she sat and watched the shadows of herself going about tending store and prostrating itself before Jody, while all the time she herself sat under a shady tree with the wind blowing through her hair and her clothes" (119).

In contrast to Janie's psychic split in which her imagination asserts itself while her body makes a show of obedience, John Pearson, trapped in a similarly constricting marriage with his second wife, Hattie, experiences not self-division but a kind of self-unification in which the past memories he has repressed seep into his consciousness and drive him to confront his life with Hattie: "Then too his daily self seemed to be wearing thin, and the past seeped thru and mastered him for increasingly

197

longer periods. He whose present had always been so bubbling that it crowded out past and future now found himself with a memory" (122). In this new state John begins to remember and visit old friends. His memories prompt him to confront Hattie and even to deny that he ever married her. Of course his memory is selective and self-serving, and quite devastating to Hattie, but it does drive him to action.

Even after Janie acquires the power of speech which allows her to stand up to Jody, Hurston continues to objectify her so that she does not take action. Immediately after Jody's death she goes to the looking glass where, she tells us, she had told her girl self to wait for her, and there she discovers that a handsome woman has taken her place. She tears off the kerchief Jody has forced her to wear and lets down her plentiful hair: "The weight, the length, the glory was there. She took careful stock of herself, then combed her hair and tied it back up again" (135). In her first moment of independence Janie is not seen as autonomous subject but again as visual object, "seeing herself seeing herself," draping before herself that "hidden mystery" which attracts men and makes her superior to women. Note that when she turns to the mirror, it is not to experience her own sensual pleasure in her hair. She does not tell us how her hair felt to her—did it tingle at the roots? Did she shiver with delight?—no, she takes stock of herself, makes an assessment of herself. What's in the mirror that she cannot experience without it: that imaginary other whom the mirror represents, looking on in judgment, recording, not her own sensations, but the way others see her.

Barbara Johnson's reading of *Their Eyes* suggests that once Janie is able to identify the split between her inside and outside selves, incorporating and articulating her own sense of self-division, she develops an increasing ability to speak.[10] I have come to different conclusions: that Hurston continues to subvert Janie's voice, that in crucial places where we need to hear her speak she is curiously silent, that even when Hurston sets out to explore Janie's internal consciousness, her internal speech, what we actually hear are the voices of men. Once Tea Cake enters the narrative his name and his voice are heard nearly twice as often as Janie's. He walks into Janie's life with a guitar and a grin and tells her, "Honey since you loose me and

gimme privelege tuh tell yuh all about mahself. Ah'll tell yuh."
(187). And from then on it is Tea Cake's tale, the only reason
for Janie's account of her life to Pheoby being to vindicate Tea
Cake's name. Insisting on Tea Cake's innocence as well as his
central place in her story, Janie tells Pheoby, "Teacake ain't
wasted no money of mine, and he ain't left me for no young gal,
neither. He give me every consolation in the world. He'd tell
'em so too, if he was here. If he wasn't gone" (18).

As many feminist critics have pointed out, women do get
silenced, even in texts by women, and there are critical places
in *Their Eyes* where Janie's voice needs to be heard and is not,
places where we would expect her as the subject of the story
to speak. Perhaps the most stunning silence in the text occurs
after Tea Cake beats Janie. The beating is seen entirely through
the eyes of the male community, while Janie's reaction is never
given. Tea Cake becomes the envy of the other men for having
a woman whose flesh is so tender that one can see every place
she's been hit. Sop-de-Bottom declares in awe, "Wouldn't Ah
love tuh whip uh tender woman lak Janie!" Janie is silent, so
thoroughly repressed in this section that all that remains of her
is what Tea Cake and the other men desire.

Passages which are supposed to represent Janie's interior consciousness begin by marking some internal change in
Janie, then gradually or abruptly shift so that a male character
takes Janie's place as the subject of the discourse; at the conclusion of these passages, ostensibly devoted to the revelation of
Janie's interior life, the male voice predominates. Janie's life
just before and after Jody's death is a fertile period for such self-
reflection, but Hurston does not focus the attention of the text
on Janie even in these significant turning points in Janie's life.
In the long paragraph that tells us how she has changed in the
six months after Jody's death, we are told that Janie talked and
laughed in the store at times and was happy except for the store.
To solve the problem of the store she hires Hezikiah "who was
the best imitation of Joe that his seventeen years could make."
At this point, the paragraph shifts its focus from Janie and her
growing sense of independence to Hezikiah and his imitation of
Jody, describing Hezikiah in a way that evokes Jody's presence
and obliterates Janie. We are told at the end of the paragraph,
in tongue-in-cheek humor, that because "managing stores and

199

women store-owners was trying on a man's nerves," Hezikiah "needed to take a drink of liquor now and then to keep up." Thus Janie is not only removed as the subject of this passage but is subsumed under the male-defined category of worrisome women. Even the much-celebrated description of Janie's discovery of her split selves: "She had an inside and an outside now and suddenly she knew how not to mix them" (112) represents her internal life as divided between two men: her outside self exists for Joe and her inside self is "saving up" for "some man she had never seen."[11]

Critic Robert Stepto was the first to raise the question about Janie's lack of voice in *Their Eyes*. In his critique of Afro-American narrative he claims that Hurston creates only the illusion that Janie has achieved her voice, that Hurston's strategy of having much of Janie's tale told by an omniscient third person rather than by a first person narrator undercuts the development of Janie's "voice."[12] While I was initially resistant to this criticism of *Their Eyes*, my reading of *Jonah's Gourd Vine* suggests that Hurston was indeed ambivalent about giving a powerful voice to a woman like Janie who is already in rebellion against male authority and against the roles prescribed for women in a male dominated society. As Stepto notes, Janie's lack of voice is particularly disturbing in the courtroom scene, which comes at the end of her tale and, presumably, at a point where she has developed her capacity to speak. Hurston tells us that down in the Everglades "She got so she could tell big stories herself," but in the courtroom scene the story of Janie and Tea Cake is told entirely in third person: "She had to go way back to let them know how she and Tea Cake had been with one another." We do not hear Janie speaking in her own voice until we return to the frame where she is speaking to her friend, Pheoby.[13]

There is a similar courtroom scene in *Jonah's Gourd Vine*, and there is also a silence, not an enforced silence, but the silence of a man who deliberately chooses not to speak. John is hauled into court by his second wife, Hattie, on the grounds of adultery. Like the court system in *Their Eyes*, this too is one where "de laws and de cote houses and de jail houses all b'longed tuh white folks" and, as in Janie's situation, the black community is united against John. His former friends take the stand against him, testifying on Hattie's behalf in order to spite John, but John refuses to call any witnesses for his defense. After he has lost the trial, his friend Hambo angrily asks him why he didn't allow him to testify. John's eloquent answer explains his silence in the courtroom, but more than that, it shows that he has such power over his own voice that he can choose when and where to use it, in this case to defy a hypocritical, racist system and to protect the black community:

> Ah didn't want de white folks tuh hear 'bout nothin' lak dat. Dey knows too much 'bout us as it is, but dey some things dey ain't tuh know. Dey's some strings on our harp fuh us tuh play on and sing all tuh ourselves. Dey thinks wese all ignorant as it is, and dey thinks wese all alike, and dat dey knows us inside and out, but you know better. Dey wouldn't make no great 'miration if you had uh tole 'em Hattie had all dem mens. Dey wouldn't zarn 'tween uh woman lak Hattie and one lak Lucy, uh yo' wife befo' she died. Dey thinks all colored folks is de same dat way. (261–262)

John's deliberate silence is motivated by his political consciousness. In spite of the community's rejection of him, he is still their defender, especially in the face of common adversary. Hurston does not allow Janie the insight John has, nor the voice, nor the loyalty to her people. To Mrs. Turner's racial insults, Janie is nearly silent, offering only a cold shoulder to show her resistance to the woman's bigotry. In the courtroom scene Janie is divorced from the other blacks and surrounded by a "protecting wall of white women." She is vindicated, and the black community humbled. Janie is the outsider; John is the culture's hero, their "inspired artist," the traditional male hero in possession of traditional male power.

But John's power in the community and his gift for words do not always serve him well. As Robert Hemenway asserts in his critical biography of Hurston, John is "a captive of the community's need for a public giver of words."

> His language does not serve to articulate his personal problems because it is directed away from the self toward the communal celebration. John, the man of words, becomes the victim of his

bardic function. He is the epic poet of the community who sac-
rifices himself for the group vision.[14]

For John, words mean power and status rather than the expression of feeling. When he first discovers the power of his voice,
he thinks immediately of how good he sounds and how his voice
can be exploited for his benefits:

> Dat sho sound good . . . If mah voice sound *dat* good de first
> time Ah ever prayed in, de church house, it sho won't be de
> las'. (93)

John never feels the call to preach until the day on Joe Clarke's
porch when the men tease John about being a "wife-made
man." One of his buddies tells him that with a wife like Lucy
any man could get ahead in life: "Anybody could put hisself
on de ladder wid her in de house." The following Sunday in
his continuing quest for manhood and power, John turns to
preaching. The dramatic quality of his preaching and his show-
manship easily make him the most famous preacher and the
most powerful man in the area. John's inability to achieve
maturity and his sudden death at the moment of his greatest
insight suggest a great deal about Hurston's discomfort with the
traditional male hero, with the values of the community he
represents, with the culture's privileging of orality over inward
development. Janie Starks is almost the complete antithesis of
John Pearson, "She assumes heroic stature not by externals,
but by her own struggle for self-definition, for autonomy, for
liberation from the illusions that others have tried to make her
live by or that she has submitted to herself." [15]

While Janie's culture honors the oral art, "this picture
making with words," Janie's final speech in *Their Eyes* actually
casts doubt on the relevance of oral speech:

> Talkin' don't amount tuh uh hill uh beans when yuh can't do
> nothin else . . . Pheoby you got tuh *go* there tuh *know* there. Yo
> papa and yo' mama and nobody else can't tell yuh and show
> yuh. Two things everybody's got tuh do fuh theyselves. They got
> tuh go tuh God, and they got tuh find out about livin' fuh they-
> selves. (285)

202

Janie's final comment that experience is more important than words is an implicit criticism of the culture that celebrates orality to the exclusion of inner growth. The language of men in *Their Eyes* and in *Jonah's Gourd Vine* is almost always divorced from any kind of interiority. The men are rarely shown in the process of growth. Their talking is a game. Janie's life is about the experience of relationships. Logan, Jody, and Tea Cake and John Pearson are essentially static characters, whereas Pheoby and Janie allow experience to change them. John, who seems almost constitutionally unfitted for self-examination, is killed at the end of the novel by a train, that very symbol of male power he has been seduced by all of his life.[16]

Vladimir Propp, in his study of folklore and narrative, cautions us not to think that plots directly reflect a given social order but "rather emerge out of the conflict, the contradictions of different social orders as they succeed or replace one another." What is manifested in the tensions of plots is "the difficult coexistence of different orders of historical reality in the long period of transition from one to the other."[17]

Hurston's plots may very well reflect such a tension in the social order, a period of transition in which the conflictual coexistence of a predominantly male and a more egalitarian culture is inscribed in these two forms of culture heroes. Both novels end in an ambiguous stance: John dies alone, so dominated by the ideals of his community that he is completely unable to understand his spiritual dilemma. And Janie, having returned to the community she once rejected, is left in a position of interiority so total it seems to represent another structure of confinement. Alone in her bedroom she watches pictures of "love and light against the walls," almost as though she is a spectator at a film. She pulls in the horizon and drapes it over her shoulder and calls in her soul to come and see. The language of this section gives us the illusion of growth and development, but the language is deceptive. The horizon represents the outside world—the world of adventure where Janie journeyed in search of people and a value system that would allow her real self to shine. If the horizon is the world of possibility, of journeys, of meeting new people and eschewing materialistic values, then Janie seems to be canceling out any further exploration of that world. In Eatonville she is a landlady with a fat bank account and a scorn for the people that ensures her alienation. Like the heroine of romantic fiction, left without a man she exists in a position of stasis with no suggestion of how she will employ her considerable energies in her now—perhaps temporarily—manless life.

Hurston was obviously comfortable with the role of the traditional male hero in *Jonah's Gourd Vine*, but *Their Eyes* presented Hurston with a problem she could not solve—the questing hero as woman. That Hurston intended Janie to be such a hero—at least on some level—is undeniable. She puts Janie on the track of autonomy, self-realization, and independence. She allows her to put on the outward trappings of male power: Janie dresses in overalls, goes on the muck, learns to shoot—even better than Tea Cake—and her rebellion changes her and potentially her friend Pheoby. If the rightful end of the romantic heroine is marriage, then Hurston has certainly resisted the script of romance by having Janie kill Tea Cake. (Though he exists in death in a far more mythical and exalted way than in life.) As Rachel Blau Du Plessis argues, when the narrative resolves itself in the repression of romance and the reassertion of quest, the result is a narrative that is critical of those patriarchal rules that govern women and deny them a role outside of the boundaries of patriarchy.[18]

While such a critique of patriarchal norms is obvious in *Their Eyes,* we still see Hurston's ambivalence about Janie's role as "hero" as opposed to "heroine." [19] Like all romantic *heroines*, Janie follows the dreams of men. She takes off after Jody because "he spoke for far horizon," and she takes off after Tea Cake's dream of going "on de muck." By the rules of romantic fiction, the *heroine* is extremely feminine in looks. Janie's long, heavy, Caucasianlike hair is mentioned so many times in *Their Eyes* that, as one of my students said, it becomes another character in the novel. A "hidden mystery," Janie's hair is one of the most powerful forces in her life, mesmerizing men and alienating the women. As a trope straight out of the turn-of-the-century "mulatto" novel (*Clotel, Iola Leroy, The House Behind the Cedars*), the hair connects Janie inexorably to the conventional romantic heroine. Employing other standard devices of romantic fiction, Hurston creates the excitement and tension of romantic seduction. Tea Cake—a tall, dark, mysterious stranger—strides into the novel and wrenches Janie away from her prim and proper life. The age and class differences between Janie and Tea Cake, the secrecy of their affair, the town's disapproval, the sense of risk and helplessness as Janie discovers passionate love and the fear, desire, even the potential violence of becoming the possessed are all standard features of romance fiction. Janie is not the subject of these romantic episodes, she is the object of Tea Cake's quest, subsumed under his desires, and, at times so subordinate to Tea Cake that even her interior consciousness reveals more about him than it does about her.

In spite of his infidelities, his arrogance, and his incapacity for self-reflection, John Pearson is unambiguously the heroic center of *Jonah's Gourd Vine*. He inhabits the entire text, his voice is heard on nearly every page, he follows his own dreams, he is selected by the community to be its leader and is recognized by the community for his powers and chastised for his shortcomings. The preacher's sermon as he eulogized John at his funeral is not so much a tribute to the man as it is a recognition that the narrative exists to assert the power of the male story and its claim to our attention. Janie has, of course, reformed her community simply by her resistance to its values. The very fact of her status as outsider makes her seem heroic by contemporary standards. Unable to achieve the easy integration into the society that John Pearson assumes, she stands on the outside and calls into question her culture's dependence on externals, its lack of self-reflection, and its treatment of women. Her rebellion changes her and her friend Pheoby, and, in the words of Lee Edwards, her life becomes "a compelling model of possibility for anyone who hears her tale."[20]

☐ Notes ∎

1. Zora Neale Hurston, *Their Eyes Were Watching God* (Urbana: University of Illinois Press, 1978).

2. Robert Hemenway, *Zora Neale Hurston: A Literary Biography* (Urbana: University of Illinois Press, 1977), p. 239. Hemenway says that Janie's "blossoming" refers personally to "her discovery of self and ultimately to her meaningful participation in black tradition." But

at the end of *Their Eyes,* Janie does not return to an accepting community. She returns to Eatonville as an outsider, and even in the Everglades she does not have an insider's role in the community as Tea Cake does.

3. Zora Neale Hurston, *Jonah's Gourd Vine* (Philadelphia: J. B. Lippincott, 1971).

4. Ibid., p. 7.

5. Henry Louis Gates, Jr., "Zora Neale Hurston and the Speakerly Text," in *The Signifying Monkey* (New York: Oxford University Press, 1987). Gates argues that *Their Eyes* resolves the implicit tension between standard English and black dialect, that Hurston's rhetorical strategies create a kind of new language in which Janie's thoughts are cast—not in black dialect per se but a colloquial form of standard English that is informed by the black idiom. By the end of the novel this language (or free indirect discourse) makes Janie's voice almost inseparable from the narrator's—a synthesis that becomes a trope for the self-knowledge Janie has achieved. While Gates sees the language of *Their Eyes* representing the collective black community's speech and thoughts in this "dialect-informed" colloquial idiom that Hurston has invented, I read the text in a much more literal way and continue to maintain that however inventive this new language might be it is still often used to invoke the thoughts, ideas, and presence of men.

6. Margaret Homans, "Her Very Own Howl," *SIGNS* 9 (Winter 1983): 186–205.

7. One of the ways women's sexuality is made to seem less dignified than men's is to have a woman's sexual experience seen or described by an unsympathetic observer. A good example of the double standard in reporting sexual behavior occurs in Ann Petry's "In Darkness and Confusion" in *Black Voices: An Anthology of Afro-American Literature,* ed. Abraham Chapman (New York: New American Library 1968), pp. 161–191. The young Annie Mae is observed by her uncle-in-law who reports that her sexual behavior is indecent. In contrast, his son's sexual adventures are alluded to respectfully as activities a father may not pry into.

8. The image of the train as fearsome and threatening occurs in Hurston's autobiography, *Dust Tracks on a Road: An Autobiography,* ed. Robert Hemenway (Urbana: University of Illinois Press, 1984). When she is a young girl on her way to Jacksonville, Zora, like John Pearson, is at first terrified of its "big, mean-looking eye" and has to be

dragged on board "kicking and screaming to the huge amusement of everybody but me." Later when she is inside the coach and sees the "glamor of the plush and metal," she calms down and begins to enjoy the ride which, she says "didn't hurt a bit." In both *Dust Tracks* and *Jonah's Gourd Vine* the imagery of the train is clearly sexual, but, while Zora sees the train as something external to herself, something that is powerful but will not hurt her, John imagines the train as an extension of his own power.

9. Teresa De Lauretis, *Alice Doesn't: Feminism, Semiotics, Cinema* (Bloomington: Indiana University Press, 1984), p. 143. De Lauretis notes that the movement of narrative discourse specifies and produces the masculine position as that of mythical subject and the feminine position as mythical obstacle, or, simply "the space in which that movement occurs."

10. I am indebted to Barbara Johnson for this insight which she suggested when I presented an early version of this paper to her class on Afro-American women writers at Harvard in the fall of 1985. I was struck by her comment that Jody's vulnerability makes him like a woman and therefore subject to this kind of attack.

11. Barbara Johnson, "Metaphor, metonymy and voice in *Their Eyes Were Watching God,*" in *Black Literature and Literary Theory,* ed. Henry Louis Gates, Jr. (New York: Methuen, 1984), pp. 204–219. Johnson's essay probes very carefully the relation between Janie's ability to speak and her ability to recognize her own self-division. Once Janie is able "to assume and articulate the incompatible forces involved in her own division," she begins to achieve an authentic voice. Arguing for a more literal reading of *Their Eyes,* I maintain that we hear precious little of Janie's voice even after she makes this pronouncement of knowing that she has "an inside and an outside self." A great deal of the "voice" of the text is devoted to the men in the story even after Janie's discovery of self-division.

12. Robert Stepto, *From Behind the Veil: A Study of Afro-American Narrative* (Urbana: University of Illinois Press, 1979), pp. 164–167. When Robert Stepto raised this issue at the 1979 Modern Language Association Meeting, he set off an intense debate. While I do not totally agree with his reading of *Their Eyes* and I think he short-changes Hurston by allotting so little space to her in *From Behind the Veil,* I do think he is right about Janie's lack of voice in the courtroom scene.

13. More accurately the style of this section should be called

free indirect discourse because both Janie's voice and the narrator's voice are evoked here. In his *Introduction to Poetics: Theory and History of Literature,* vol. I (Minneapolis: University of Minnesota Press, 1982), Tzvetan Todorov explains Gerard Genette's definition of free indirect discourse as a grammatical form that adopts the indirect style but retains the "semantic nuances of the 'original' discourse." (p. 28)

14. Hemenway, *Zora Neale Hurston,* p. 198.

15. Mary Helen Washington, "Zora Neale Hurston: A Woman Half in Shadow," in *I Love Myself When I Am Laughing . . . And Then Again When I Am Looking Mean and Impressive: A Zora Neale Hurston Reader,* ed. Alice Walker (Old Westbury, N.Y.: Feminist Press, 1979), p. 16. In the original version of this essay, I showed how Joseph Campbell's model of the hero, though it had been applied to Ralph Ellison's invisible man, could more appropriately be applied to Janie, who defies her status as the mule of the world, and, unlike Ellison's antihero, does not end up in an underground hideout.

Following the pattern of the classic mythological hero, defined by Campbell in *The Hero with a Thousand Faces* (Princeton, N.J.: Princeton University Press, 1968), Janie leaves her everyday world to proceed to the threshold of adventure (leaves Nanny and Logan to run off with Jody to Eatonville); she is confronted by a power that threatens her spiritual life (Jody Starks and his efforts to make her submissive to him); she goes beyond that threat to a world of unfamiliar forces some of which threaten her and some of which give aid (Tea Cake, his wild adventures, and his ability to see her as an equal); she descends into an underworld where she must undergo the supreme ordeal (the journey to the Everglades; the killing of Tea Cake and the trial); and the final work is that of the return when the hero reemerges from the kingdom of dread and brings a gift that restores the world (Janie returns to Eatonville and tells her story to her friend Pheoby who recognizes immediately her communion with Janie's experience "Ah done growed ten feet higher from jus' listenin' tuh you, Janie").

16. Anne Jones, "Pheoby's Hungry Listening: Zora Neale Hurston's *Their Eyes Were Watching God*" (Paper presented at the National Women's Studies Association, Humboldt State University, Arcata, California, June 1982).

17. De Lauretis, *Alice Doesn't,* p. 113. In the chapter, "Desire in Narrative," De Lauretis refers to Vladimir Propp's essay, "Oedipus in the Light of Folklore," which studies plot types and their diachronic or historical transformations.

18. Rachel Blau Du Plessis, *Writing Beyond the Ending: Narrative Strategies of Twentieth-Century Women Writers* (Bloomington: Indiana University Press, 1985). Du Plessis asserts that "it is the project of twentieth-century women writers to solve the contradiction between love and quest and to replace the alternate endings in marriage and death that are their cultural legacy from nineteenth-century life and letters by offering a different set of choices" (p. 4).

19. Du Plessis distinguishes between *hero* and *heroine* in this way: "the female hero is a central character whose activities, growth, and insight are given much narrative attention and authorial interest." By *heroine* she means "the object of male attention or rescue." (*Writing Beyond the Ending,* n. 22, p. 200) Hurston oscillates between these two positions, making Janie at one time a conventional romantic heroine, at other times a woman whose quest for independence drives the narrative.

20. Lee R. Edwards, *Psyche As Hero: Female Heroism and Fictional Form* (Middletown, Conn.: Wesleyan University Press, 1984), p. 212.

Looking
for Zora

On January 16, 1959, Zora Neale Hurston,
suffering from the effects of a stroke and writing
painfully in longhand, composed a letter to the
"editorial department" of Harper & Brothers
inquiring if they would be interested in seeing
"the book I am laboring upon at present—a life of
Herod the Great." One year and twelve days later,
Zora Neale Hurston died without funds to provide
for her burial, a resident of the St. Lucie County,
Florida, Welfare Home. She lies today in an
unmarked grave in a segregated cemetery in Fort
Pierce, Florida, a resting place generally symbolic
of the black writer's fate in America.
Zora Neale Hurston is one of the most significant
unread authors in America, the author of two
minor classics and four other major books.
—ROBERT HEMENWAY, "Zora Hurston and the
Eatonville Anthropology," in *The Harlem
Renaissance Remembered*

On August 15, 1973, I wake up just as the plane is lowering over
Sanford, Florida, which means I am also looking down on Eatonville, Zora Neale Hurston's birthplace. I recognize it from
Zora's description in *Mules and Men:* "the city of five lakes,
three croquet courts, three hundred brown skins, three hundred good swimmers, plenty guavas, two schools, and no jail-
house." Of course I cannot see the guavas, but the five lakes are
still there, and it is the lakes I count as the plane prepares to
land in Orlando.

From *In Search of Our Mothers' Gardens: Womanist Prose* (New York: Harcourt
Brace Jovanovich, 1983).

From the air, Florida looks completely flat, and as we near the ground this impression does not change. This is the first time I have seen the interior of the state, which Zora wrote about so well, but there are the acres of orange groves, the sand, mangrove trees, and scrub pine that I know from her books. Getting off the plane I walk through the humid air of midday into the tacky but air-conditioned airport. I search for Charlotte Hunt, my companion on the Zora Hurston expedition. She lives in Winter Park, Florida, very near Eatonville, and is writing her graduate dissertation on Zora. I see her waving—a large, pleasant-faced white woman in dark glasses. We have written to each other for several weeks, swapping our latest finds (mostly hers) on Zora, and trying to make sense out of the mass of information obtained (often erroneous or simply confusing) from Zora herself—through her stories and autobiography—and from people who wrote about her.

Eatonville has lived for such a long time in my imagination that I can hardly believe it will be found existing in its own right. But after twenty minutes on the expressway, Charlotte turns off and I see a small settlement of houses and stores set with no particular pattern in the sandy soil off the road. We stop in front of a neat gray building that has two fascinating signs: EATONVILLE POST OFFICE and EATONVILLE CITY HALL.

Inside the Eatonville City Hall half of the building, a slender, dark-brown-skin woman sits looking through letters on a desk. When she hears we are searching for anyone who might have known Zora Neale Hurston, she leans back in thought. Because I don't wish to inspire foot-dragging in people who might know something about Zora they're not sure they should tell, I have decided on a simple, but I feel profoundly *useful,* lie.

"I am Miss Hurston's niece," I prompt the young woman, who brings her head down with a smile.

"I think Mrs. Moseley is about the only one still living who might remember her," she says.

"Do you mean *Mathilda* Moseley, the woman who tells those 'woman-is-smarter-than-man' lies in Zora's book?"

"Yes," says the young woman. "Mrs. Moseley is real old now, of course. But this time of day, she should be at home."

I stand at the counter looking down on her, the first Eatonville resident I have spoken to. Because of Zora's books, I

212

feel I know something about her; at least I know what the town she grew up in was like years before she was born.

"Tell me something," I say. "Do the schools teach Zora's books here?"

"No," she says, "they don't. I don't think most people know anything about Zora Neale Hurston, or know about any of the great things she did. She was a fine lady. I've read all of her books myself, but I don't think many other folks in Eatonville have."

"Many of the church people around here, as I understand it," says Charlotte in a murmured aside, "thought Zora was pretty loose. I don't think they appreciated her writing about them."

"Well," I say to the young woman, "thank you for your help." She clarifies her directions to Mrs. Moseley's house and smiles as Charlotte and I turn to go.

> The letter to Harper's does not expose a publisher's rejection of an unknown masterpiece, but it does reveal how the bright promise of the Harlem Renaissance deteriorated for many of the writers who shared in its exuberance. It also indicates the personal tragedy of Zora Neale Hurston: Barnard graduate, author of four novels, two books of folklore, one volume of autobiography, the most important collector of Afro-American folklore in America, reduced by poverty and circumstance to seek a publisher by unsolicited mail.
> —ROBERT HEMENWAY

> Zora Hurston was born in 1901, 1902, or 1903—depending on how old she felt herself to be at the time someone asked.
> —LIBRARIAN, Beinecke Library, Yale University

The Moseley house is small and white and snug, its tiny yard nearly swallowed up by oleanders and hibiscus bushes. Charlotte and I knock on the door. I call out. But there is no answer. This strikes us as peculiar. We have had time to figure out an age for Mrs. Moseley—not dates or a number, just old. I am thinking of a quivery, bedridden invalid when we hear the car. We look behind us to see an old black-and-white Buick—paint peeling and grillwork rusty—pulling into the drive. A neat old lady in a purple dress and with white hair is straining at the wheel. She is frowning because Charlotte's car is in the way.

Mrs. Moseley looks at us suspiciously. "Yes, I knew Zora Neale," she says, unsmilingly and with a rather cold stare at Charlotte (who, I imagine, feels very *white* at that moment), "but that was a long time ago, and I don't want to talk about it."

"Yes, ma'am," I murmur, bringing all my sympathy to bear on the situation.

"Not only that," Mrs. Moseley continues, "I've been sick. Been in the hospital for an operation. Ruptured artery. The doctors didn't believe I was going to live, but you see me alive, don't you?"

"Looking well, too," I comment.

Mrs. Moseley is out of her car. A thin, sprightly woman with nice gold-studded false teeth, uppers and lowers. I like her because she stands there *straight* beside her car, with a hand on her hip and her straw pocketbook on her arm. She wears white T-strap shoes with heels that show off her well-shaped legs.

"I'm eighty-two years old, you know," she says. "And I just can't remember things the way I used to. Anyhow, Zora Neale left here to go to school and she never really came back to live. She'd come here for material for her books, but that was all. She spent most of her time down in South Florida."

"You know, Mrs. Moseley, I saw your name in one of Zora's books."

"You did?" She looks at me with only slightly more interest. "I read some of her books a long time ago, but then people got to borrowing and borrowing and they borrowed them all away."

"I could send you a copy of everything that's been reprinted," I offer. "Would you like me to do that?"

"No," says Mrs. Moseley promptly. "I don't read much any more. Besides, all of that was *so* long ago . . ."

Charlotte and I settle back against the car in the sun. Mrs. Moseley tells us at length and with exact recall every step

214

in her recent operation, ending with: "What those doctors didn't know—when they were expecting me to die (and they didn't even think I'd live long enough for them to have to take out my stitches!)—is that Jesus is the best doctor, and if *He* says for you to get well, that's all that counts."

With this philosophy, Charlotte and I murmur quick assent: being Southerners and church bred, we have heard that belief before. But what we learn from Mrs. Moseley is that she does not remember much beyond the year 1938. She shows us a picture of her father and mother and says that her father was Joe Clarke's brother. Joe Clarke, as every Zora Hurston reader knows, was the first mayor of Eatonville; his fictional counterpart is Jody Starks of *Their Eyes Were Watching God.* We also get directions to where Joe Clarke's store *was*—where Club Eaton is now. Club Eaton, a long orange-beige nightspot we had seen on the main road, is apparently famous for the good times in it regularly had by all. It is, perhaps, the modern equivalent of the store porch, where all the men of Zora's childhood came to tell "lies," that is, black folk tales, that were "made and used on the spot," to take a line from Zora. As for Zora's exact birthplace, Mrs. Moseley has no idea.

After I have commented on the healthy growth of her hibiscus bushes, she becomes more talkative. She mentions how much she *loved* to dance, when she was a young woman, and talks about how good her husband was. When he was alive, she says, she was completely happy because he allowed her to be completely free. "I was so free I had to pinch myself sometimes to tell if I was a married woman."

Relaxed now, she tells us about going to school with Zora. "Zora and I went to the same school. It's called Hungerford High now. It *was* only to the eighth grade. But our teachers were so good that by the time you left you knew college subjects. When I went to Morris Brown in Atlanta, the teachers there were just teaching me the same things I had already learned right in Eatonville. I wrote Mama and told her I was going to come home and help her with her babies. I wasn't learning anything new."

"Tell me something, Mrs. Moseley," I ask. "Why do you suppose Zora was against integration? I read somewhere that she was against school desegregation because she felt it was an insult to black teachers."

"Oh, one of them [white people] came around asking me about integration. One day I was doing my shopping. I heard 'em over there talking about it in the store, about the schools. And I got on out of the way because I knew if they asked me, they wouldn't like what I was going to tell 'em. But they came up and asked me anyhow. 'What do you think about this integration?' one of them said. I acted like I thought I had heard wrong. 'You're asking *me* what *I* think about integration?' I said. 'Well, as you can see, I'm just an old colored woman'—I was seventy-five or seventy-six then—'and this is the first time anybody ever asked me about integration. And nobody asked my grandmother what she thought, either, but her daddy was one of you all.'" Mrs. Moseley seems satisfied with this memory of her rejoinder. She looks at Charlotte. "I have the blood of three races in my veins," she says belligerently, "white, black, and Indian, and nobody asked me *anything* before."

"Do you think living in Eatonville made integration less appealing to you?"

"Well, I can tell you this: I have lived in Eatonville all my life, and I've been in the governing of this town. I've been everything but mayor and I've been *assistant* mayor. Eatonville was and is an all-black town. We have our own police department, post office, and town hall. Our own school and good teachers. Do I need integration?

"They took over Goldsboro, because the black people who lived there never incorporated, like we did. And now I don't even know if any black folks live there. They built big houses up there around the lakes. But we didn't let that happen in Eatonville, and we don't sell land to just anybody. And you see, we're still here."

When we leave, Mrs. Moseley is standing by her car, waving. I think of the letter Roy Wilkins wrote to a black newspaper blasting Zora Neale for her lack of enthusiasm about the integration of schools. I wonder if he knew the experience of Eatonville she was coming from. Not many black people in America have come from a self-contained, all-black community where loyalty and unity are taken for granted. A place where black pride is nothing new.

216

There is, however, one thing Mrs. Moseley said that bothered me.

"Tell me, Mrs. Moseley," I had asked, "why is it that thirteen years after Zora's death, no marker has been put on her grave?"

And Mrs. Moseley answered: "The reason she doesn't have a stone is because she wasn't buried here. She was buried down in South Florida somewhere. I don't think anybody really knew where she was."

> Only to reach a wider audience, need she ever write books—because she is a perfect book of entertainment in herself. In her youth she was always getting scholarships and things from wealthy white people, some of whom simply paid her just to sit around and represent the Negro race for them, she did it in such a racy fashion. She was full of sidesplitting anecdotes, humorous tales, and tragicomic stories, remembered out of her life in the South as a daughter of a traveling minister of God. She could make you laugh one minute and cry the next. To many of her white friends, no doubt, she was a perfect "darkie," in the nice meaning they give the term—that is, a naïve, childlike, sweet, humorous, and highly colored Negro.
>
> But Miss Hurston was clever, too—a student who didn't let college give her a broad "a" and who had great scorn for all pretensions, academic or otherwise. That is why she was such a fine folklore collector, able to go among the people and never act as if she had been to school at all. Almost nobody else could stop the average Harlemite on Lenox Avenue and measure his head with a strange-looking, anthropological device and not get bawled out for the attempt, except Zora, who used to stop anyone whose head looked interesting, and measure it.
> —LANGSTON HUGHES,
> *The Big Sea*

> What does it matter what white folks must have thought about her?
> —STUDENT, black women writers class
> Wellesley College

217

Mrs. Sarah Peek Patterson is a handsome, red-haired woman in her late forties, wearing orange slacks and gold earrings. She is the director of Lee-Peek Mortuary in Fort Pierce, the establishment that handled Zora's burial. Unlike most black funeral homes in Southern towns that sit like palaces among the general poverty, Lee-Peek has a run-down, *small* look. Perhaps this is because it is painted purple and white, as are its Cadillac chariots. These colors do not age well. The rooms are cluttered and grimy, and the bathroom is a tiny, stale-smelling prison, with a bottle of black hair dye (apparently used to touch up the hair of the corpses) dripping into the face bowl. Two pine burial boxes are resting in the bathtub.

Mrs. Patterson herself is pleasant and helpful.

"As I told you over the phone, Mrs. Patterson," I begin, shaking her hand and looking into her penny-brown eyes, "I am Zora Neale Hurston's niece, and I would like to have a marker put on her grave. You said, when I called you last week, that you could tell me where the grave is."

By this time I am, of course, completely into being Zora's niece, and the lie comes with perfect naturalness to my lips. Besides, as far as I'm concerned, she *is* my aunt—and that of all black people as well.

"She was buried in 1960," exclaims Mrs. Patterson. "That was when my father was running this funeral home. He's sick now or I'd let you talk to him. But I know where she's buried. She's in the old cemetery, the Garden of the Heavenly Rest, on Seventeenth Street. Just when you go in the gate there's a circle, and she's buried right in the middle of it. Hers is the only grave in that circle—because people don't bury in that cemetery any more."

She turns to a stocky, black-skinned woman in her thirties, wearing a green polo shirt and white jeans cut off at the knee. "This lady will show you where it is," she says.

"I can't tell you how much I appreciate this," I say to Mrs. Patterson, as I rise to go. "And could you tell me something else? You see, I never met my aunt. When she died, I was still a junior in high school. But could you tell me what she died of, and what kind of funeral she had?"

"I don't know exactly what she died of," Mrs. Patterson

says. "I know she didn't have any money. Folks took up a collection to bury her. I believe she died of malnutrition."

"*Malnutrition?*"

Outside, in the blistering sun, I lean my head against Charlotte's even more blistering car top. The sting of the hot metal only intensifies my anger "*Malnutrition,*" I manage to mutter. "Hell, our condition hasn't changed *any* since Phillis Wheatley's time. *She* died of malnutrition!"

"Really?" says Charlotte. "I didn't know that."

> One cannot overemphasize the extent of her commitment. It was so great that her marriage in the spring of 1927 to Herbert Sheen was short-lived. Although divorce did not come officially until 1931, the two separated amicably after only a few months, Hurston to continue her collecting, Sheen to attend Medical School. Hurston never married again.
> —ROBERT HEMENWAY

"What is your name?" I ask the woman who has climbed into the back seat.

"Rosalee," she says. She has a rough, pleasant voice, as if she is a singer who also smokes a lot. She is homely, and has an air of ready indifference.

"Another woman came by here wanting to see the grave," she says, lighting up a cigarette. "She was a little short, dumpty white lady from one of these Florida schools. Orlando or Daytona. But let me tell you something before we gets started. All I know is where the cemetery is. I don't know one thing about that grave. You better go back in and ask her to draw you a map."

A few moments later, with Mrs. Patterson's diagram of where the grave is, we head for the cemetery.

We drive past blocks of small, pastel-colored houses and turn right onto Seventeenth Street. At the very end, we reach a tall curving gate, with the words "Garden of the Heavenly Rest" fading into the stone. I expected, from Mrs. Patterson's small drawing, to find a small circle—which would have placed Zora's grave five or ten paces from the road. But the "circle" is over an acre large and looks more like an abandoned field. Tall weeds choke the dirt road and scrape against the sides of the car. It doesn't help either that I step out into an active ant hill.

"I don't know about y'all," I say, "but I don't even believe this." I am used to the haphazard cemetery-keeping that is traditional in most Southern black communities, but this neglect is staggering. As far as I can see there is nothing but bushes and weeds, some as tall as my waist. One grave is near the road, and Charlotte elects to investigate it. It is fairly clean, and belongs to someone who died in 1963.

Rosalee and I plunge into the weeds; I pull my long dress up to my hips. The weeds scratch my knees, and the insects have a feast. Looking back, I see Charlotte standing resolutely near the road.

"Aren't you coming?" I call.

"No," she calls back. "I'm from these parts and I know what's out there." She means snakes.

"Shit," I say, my whole life and the people I love flashing melodramatically before my eyes. Rosalee is a few yards to my right.

"How're you going to find anything out here?" she asks. And I stand still a few seconds, looking at the weeds. Some of them are quite pretty, with tiny yellow flowers. They are thick and healthy, but dead weeds under them have formed a thick gray carpet on the ground. A snake could be lying six inches from my big toe and I wouldn't see it. We move slowly, very slowly, our eyes alert, our legs trembly. It is hard to tell where the center of the circle is since the circle is not really round, but more like half of something round. There are things crackling and hissing in the grass. Sandspurs are sticking to the inside of my skirt. Sand and ants cover my feet. I look toward the road and notice that there are, indeed, *two* large curving stones, making an entrance and exit to the cemetery. I take my bearings from them and try to navigate to exact center. But the center of anything can be very large, and a grave is not a pinpoint. Finding the grave seems positively hopeless. There is only one thing to do:

"Zora!" I yell, as loud as I can (causing Rosalee to jump). "Are you out here?"

"If she is, I sho hope she don't answer you. If she do, I'm gone."

"Zora!" I call again. "I'm here. Are you?"

"If she is," grumbles Rosalee, "I hope she'll keep it to herself."

"Zora!" Then I start fussing with her. "I hope you don't think I'm going to stand out here all day, with these snakes watching me and these ants having a field day. In fact, I'm going to call you just one or two more times." On a clump of dried grass, near a small bushy tree, my eye falls on one of the largest bugs I have ever seen. It is on its back, and is as large as three of my fingers. I walk toward it, and yell "Zo-ra!" and my foot sinks into a hole. I look down. I am standing in a sunken rectangle that is about six feet long and about three or four feet wide. I look up to see where the two gates are.

"Well," I say, "this is the center, or approximately anyhow. It's also the only sunken spot we've found. Doesn't this look like a grave to you?"

"For the sake of not going no farther through these bushes," Rosalee growls, "yes, it do."

"Wait a minute," I say, "I have to look around some more to be sure this is the only spot that resembles a grave. But you don't have to come."

Rosalee smiles—a grin, really—beautiful and tough.

"Naw," she says, "I feels sorry for you. If one of these snakes got ahold of you out here by yourself I'd feel *real* bad." She laughs. "I done come this far, I'll go on with you."

"Thank you, Rosalee," I say. "Zora thanks you too."

"Just as long as she don't try to tell me in person," she says, and together we walk down the field.

The gusto and flavor of Zora Neal[e] Hurston's storytelling, for example, long before the yarns were published in "Mules and Men" and other books, became a local legend which might . . . have spread further under different conditions. A tiny shift in the center of gravity could have made them best-sellers.
—ARNA BONTEMPS,
Personals

221

> Bitter over the rejection of her folklore's value, especially in the black community, frustrated by what she felt was her failure to convert the Afro-American world view into the forms of prose fiction, Hurston finally gave up.
> —ROBERT HEMENWAY

When Charlotte and I drive up to the Merritt Monument Company, I immediately see the headstone I want.

"How much is this one?" I ask the young woman in charge, pointing to a tall black stone. It looks as majestic as Zora herself must have been when she was learning voodoo from those root doctors down in New Orleans.

"Oh, *that* one," she says, "that's our finest. That's Ebony Mist."

"Well, how much is it?"

"I don't know. But wait," she says, looking around in relief, "here comes somebody who'll know."

A small, sunburned man with squinty green eyes comes up. He must be the engraver, I think, because his eyes are contracted into slits, as if he has been keeping stone dust out of them for years.

"That's Ebony Mist," he says. "That's our best."

"How much is it?" I ask, beginning to realize I probably *can't* afford it.

He gives me a price that would feed a dozen Sahelian drought victims for three years. I realize I must honor the dead, but between the dead great and the living starving, there is no choice.

"I have a lot of letters to be engraved," I say, standing by the plain gray marker I have chosen. It is pale and ordinary, not at all like Zora, and makes me momentarily angry that I am not rich.

We go into his office and I hand him a sheet of paper that has:

ZORA NEALE HURSTON

"A GENIUS OF THE SOUTH"

NOVELIST   FOLKLORIST

ANTHROPOLOGIST

1901   1960

"A genius of the South" is from one of Jean Toomer's poems.

"Where is this grave?" the monument man asks. "If it's in a new cemetery, the stone has to be flat."

"Well, it's not a new cemetery and Zora—my aunt—doesn't need anything flat, because with the weeds out there, you'd never be able to see it. You'll have to go out there with me."

He grunts.

"And take a long pole and 'sound' the spot," I add. "Because there's no way of telling it's a grave, except that it's sunken."

"Well," he says, after taking my money and writing up a receipt, in the full awareness that he's the only monument dealer for miles, "you take this flag" (he hands me a four-foot-long pole with a red-metal marker on top) "and take it out to the cemetery and put it where you think the grave is. It'll take us about three weeks to get the stone out there."

I wonder if he knows he is sending me to another confrontation with the snakes. He probably does. Charlotte has told me she will cut my leg and suck out the blood if I am bit.

"At least send me a photograph when it's done, won't you?"

He says he will.

Hurston's return to her folklore-collecting in December of 1927 was made possible by Mrs. R. Osgood Mason, an elderly white patron of the arts, who at various times also helped Langston Hughes, Alain Locke, Richmond Barthe, and Miguel Covarrubias. Hurston apparently came to her attention through the intercession of Locke, who frequently served as a kind of liaison between the young black talent and Mrs. Mason. The entire relationship between this woman and the Harlem Renaissance deserves extended study, for it represents much of the ambiguity involved in white patronage of black artists. All her artists were instructed to call her "Godmother"; there was a decided emphasis on the "primitive" aspects of black culture, apparently a holdover from Mrs. Mason's interest in the Plains Indians. In

223

Hurston's case there were special restrictions imposed by her patron: although she was to be paid
a handsome salary for her folklore collecting, she
was to limit her correspondence and publish
nothing of her research without prior approval.
—ROBERT HEMENWAY

You have to read the chapters Zora *left out*
of her autobiography.
—STUDENT, Special Collections Room
Beinecke Library, Yale University

Dr. Benton, a friend of Zora's and a practicing M.D. in
Fort Pierce, is one of those old, good-looking men whom I always have trouble not liking. (It no longer bothers me that I may
be constantly searching for father figures; by this time, I have
found several and dearly enjoyed knowing them all.) He is
shrewd, with steady brown eyes under hair that is almost white.
He is probably in his seventies, but doesn't look it. He carries
himself with dignity, and has cause to be proud of the new clinic
where he now practices medicine. His nurse looks at us with
suspicion, but Dr. Benton's eyes have the penetration of a scal-
pel cutting through skin. I guess right away that if he knows
anything at all about Zora Hurston, he will not believe I am her
niece. "Eatonville?" Dr. Benton says, leaning forward in his
chair, looking first at me, then at Charlotte. "Yes, I know Eatonville; I grew up not far from there. I knew the whole bunch of
Zora's family." (He looks at the shape of my cheekbones, the
size of my eyes, and the nappiness of my hair.) "I knew her
daddy. The old man. He was a hard-working, Christian man.
Did the best he could for his family. He was the mayor of Eatonville for a while, you know.

"My father was the mayor of Goldsboro. You probably
never heard of it. It never incorporated like Eatonville did, and
has just about disappeared. But Eatonville, is still all black."

He pauses and looks at me. "And you're Zora's niece,"
he says wonderingly.

"Well," I say with shy dignity, yet with some tinge, I hope,
of a nineteenth-century blush, "I'm illegitimate. That's why I
never knew Aunt Zora."

I love him for the way he comes to my rescue. "You're *not* illegitimate!" he cries, his eyes resting on me fondly. "All of us are God's children! Don't you even *think* such a thing!"

And I hate myself for lying to him. Still, I ask myself, would I have gotten this far toward getting the headstone and finding out about Zora Hurston's last days without telling my lie? Actually, I probably would have. But I don't like taking chances that could get me stranded in central Florida.

"Zora didn't get along with her family. I don't know why. Did you read her autobiography, *Dust Tracks on a Road?*"

"Yes, I did," I say. "It pained me to see Zora pretending to be naïve and grateful about the old white 'Godmother' who helped finance her research, but I loved the part where she ran off from home after falling out with her brother's wife."

Dr. Benton nods. "When she got sick, I tried to get her to go back to her family, but she refused. There wasn't any real hatred; they just never had gotten along and Zora wouldn't go to them. She didn't want to go to the county home, either, but she had to, because she couldn't do a thing for herself."

"I was surprised to learn she died of malnutrition."

Dr. Benton seems startled. "Zora *didn't* die of malnutrition," he says indignantly. "Where did you get that story from? She had a stroke and she died in the welfare home." He seems peculiarly upset, distressed, but sits back reflectively in his chair. "She was an incredible woman," he muses. "Sometimes when I closed my office, I'd go by her house and just talk to her for an hour or two. She was a well-read, well-traveled woman and always had her own ideas about what was going on. . . ."

"I never knew her, you know. Only some of Carl Van Vechten's photographs and some newspaper photographs. . . . What did she look like?"

"When I knew her, in the fifties, she was a big woman, *erect*. Not quite as light as I am [Dr. Benton is dark beige], and about five foot, seven inches, and she weighed about two hundred pounds. Probably more. She . . ."

"What! Zora was *fat!* She wasn't, in Van Vechten's pictures!"

"Zora loved to eat," Dr. Benton says complacently. "She

could sit down with a mound of ice cream and just eat and talk till it was all gone."

While Dr. Benton is talking, I recall that the Van Vechten pictures were taken when Zora was still a young woman. In them she appears tall, tan, and healthy. In later newspaper photographs—when she was in her forties—I remembered that she seemed heavier and several shades lighter. I reasoned that the earlier photographs were taken while she was busy collecting folklore materials in the hot Florida sun.

"She had high blood pressure. Her health wasn't good. . . . She used to live in one of my houses—on School Court Street. It's a block house. . . . I don't recall the number. But my wife and I used to invite her over to the house for dinner. *She always ate well,*" he says emphatically.

"That's comforting to know," I say, wondering where Zora ate when she wasn't with the Bentons.

"Sometimes she would run out of groceries—after she got sick—and she'd call me. 'Come over here and see 'bout me,' she'd say. And I'd take her shopping and buy her groceries.

"She was always studying. Her mind—before the stroke—just worked all the time. She was always going somewhere, too. She once went to Honduras to study something. And when she died, she was working on that book about Herod the Great. She was so intelligent! And really had perfect expressions. Her English was beautiful." (I suspect this is a clever way to let me know Zora herself didn't speak in the "black English" her characters used.)

"I used to read all of her books," Dr. Benton continues, "but it was a long time ago. I remember one about . . . it was called, I think, 'The Children of God' [*Their Eyes Were Watching God*], and I remember Janie and Teapot [Teacake] and the mad dog riding on the cow in that hurricane and bit old Teapot on the cheek. . . ."

I am delighted that he remembers even this much of the story, even if the names are wrong, but seeing his affection for Zora I feel I must ask him about her burial. "Did she *really* have a pauper's funeral?"

"She *didn't* have a pauper's funeral!" he says with great heat. "Everybody around here *loved* Zora."

226

"We just came back from ordering a headstone," I say quietly, because he *is* an old man and the color is coming and going on his face, "but to tell the truth, I can't be positive what I found is the grave. All I know is the spot I found was the only grave-size hole in the area."

"I remember it wasn't near the road," says Dr. Benton, more calmly. "Some other lady came by here and we went out looking for the grave and I took a long iron stick and poked all over that part of the cemetery but we didn't find anything. She took some pictures of the general area. Do the weeds still come up to your knees?"

"And beyond," I murmur. This time there isn't any doubt Dr. Benton feels ashamed.

As he walks us to our car, he continues to talk about Zora. "She couldn't really write much near the end. She had the stroke and it left her weak; her mind was affected. She couldn't think about anything for long.

"She came here from Daytona, I think. She owned a houseboat over there. When she came here, she sold it. She lived on that money, then she worked as a maid—for an article on maids she was writing—and she worked for the *Chronicle* writing the horoscope column.

"I think black people here in Florida got mad at her because she was for some politician they were against. She said this politician *built* schools for blacks while the one they wanted just talked about it. And although Zora wasn't egotistical, what she thought, she thought; and generally what she thought, she said."

When we leave Dr. Benton's office, I realize I have missed my plane back home to Jackson, Mississippi. That being so, Charlotte and I decide to find the house Zora lived in before she was taken to the county welfare home to die. From among her many notes, Charlotte locates a letter of Zora's she has copied that carries the address: 1734 School Court Street. We ask several people for directions. Finally, two old gentlemen in a dusty gray Plymouth offer to lead us there. School Court Street is not paved, and the road is full of mud puddles. It is dismal and squalid, redeemed only by the brightness of the late afternoon sun. Now I can understand what a "block" house is. It is a house shaped like a block, for one thing, surrounded by others just like it. Some houses are blue and some are green or yellow. Zora's is light green. They are tiny—about fifty by fifty feet, squatty with flat roofs. The house Zora lived in looks worse than the others, but that is its only distinction. It also has three ragged and dirty children sitting on the steps.

"Is this where y'all live?" I ask, aiming my camera.

"No, ma'am" they say in unison, looking at me earnestly. "We live over yonder. This Miss So-and-So's house; but she in the horspital."

We chatter inconsequentially while I take more pictures. A car drives up with a young black couple in it. They scowl fiercely at Charlotte and don't look at me with friendliness, either. They get out and stand in their doorway across the street. I go up to them to explain. "Did you know Zora Hurston used to live right across from you?" I ask.

"Who?" They stare at me blankly, then become curiously attentive, as if they think I made the name up. They are both Afroed and he is somberly dashikied.

I suddenly feel frail and exhausted. "It's too long a story," I say, "but tell me something: is there anybody on this street who's lived here for more than thirteen years?"

"That old man down there," the young man says, pointing. Sure enough, there is a man sitting on his steps three houses down. He has graying hair and is very neat, but there is a weakness about him. He reminds me of Mrs. Turner's husband in *Their Eyes Were Watching God*. He's rather "vanishing"-looking, as if his features have been sanded down. In the old days, before black was beautiful, he was probably considered attractive, because he has wavy hair and light-brown skin; but now, well, light skin has ceased to be its own reward.

After the preliminaries, there is only one thing I want to know: "Tell me something," I begin, looking down at Zora's house. "Did Zora like flowers?"

He looks at me queerly. "As a matter of fact," he says, looking regretfully at the bare, rough yard that surrounds her former house, "she was crazy about them. And she was a great gardener. She loved azaleas, and that running and blooming vine [morning-glories], and she really loved that night-smelling flower [gardenia]. She kept a vegetable garden year-round, too. She raised collards and tomatoes and things like that.

"Everyone in this community thought well of Miss Hurston. When she died, people all up and down this street took up a collection for her burial. We put her away nice."

"Why didn't somebody put up a headstone?"

"Well, you know, one was never requested. Her and her family didn't get along. They didn't even come to the funeral."

"And did she live down there by herself?"

"Yes, until they took her away. She lived with—just her and her companion, Sport."

My ears perk up. "Who?"

"Sport, you know, her dog. He was her only companion. He was a big brown-and-white dog."

When I walk back to the car, Charlotte is talking to the young couple on their porch. They are relaxed and smiling.

"I told them about the famous lady who used to live across the street from them," says Charlotte as we drive off. "Of course they had no idea Zora ever lived, let alone that she lived across the street. I think I'll send some of her books to them."

"That's real kind of you," I say.

> I am not tragically colored. There is no great sorrow dammed up in my soul, nor lurking behind my eyes. I do not mind at all. I do not belong to the sobbing school of Negrohood who hold that nature somehow has given them a lowdown dirty deal and whose feelings are all hurt about it. . . . No, I do not weep at the world—I am too busy sharpening my oyster knife.
> —ZORA NEALE HURSTON, "How It Feels To Be Colored Me," *World Tomorrow,* 1928

There are times—and finding Zora Hurston's grave was one of them—when normal responses of grief, horror, and so on do not make sense because they bear no real relation to the depth of the emotion one feels. It was impossible for me to cry when I saw the field full of weeds where Zora is. Partly this is because I have come to know Zora through her books and she was not a teary sort of person herself; but partly, too, it is because there is a point at which even grief feels absurd. And at this point, laughter gushes up to retrieve sanity.

It is only later, when the pain is not so direct a threat to one's own existence, that what was learned in that moment of comical lunacy is understood. Such moments rob us of both youth and vanity. But perhaps they are also times when greater disciplines are born.

❑ Selected Bibliography ∎

Works by Zora Neale Hurston

Dust Tracks on a Road. 1942. Reprint. New York: HarperCollins, 1991.

I Love Myself: A Zora Neale Hurston Reader. Edited by Alice Walker. New York: The Feminist Press, 1979.

Jonah's Gourd Vine. 1935. Reprint. New York: HarperCollins, 1990.

Moses, Man of the Mountain. 1938. Reprint. New York: HarperCollins, 1991.

Mules and Men. 1935. Reprint. New York: HarperCollins, 1990.

Mule Bone: A Comedy of Negro Life. With Langston Hughes. New York: HarperCollins, 1991.

The Sanctified Church. Berkeley, CA: Turtle Island, 1981.

Seraph on the Suwanee. 1948. Reprint. New York: HarperCollins, 1991.

Spunk: The Collected Short Stories of Zora Neale Hurston. Berkeley, California: Turtle Island, 1985.

Tell My Horse. 1938. Reprint. New York: HarperCollins, 1990.

Their Eyes Were Watching God. 1937. Reprint. New York: HarperCollins, 1990.

Zora Neale Hurston: Novels and Stories. Edited by Cheryl A. Wall. New York: Library of America, 1995.

Zora Neale Hurston: Folklore, Memoirs, and Other Writings. Edited by Cheryl A. Wall. New York: Library of America, 1995.

Suggested Further Reading

Awkward, Michael. *Inspiriting Influences: Tradition, Revision and Afro-American Women's Novels.* New York: Columbia University Press, 1989.

———, editor. *New Essays on Their Eyes Were Watching God.* New York: Cambridge University Press, 1990.

Baker, Houston. *Blues, Ideology and Afro-American Literature.* Chicago: University of Chicago Press, 1984.

Callahan, John. *In the African American Grain: The Pursuit of Voice in Twentieth-Century Fiction.* Urbana: University of Illinois Press, 1988.

Carby, Hazel. *Reconstructing Womanhood: The Emergence of the Afro-American Woman Novelist.* New York: Oxford University Press, 1987.

Christian, Barbara. *Black Women Novelists.* Westport, Connecticut: Greenwood Press, 1980.

duCille, Ann. *The Coupling Convention: Sex, Text, and Tradition in Black Women's Fiction.* New York: Oxford University Press, 1993.

DuPlessis, Rachel. *Writing Beyond the Ending: Narrative Strategies of Twentieth-Century Women Writers.* Bloomington: Indiana University Press, 1985.

Gates, Henry Louis, Jr. *The Signifying Monkey: A Theory of Afro-American Literary Criticism.* New York: Oxford University Press, 1988.

——— and K. A. Appiah, editors. *Zora Neale Hurston: Critical Perspectives Past and Present.* New York: Amistad Press, 1993.

Glassman, Steve and Kathryn Seidel, editors. *Zora in Florida.* Orlando: University of Central Florida Press, 1991.

Hemenway, Robert. *Zora Neale Hurston: A Literary Biography.* Urbana: University of Illinois Press, 1977.

Hill, Lynda. *Social Rituals and the Verbal Art of Zora Neale Hurston.* Washington, D.C.: Howard University Press, 1996.

Holloway, Karla. *The Character of the Word: The Texts of Zora Neale Hurston.* Westport, Connecticut: Greenwood, 1987.

hooks, bell. *Talking Back.* Boston: South End Press, 1989.

Howard, Lillie P. *Zora Neale Hurston.* Boston: Twayne, 1980.

Huggins, Nathan. *Harlem Renaissance.* New York: Oxford University Press, 1971.

Jones, Gayl. *Liberating Voices: Oral Tradition in African American Literature.* Cambridge: Harvard University Press, 1991.

Lewis, David Levering. *When Harlem Was in Vogue.* New York: Alfred A. Knopf, 1981.

Lowe, John. *Jump At the Sun: Zora Neale Hurston's Cosmic Comedy.* Urbana: University of Illinois Press, 1994.

Nathiri, N. Y. *Zora! Zora Neale Hurston: A Woman and Her Community.* Orlando: Sentinel Communications, 1991.

Walker, Alice. *In Search of Our Mothers' Gardens.* New York: Harcourt Brace Jovanovich, 1983.

Wall, Cheryl A. *Women of the Harlem Renaissance.* Bloomington: Indiana University Press, 1995.

Washington, Mary Helen. *Invented Lives: Narratives of Black Women.* New York: Anchor Press, 1987.

Willis, Susan. *Specifying: Black Women Writing the American Experience.* Madison: University of Wisconsin Press, 1987.

Wolfe, George C. *Spunk: Three Tales by Zora Neale Hurston,* adapted by George C. Wolfe. New York: Theatre Communications Group, 1991.

❏ Permissions ■